Voyages in English

Writing and Grammar

Carolyn Marie Dimick
General Editor

Marie T. McVey
Revision Editor

Jeanne M. Baker
Carolyn Marie Dimick
Jeannine M. Norton
Susan Mary Platt
Authors

Editorial
Margaret O'Leary Coyle
Catherine Marcic Joyce

Contributors
Beth Duncan
Elizabeth Cook Fresen
Diane Gonciarz
Cathy Ann Tell
Patricia Walsh
Richard Weisenseel

Production
Mary Bowers
Genevieve Kelley
Ellie Knepler
Anne Marie Mastandrea
Carla Jean Mayer
Julia Mayer
Molly O'Halloran
Jill Smith
Leslie Uriss

Cover Design
Steve Straus, Think Design

Cover Art
Konstantin Rodko, *Train Station*

3441 North Ashland Avenue
Chicago, Illinois 60657
1-800-621-1008

ISBN 0-8294-0986-6

Printed in the United States of America

00 01 02 5 4 3

Table of Contents

Part I Written and Oral Communication

CHAPTER 1 Personal Narrative

Excerpts from *My Little Island* by Frané Lessac 11

Writer's Craft....14

The Writing Process....16

Prewriting 17

Drafting 20

Listening and Speaking: Tips for a Peer Conference 22

Revising....23

Proofreading 26

Editor's Workshop: Proofreading for Punctuation and Capitalization 28

Publishing....30

Listening and Speaking: Making Introductions....32

CHAPTER 2 Writing a Paragraph

Lesson 1 Finding and Organizing an Idea 35

Lesson 2 Understanding the Paragraph....41

Lesson 3 Writing Beginning Sentences....44

Lesson 4 Writing Middle Sentences 47

Lesson 5 Writing Ending Sentences....50

Lesson 6 Giving the Paragraph a Title 54

Word Study: Exploring Words....56

Writer's Workshop 62

Editor's Workshop 64

CHAPTER 3

Making the Paragraph Better

Lesson 1 Using Strong Verbs....67
Lesson 2 Using Colorful Adjectives....70
Lesson 3 Combining Subjects....72
Lesson 4 Combining Predicates....75
Lesson 5 Combining Sentences....78
Lesson 6 Revising the Paragraph....81
Word Study: Exploring Words....84
Writer's Workshop....90
Editor's Workshop....92

CHAPTER 4

Writing a Report

Lesson 1 Choosing an Idea and Finding Facts....95
Lesson 2 Planning the Report....98
Lesson 3 Writing the Report....102
Lesson 4 Revising the Report....106
Word Study: Exploring Words....110
Writer's Workshop....116
Editor's Workshop....118

More to Explore About Writing

Lesson 1 Writing a News Story 121
Lesson 2 Writing a How-To Paragraph 124
Lesson 3 Writing About Yourself..........................127
Lesson 4 Writing a Book Report 131
Lesson 5 Writing About a Book Character 133
Word Study: Exploring Words 136
Writer's Workshop 142
Editor's Workshop 144

Writing Letters

Lesson 1 A Friendly Letter 147
Lesson 2 Letters of Invitation and Acceptance 154
Lesson 3 A Thank-You Letter 160
Lesson 4 Addressing the Envelope 163
Lesson 5 Filling Out Forms 166
Word Study: Exploring Words 170
Writer's Workshop 176
Editor's Workshop 178

Speaking and Listening Skills

Lesson 1 Oral Presentations 181

Lesson 2 Choral Speaking....................................184

Lesson 3 Listening for Sequence 192

Lesson 4 Listening to Directions 194

Lesson 5 Listening to Poetry 196

Word Study: Exploring Words 202

Writer's Workshop 208

Editor's Workshop 210

Dictionary and Library Skills

Lesson 1 Dictionary Skills—Alphabetical Order 213

Lesson 2 Dictionary Skills—Guide Words 216

Lesson 3 Dictionary Skills—Word Meaning....................................218

Lesson 4 Library Skills—Cover, Spine, Title Page 221

Lesson 5 Library Skills—Table of Contents, Index, Glossary 224

Lesson 6 Library Skills—Reference Books: The Encyclopedia and the Atlas....................................229

Lesson 7 Library Skills—Kinds of Books 232

Lesson 8 Library Skills—The Card Catalog....................................234

Writer's Workshop 236

Editor's Workshop 238

Part II Grammar, Usage, and Mechanics

Sentences

Lesson 1 What Is a Sentence? 243

Lesson 2 Telling and Asking Sentences 246

Lesson 3 Commanding Sentences 251

Lesson 4 Exclaiming Sentences 256

Lesson 5 The Four Kinds of Sentences 260

Lesson 6 Subject Nouns and Predicate Verbs 263

Chapter Challenge 267

Creative Space 268

CHAPTER 10

Nouns

Lesson 1 Identifying Nouns 271

Lesson 2 Proper and Common Nouns 276

Lesson 3 Singular and Plural Nouns 278

Lesson 4 Irregular Plurals 281

Lesson 5 Singular Possessives 283

Lesson 6 Plural and Irregular Plural Possessives 286

Chapter Challenge 291

Creative Space 292

CHAPTER 11 Pronouns

Lesson 1 Identifying Pronouns 295
Lesson 2 Pronouns as Subjects 299
Lesson 3 Pronouns Used After Verbs 302
Lesson 4 Possessive Pronouns 305
Lesson 5 The Correct Use of *I* and *Me* 308
Chapter Challenge 313
Creative Space 314

CHAPTER 12 Verbs

Lesson 1 Action Verbs 317
Lesson 2 Being Verbs 321
Lesson 3 Helping Verbs 324
Lesson 4 Forms of Verbs 327
Lesson 5 Regular and Irregular Verbs 331
Lesson 6 Present Tense 346
Lesson 7 Past Tense 349
Lesson 8 Correct Use of *Is* and *Are,* *Was* and *Were* 351
Chapter Challenge 353
Creative Space 354

Adjectives

Lesson 1 Adjectives That Describe 357
Lesson 2 Adjectives That Compare 363
Lesson 3 Adjectives That Tell Number 368
Lesson 4 Articles 372
Lesson 5 Adjectives That Point Out 376
Chapter Challenge 380
Creative Space 382

Adverbs

Lesson 1 Kinds of Adverbs 385
Lesson 2 Using Words Correctly 393
Chapter Challenge 399
Creative Space 400

Punctuation and Capitalization

Lesson 1 End Punctuation 403
Lesson 2 Capital Letters 407
Lesson 3 Abbreviations 412
Lesson 4 Titles and Initials 415
Lesson 5 Titles of Books and Poems 418
Lesson 6 Commas 420
Lesson 7 Direct Quotations 424
Chapter Challenge 428

Grammar and Writing Handbook 430
Index 446
Acknowledgments 453

PART 1

Written and Oral Communication

938
SAVITSKY

CHAPTER

1

Personal Narrative

The selection on the next page is from the book *My Little Island.* It tells the story of a boy's visit to the Caribbean island where he was born. The sights and sounds of the island make the trip exciting for the boy and his best friend, Lucca.

Because the boy tells the story, it is called a personal narrative. The interesting and unusual details of the events, people, and things make this personal narrative one you won't forget.

As you read, pay attention to the details that help you share in the visit to the island. Look for words that tell what the boy sees, hears, smells, tastes, and touches. Look for the story's beginning, middle, and end. All this will help you to write your own personal narrative as you follow the steps in the writing process.

excerpts from

My Little Island

by Frané Lessac

It can be exciting to take a trip to visit family far away and to do unusual things. Read this boy's account of his visit to the island where he was born. As you read, think about how he tries to help you share his experiences.

My best friend, Lucca, and I are going to visit the little Caribbean island where I was born. From the air it looks like a giant green turtle swimming in the sea.

When our plane lands, we see dozens of smiling faces welcoming us.

It's good to be home again!

On the way to my aunt's house we pass dozens of brightly painted wooden houses.

From the road they look like little rainbows sitting on the hills.

As we drive up a mountainside, a breeze begins to blow. It smells so sweet.

Lucca wants to know the names of all the beautiful trees and flowers. I know only some of them: frangipani and jasmine flowers, yellow poui and red flamboyant trees, pink coral and sweet bay-rum trees.

My aunt has lunch ready for us when we arrive.

It is too hot to cook indoors, so my aunt cooked the food outside in old coal-pots.

My cousins and I gobble up pumpkin soup, pigeon peas, goat-water stew, red snapper fish, and fried bananas topped with guava ice cream.

Lucca makes funny faces but eats it all.

After lunch lots of children come to play with us.

Donkeys and goats, cats and dogs, birds and cows are everywhere. We even see iguanas that are three feet long, and giant barking frogs. Our friends call the barking frogs "mountain chickens."

Lucca and I laugh.

Who will believe us back home?

The next day we take a walk along the seashore.

Fathers and sons are rowing brightly painted wooden boats with names like *Frangelica, Annipani,* and *Shonabee.* They catch mackerel, parrot fish, tuna fish, trunkfish, and picasso fish in their huge nets.

When their boats are filled with flipping and flopping fish, they row back to shore.

A fisherman blows a conch shell. People hear the "Tootle-tu-whooo!" and run to the beach to buy nice, fresh fish for supper.

My island has its own volcano.

Sometimes it sends puffs of smoke and fire into the air.

I wonder what it would look like if it erupted—but I wouldn't want to be nearby if it did.

Not far from the volcano is a wild, wild forest where we go fishing.

We don't want to scare the fish, so we stand there quietly and just listen to the bird songs and frogs and insects and the sound of the bubbling mountain stream.

On the night before we go home, we get to stay up late. It's carnival!

Jump up! . . . Jump up!

Our toes barely touch the ground as we dance to the carnival songs that play all night long.

When morning comes, our visit to my little island is over.

Lucca and I don't want to say good-bye to my aunt and cousins and all our friends.

We just say, "We'll come back. Soon!"

TALK IT OVER

1. How does the boy feel about his island home? How do you know?
2. The boy tells about many of his experiences during the trip. Which ones would you like to share in, if you could? Why?
3. The boy makes you feel as if you are right there on the island with him. How does he do this?

WRITER'S CRAFT

Personal Narrative

A personal narrative is a story about you. It might tell about something you did, something that happened to you, or how you feel about something.

Did you notice how the boy who is telling the story in *My Little Island* is always in the middle of the action? Go back and count the number of times you find the words *I, me, my,* and *we.* These words are signals that you're reading a personal narrative.

A well-crafted personal narrative also has

- just one topic.
- a beginning that grabs the reader's attention.
- a middle that includes events told in order.
- details to help the reader share the writer's experience.
- an ending that pulls the story together.

Take a Closer Look

REREAD **Reread *My Little Island.* Look for the answers to these questions as you read.**

1. What is the topic?
2. How is the beginning of the story interesting?
3. Are the story events in an order that makes sense?
4. Did any of the details surprise you? Which ones?
5. Does the story's ending make sense?

DISCUSS **Talk over your answers to the questions on page 14 with a partner or in a small group. Compare your thinking with the notes in the following chart.**

Topic	A homecoming visit to a Caribbean island *When our plane lands, we see dozens of smiling faces welcoming us.* *It's good to be home again!*
Story beginning	In the story opening, the writer sets a happy, warm mood. The reader feels welcome to come along. *We even see iguanas that are three feet long, and giant barking frogs.*
Middle with events in order	Phrases like *after lunch* and *the next day* signal that the events are in correct time order. *After lunch lots of children come to play with us.* *The next day we take a walk along the seashore.*
Attention-getting details	Details, such as pumpkin soup and barking frogs, appeal to the senses. *When their boats are filled with flipping and flopping fish, they row back to shore.*
Ending	The story ends when the trip is over. *When morning comes, our visit to my little island is over.*

WRITE **Read this personal narrative. Make notes in a chart like the one above. Talk about your notes with a partner.**

It was the worst day of my life. My pet snake was missing. I started a search.

I began by looking in the living room. I heard little shooshing noises but saw no sign of the snake. Then I looked in the closet. I saw something long and slithery, but it was only some ribbon. Then I went to the laundry room. There was my little snake, sleeping on top of the warm dryer!

Prewriting
Drafting
Revising
Proofreading
Publishing

Personal Narrative

Here's a personal narrative written by Keisha, a third grader.

This is her final version of the story. Read it. Then take a look on the following pages to see how Keisha worked through the steps of the writing process to get to this point.

Fishing for Fun

"Fishing?" I asked. I had never fished before, so I didn't know if I would like it. I was visiting with my older cousin, Leila. She wanted to go fishing at the lake where she lives.

We sat on the wobbly dock. It was so hot, and there were giant bugs everywhere. The heat and the bugs didn't seem to bother Leila. We fished for a long time. I was starting to get kind of bored. Then, suddenly, I felt a tug on my line. I had caught a huge fish!

We had fresh fish for lunch. Then Leila asked, "What would you like to do next?" I said I would like to fish some more!

Prewriting
Drafting
Revising
Proofreading
Publishing

STEP 1

Prewriting

Keisha began by making a list of topics for a story about herself.

None of the topics on her list seemed very interesting to Keisha. She could barely remember how she met her best friend, Tania. Most report card days were the same. She usually got good grades. But, what about the family?

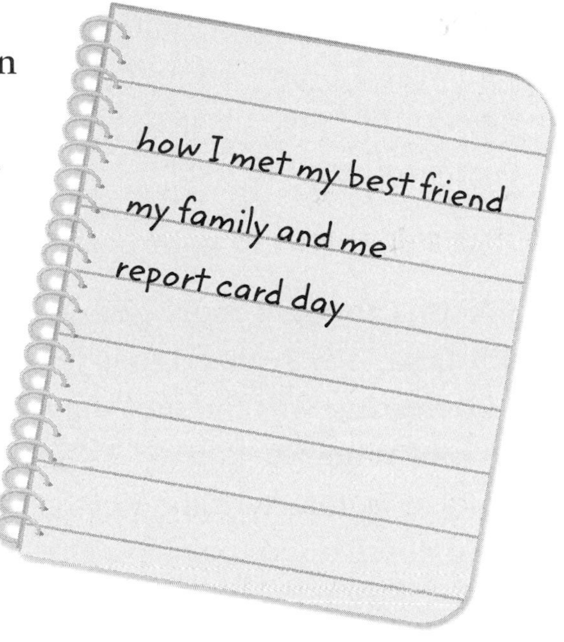

Keisha made a second list, a list of her relatives. She jotted down some interesting or funny things that happened when she was with them. When she got to her cousin Leila's name, she remembered the day they went fishing. It made her laugh to think about it. "Fishing with Leila" seemed to be a good topic. Here's why:

- Keisha had vivid memories of what happened, so she could give lots of details.
- It involved something interesting or funny.
- Students Keisha's age, her readers, would probably be familiar with her feelings.

Prewriting
Drafting
Revising
Proofreading
Publishing

Try It!

▶ **Make a list of topics for a personal narrative. Review your list as Keisha did. Ask yourself:**

- Would my story hold my readers' interest?
- Would I have enough to say about my topic?
- Could I give clear details so the reader feels part of my experience?

▶ **Put a star next to your best topic idea.**

As Keisha thought more about her topic, "Fishing with Leila," she realized that what made the situation so interesting was the fact that she and Leila were so different when it came to fishing. So, to help organize her ideas before writing, Keisha made a chart. She wrote down anything that came to mind about Leila and herself that related to the topic. Take a look.

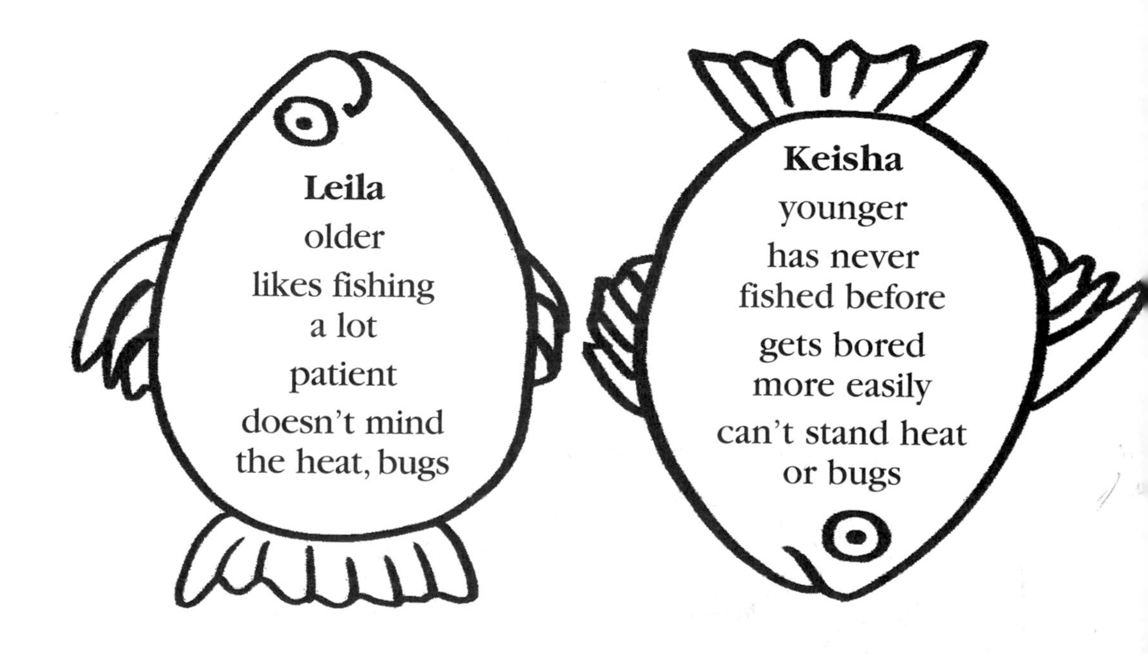

Keisha's chart gave her notes to help her write her first draft. Keisha was having fun when she made her chart in fish shapes. She could have made a two-column chart, a word map, or little pictures to help her get her ideas down on paper.

Try It!

- **Think more about the topic you starred for Try It! on page 18.**
- **Decide how you want to get your best ideas down on paper. You can make a list, a chart, a word map, or sketches.**
- **Share your topic and ideas with a partner.**

- Prewriting
- **Drafting**
- Revising
- Proofreading
- Publishing

STEP 2

Drafting

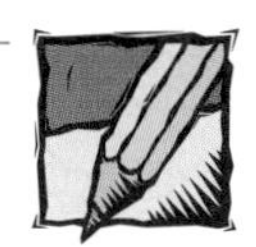

Keisha used her chart to write the first draft of her personal narrative. She wrote quickly because she wanted to get her ideas down. She knew that later she could go over what she wrote to change things, add new ideas, and check for correct spelling. She did, however, keep in mind her audience, the students in her class.

Take a look at Keisha's first draft.

Fishing

One day I went fishing. I was visiting with my cousin, Leila. she is older than me. She lives on a lake. She wanted to go fishing. I had never fished before. I didnt know if I woud like it. I wasnt sure about this fishing idea.

It was hot we sat on the dock. Thare were lots of bugs buzing around. The heat and the bugs didn't seem to bother my cousin. We fished for a long time. I was starting to get bored. then I felt a tug on my line. I caught a Fish.

We had fish for lunch. After lunch my cusin asked What I woud like to do next. I said I woud like to do it some more.

When Keisha read over her first draft, she knew she had some more work to do. But she felt that her story had definite possibilities. What do you think?

Take a Closer Look

1. Does Keisha's first draft have all the things that make up a personal narrative?
2. What do you think of Keisha's beginning? Does it grab your interest?
3. Will this story appeal to Keisha's audience, her classmates? Why?

Personal Narrative
- uses *I, me, my,* and *we*
- one topic
- events in order
- details to add interest
- ending to pull things together

Peer to Peer

Keisha asked a classmate to read her first draft. Here's what he said.

> Your story made me want to learn how to fish! I could almost see what was happening. Your opening sentence is kind of dull, though. Maybe you could put in some of the actual words you and your cousin said that day.

Keisha was pleased with her friend's comments. It was good to hear that her personal narrative
- was interesting.
- had enough details to help a reader share in the experience.

It was helpful to know that
- the opening needed more work.
- dialogue might make the event seem as if it were taking place right now.

Dialogue means the actual words as the person said them. Quotation marks signal dialogue.

DISCUSS **What would you say to Keisha? Talk it over with a friend.**

Tips for a Peer Conference

One of the best ways to get help with your writing is to have a peer conference with your classmates.

What to Do If You're the Writer

Have your writing ready. If it looks messy and is hard to read, ask your peers to listen as you read it aloud.

Remember You want help. So listen to what your peers say. You don't have to make the changes they suggest, but you *should* listen. Ask specific questions, such as "I can't think of a good ending. Any ideas?"

What to Do If You're the Helper

It's easy to say "I like this," or "I don't like that," but telling *why* is hard work. Take time to think about what the writer has written.

Remember You want to help—not hurt someone's feelings. First, tell something you like about the writing. Then, ask questions about anything you don't understand.

When to Have a Peer Conference

You can have a peer conference any time during the writing process. You can brainstorm topics during prewriting. You can get classmates' reactions to your first draft and ask for ideas to help you revise. You can have a classmate proofread your edited work.

Try It!

▶ **Make a peer conference checklist. Write down things you will need to pay attention to as you read or listen to your classmate's written work.**

STEP 3

Revising

- Prewriting
- Drafting
- **Revising**
- Proofreading
- Publishing

When you revise something, you make changes in it. Keisha felt that it was important to change the first paragraph of her story. She had to do some rewriting to grab the attention of her audience. She knew, too, that she would eventually change the title of her story to make it more interesting. To remind herself to do this, she crossed it out.

Editor's Marks

- ∧ Add
- Take out
- Move
- Replace

READ Look over Keisha's revisions to be sure you understand how the new paragraph should read. Notice the ways Keisha signals her changes.

~~Fishing~~

Fishing? I asked.

~~One day I went fishing.~~ I was visiting with my cousin, Leila. ~~She is~~ older ~~than me. She lives on a lake.~~ She wanted to go fishing at the lake where she lives. I had never fished before, so I didnt know if I woud like it. ~~I wasnt sure about this fishing idea.~~

DISCUSS How do Keisha's changes improve her paragraph? Talk it over with a partner.

Prewriting
Drafting
Revising
Proofreading
Publishing

Take a Closer Look

Now compare your ideas about Keisha's revisions with the comments in the chart below.

Keisha's First Draft	Keisha's Revision	Comments
One day I went fishing.	Fishing? I asked. I had never fished before, so I didnt know if I woud like it.	Keisha's exact words grab your attention and the next statement explains her inexperience with fishing.
she is older than me. She lives on a lake. She wanted to go fishing.	I was visiting with my older cousin, Leila. She wanted to go fishing at the lake where she lives.	Combining three short sentences makes the story sound less choppy.
I wasnt sure about this fishing idea.		By this point in the story, it is very clear that Keisha isn't sure about going fishing. The sentence is not needed, so it was taken out.

Keisha read over her revised first paragraph. She felt satisfied, so she continued working on her story. Her revisions are shown on the next page. Take a look at them. Pay careful attention to how she made changes in her ideas and how she expressed them.

Fishing

It was [so] hot we sat on the [wobbly] dock. [and] Thare were ~~lots of~~ [giant] bugs ~~buzing around.~~ [everywhere] The heat and the bugs didn't seem to bother ~~my cousin.~~ [Leila] We fished for a long time. I was starting to get [kind of] bored. then[, suddenly,] I felt a tug on my line. I [had] caught a [huge] Fish[!]

We had [fresh] fish for lunch. ~~After lunch my cusin~~ [Then Leila] asked[,] ["]What ~~I~~ [you] woud like to do next[?"] I said I woud like to ~~do it~~ [fish] some more[!]

WRITE/DISCUSS **Work with a partner to make a chart like the one on page 24. List each change Keisha made in her second and third paragraphs. Think about why she may have made each change. Make notes about how the changes helped her story.**

Editor's Marks

- ^ Add
- Take out
- Move
- Replace

Keisha used describing words, or adjectives, to help her readers experience her story. She used the words *wobbly, giant,* and *huge.*

Find out more about adjectives, beginning on page 357.

- Prewriting
- Drafting
- Revising
- **Proofreading**
- Publishing

STEP 4

Proofreading

Next Keisha proofread and edited her story. When you proofread, you look carefully for mistakes in spelling, punctuation, capitalization, and grammar. When you correct the mistakes, you are editing.

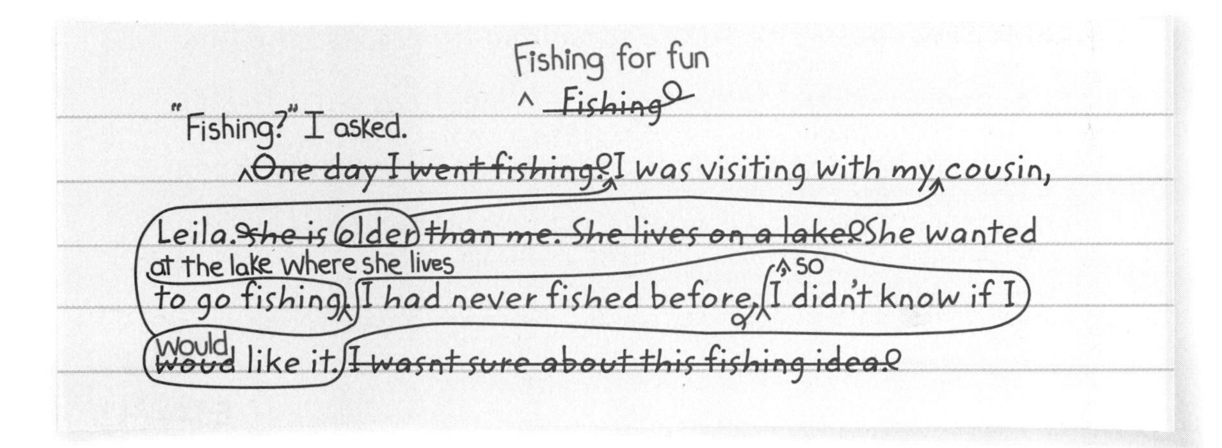

Reminder:

A contraction always has an apostrophe to replace the letter or letters that were left out.

Take a Closer Look

READ Look carefully at Keisha's paragraph. Pay attention to her newest changes. They are in red.

1. Keisha made two spelling mistakes. Find the words. What did Keisha forget when she wrote *didnt?*
2. Keisha added quotation marks at the beginning and end of her new first sentence. Tell why.
3. Keisha changed the title of her story. Why do just some words begin with capital letters? Should the *f* in *fun* be a capital letter?

PRACTICE **Here is Keisha's second paragraph. This is a typed version, so it will be easier for you to proofread and edit. Look for these things that need correcting:**

1. Find two spelling mistakes.
2. Find two words that begin with a capital letter but should begin with a lowercase letter.
3. Find two words that start sentences and need capital letters.

we sat on the wobbly dock. It was so hot, and Thare were giant bugs everywhere. The heat and the bugs didn't seem to bother Leila. We fished for a long time. I was starting to get kind of bored. then, suddenly, I felt a tug on my line. I had cought a huge Fish!

Editor's Marks

- ^ Add
- Take out
- Move
- Replace
- ≡ Use a capital letter
- / Make a lowercase letter

Try It!

▶ **Write your own proofreading checklist. Write down things you will need to check for as you proofread and edit your writing.**

Proofreading for Punctuation and Capitalization

When you proofread and edit your writing, always check your punctuation and capitalization. Remember these basics.

Use a period to end a sentence that makes a statement.
(I wrote a thank-you note to my aunt.)

Use a question mark to end a sentence that asks a question.
(Where is the book?)

Use an exclamation point to end a sentence that shows strong emotion.
(What a storm that was!)

Use a comma to separate

- items in a series.
  (Dad bought cherries, milk, and cereal at the market.)
- a speaker's exact words from other words in a sentence.
  ("It's six o'clock," Barbara said.)

Use quotation marks around a speaker's exact words.
(Dave replied, "I put it in the car.")

Capitalize

- the first word in a sentence.
  (Once upon a time, there was a special kingdom.)
- proper nouns.
  (We invited Mike and Tina to our Mexican fiesta.)
- the pronoun *I*.
  (Ben and I both like fishing.)

READ/PRACTICE **Read the following story. Tell where you would use editor's marks to show punctuation and capitalization corrections.**

Editor's Marks

- ∧ Add
- Take out
- Move
- Replace
- ≡ Use a capital letter
- / Make a lowercase letter

an Actor Is born

I decided I wanted to be an actor after my first time on stage. In Ms. taylor's class, we put on skits for our parents teachers and classmates. I played a duck in a doughnut shop I said, "I'd like a chocolate doughnut, please.

The owner asked me "Will that be cash or charge."

"Put it on my bill" I quacked. the audience laughed and laughed. I was hooked on acting. it felt great Now I'm trying out for the lead part in the next school play. No more ducks for this actor!

Try It!

▶ **Write a story in one paragraph about something interesting or funny that happened to you. It might have taken place at school or at home. Include people talking. Give a title to your story. Proofread and edit your finished story for punctuation and capitalization.**

For more about punctuation and capitalization, see Chapter 15, beginning on page 402 of *Voyages in English*.

- Prewriting
- Drafting
- Revising
- Proofreading
- **Publishing**

STEP 5

Publishing

The last step in the writing process is to publish your story. When you publish, you share your story with others.

When Keisha published, she followed these steps.

- She copied over her personal narrative neatly in her best handwriting.
- She checked to be sure nothing got left out as she copied.
- She reread to be sure there were no mistakes.
- She prepared her story to be part of a class book.

Now might be a good time for you to turn back to page 16 and take another look at Keisha's completed personal narrative.

One Publishing Plan

Keisha's whole class wrote personal narratives. The class decided to publish all the stories in one big book. The students followed these steps.

- Each student attached a picture of himself or herself to the personal narrative.
- The students made a cover for their book, gave it the title *Just Us,* and then decorated it.
- Then the students bound together all their personal narratives.

DISCUSS **As a class, talk about these questions.**

1. Do you think Keisha's class had a good publishing plan? Why?
2. Would you be interested in reading the personal narratives in the book? Why?
3. Do you think the students' title is a good one for their collection of stories? What are other possibilities?

Expanding the Publishing Plan

Sometimes libraries and bookstores invite authors to read aloud from their published works. Have you ever been to a read-aloud? One of Keisha's friends thought it would be fun for the students to read their personal narratives for an audience of listeners. At the end of each reading, there could be a short question-and-answer time.

The students in the class followed these steps.

- With the help of their teacher, a special time was set aside for the readings.
- Students interested in reading signed up. Their teacher assigned the order in which students would read.
- A student host was selected to introduce each author and to lead the question-and-answer time.
- On the day of the reading, seats were arranged for the authors and their audience.

DISCUSS The students in Keisha's class asked the student authors these questions. What questions would you ask?

- How did you choose your topic?
- Do you find it hard to think of good writing ideas?
- What do you think you'll write about next?

DISCUSS/WRITE Can you think of other fun ways to share a writing assignment? Brainstorm ideas with classmates. Then write a plan for your favorite idea.

Making Introductions

The boy in *My Little Island* introduced himself to you in his personal narrative. He told you special things about himself and his experiences. When you meet people for the first time, you need to introduce yourself, too.

Here are some things to remember when introducing yourself:

- Speak clearly and slowly so you can be heard and understood.
- Tell something about yourself—hobbies, family, or favorite things.
- Use personal pronouns such as *I, me, my,* or *mine.*

Here is an introduction given by a boy on his first day at a new school:

> My name is Carlos. I live with my parents on Maple Avenue. We moved here from California. I like to play soccer. I have a pet lizard. It's great to be in your class.

DISCUSS **What interested you most about what Carlos said? What else could he have included in his introduction?**

Here's what one of Carlos's new classmates said:

> Hello, Carlos. My name's Doug. I have lived in this town all my life. I have a twin brother and a collie.

DISCUSS **What do Carlos and Doug have in common? What are some differences?**

Try It!

▶ **Imagine it's your first day at summer camp. Write an introduction for yourself. Read your introduction to a friend or family member.**

Putting It All Together

Keisha used the steps in the writing process to create her personal narrative about fishing.

STEP 1 Prewriting

Planning your writing
- Select a subject.
- Decide on your audience.
- Collect details.

STEP 2 Drafting
- Get all your ideas on paper.
- Don't worry about mistakes.

STEP 3 Revising

Improving your writing
- Read and review your draft.
- Share your draft with someone.
- Make changes to improve your writing.

STEP 4 Proofreading
- Check your spelling, capitalization, punctuation, and grammar.
- Write a neat final copy.
- Check one last time for errors.

STEP 5 Publishing
- Share your writing.

Writer's Corner

▶ **Write your own personal narrative. Remember, a personal narrative is a story about you, so let your personality and talents shine.**

CHAPTER 2

Writing a Paragraph

LESSON 1

Finding and Organizing an Idea

A paragraph is a group of sentences.
A paragraph tells about one specific idea.

Clubhouse Surprise

My friends and I thought it would be fun to build a clubhouse. First, we chose a secret spot in the back of my yard. We put boards on the ground under a big, old pine tree. We were sure no one could see us hidden under the branches. How surprised we were when a small skunk waddled in to join our first club meeting!

This paragraph tells about one specific idea. Do you know what it is? You can find the specific idea in the first sentence.

You were right if you said the specific idea is *building a clubhouse.* The other sentences in the paragraph tell more about what happens when the friends build the clubhouse.

About the Photograph

Do you ever like to just sit by yourself and think?
What do you like to think about?

Joe wants to write a paragraph. He begins to think of ideas about which to write. His teacher suggests that he ask himself some questions.

- What things do I like to do?
- What are my favorite games?
- What do I talk about with my friends?
- Do I take any special lessons?
- What is my favorite subject?
- Did I ever make anything? How did I make it?
- Have I taken a trip with my family?
- What animals do I like?
- Has anything interesting or funny happened to me or someone in my family?

Joe thought about the answers to these questions. He wrote them down on a piece of paper. Joe now has a treasure chest of ideas. He could use any of them for a paragraph. Joe's treasure chest of ideas looks like this.

After Joe chose a specific idea, he decided what he wanted to say about it. A word map is a fun way to organize ideas. Joe looked over his treasure chest of ideas and decided to write about a day at the beach. Here is Joe's word map.

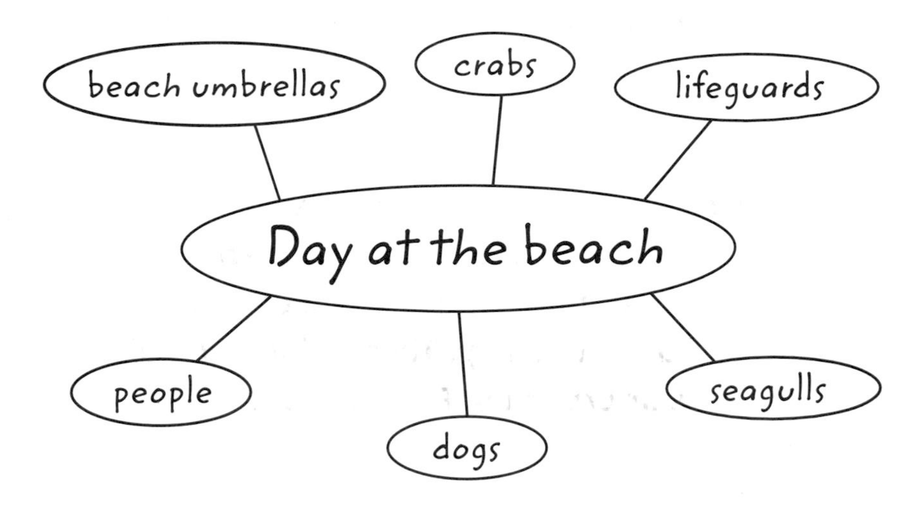

Did you notice that the specific idea is in an oval in the middle of the word map? In the other ovals are the things that Joe remembered about the beach. These are details that give more information about the specific idea.

Activity A

Think of things that interest you. Think of things about which you know. Use the questions on page 36 to help you create your own treasure chest of ideas. You can add other questions to the list if you like.

Activity B

Choose an idea from your treasure chest in Activity A and make a word map. Use Joe's word map on page 38 as a guide. First, put your specific idea in an oval in the middle of the word map. Then, think of details that give more information. Put these details in ovals around your specific idea.

Activity C

Choose another idea from your treasure chest. Make a word map, but leave the oval in the middle of the word map empty. Exchange papers with a partner. Read the details in your partner's word map, and see if you can guess the specific idea. See if your partner can guess the specific idea of your word map.

Writer's Corner

▶ **Read this paragraph. Make a word map to go with it. First find the specific idea. Place it in an oval in the middle of the word map. Then put all the details that add information around the specific idea.**

Writing Without Words

Fossils of plants and animals can help us understand the history of the earth. From a fossil of a flower found in Greenland, we learn that long ago Greenland had warm weather. Fossils of shellfish found in rocks high in the Alps and Rocky Mountains prove that these lands were once underwater. A fossil tells us that a rhinoceros is an old-timer from at least twenty million years ago! All these discoveries help us learn more and more about our amazing earth.

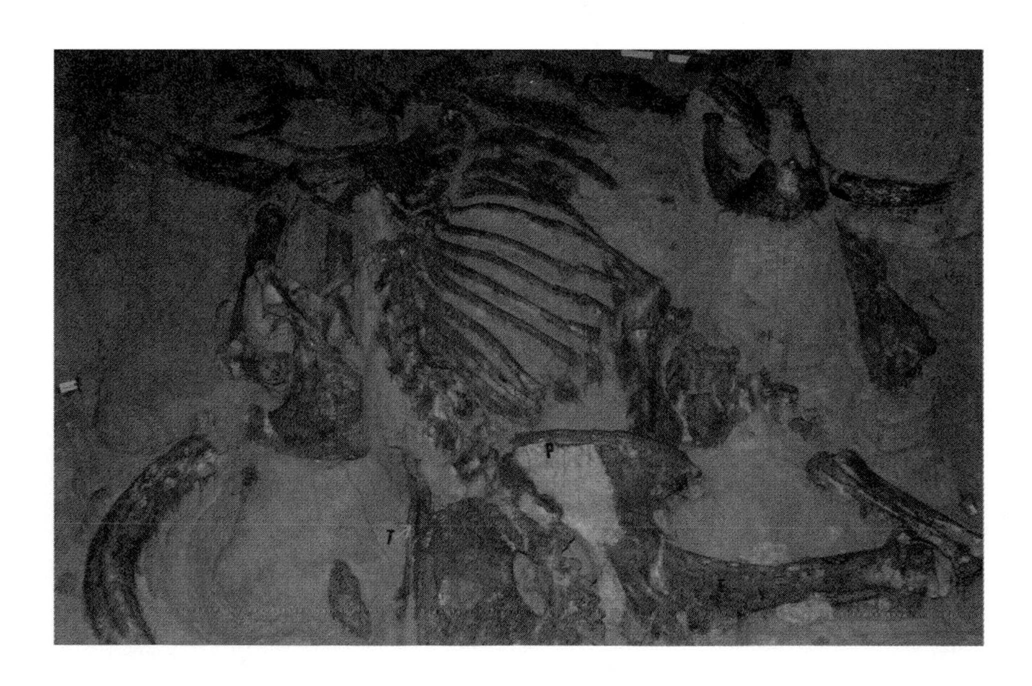

LESSON 2

Understanding the Paragraph

A paragraph is a group of sentences that tells about one specific idea. Each sentence in a paragraph has a special job.

A paragraph has three parts.

- A beginning sentence gives the specific idea of the paragraph.
- Middle sentences give more information about the specific idea.
- An ending sentence gives the last detail, asks a question, or tells how the writer feels.

Before Joe wrote his paragraph, he looked at his word map again.

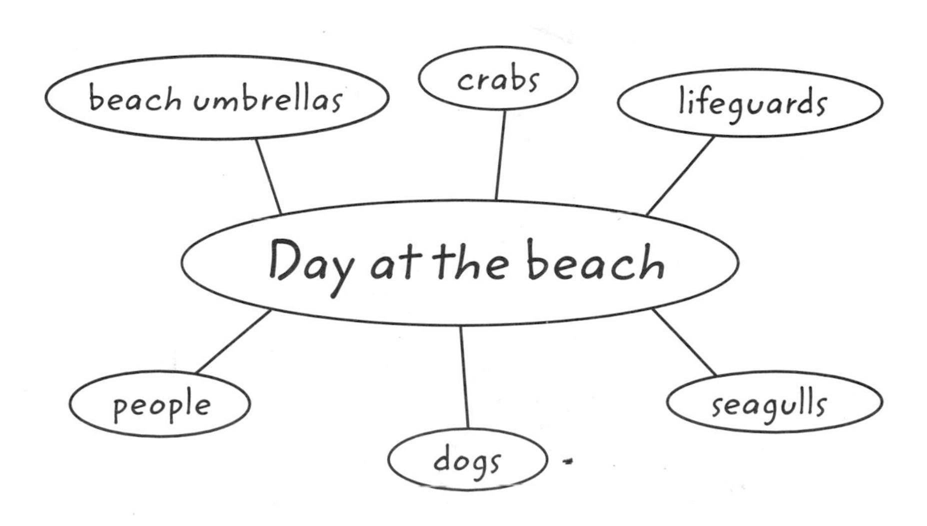

Joe used the ideas in his word map to write the paragraph "Beach Fun." Read Joe's paragraph, and then answer the questions.

Beach Fun

When you spend a day at the beach, there's always plenty to see. Bright beach umbrellas dot the sand with rainbows of color. Lifeguards, perched in high chairs, whistle at and signal to people in the water. Seagulls land and take off again. Dogs trot, crabs crawl, and joggers run past your blanket. With so much excitement all around, you could almost forget to eat.

1. How many sentences are in this paragraph?
2. What is the specific idea? Look for it in the beginning sentence.
3. What are the details in the middle sentences that give more information about the specific idea?
4. What does the ending sentence do?

Activity A

Tell the specific idea of each of these paragraphs. Then identify the beginning sentence, the middle sentences, and the ending sentence.

1

A Brown Ghost

The tree camping in my yard has changed its looks again. All the colorful leaves have fallen to the ground. The branches are brown and bare. Now it looks like a lonely ghost.

2

Windows

The windows in our classroom are like shining eyes. They watch the busy streets below. On clear days, they can see the whole town. When I come to school, I feel as if they give me a warm welcome.

3

Hard Workers

Our teeth work hard for us. They work as cutters so that we can bite off small amounts of food. Then they grind the food and make it easy to swallow. Without these hard workers, the food we eat could not be digested and used by our bodies.

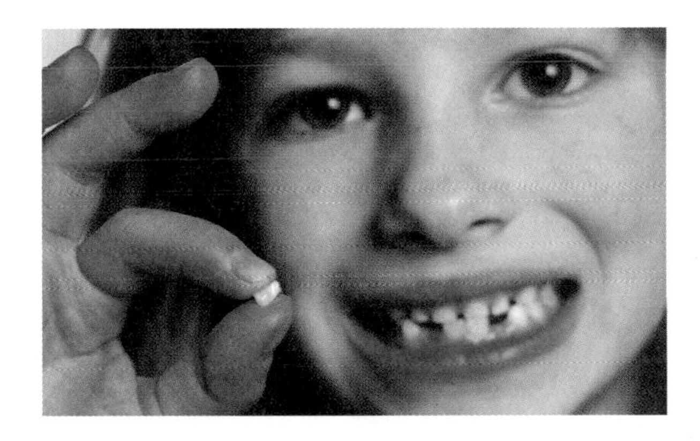

Writer's Corner

▶ **Complete the sentences in this paragraph. Remember that the beginning sentence should tell the specific idea. The middle sentences should add information. The ending sentence should give the last detail, ask a question, or tell the writer's feelings.**

School is _______ . _______ , my teacher, _______ .
My friends _______ . Every day I _______ .
Wouldn't you _______ ?

LESSON 3

Writing Beginning Sentences

The beginning sentence gives the specific idea of the paragraph. It should catch the reader's interest.

A beginning sentence

- gives the specific idea of the paragraph.
- makes the reader want to finish reading the paragraph.
- creates a picture in the reader's mind.

Springtime

The world wakes in spring after sleeping all winter. Trees, plants, and grass turn a vibrant green. Curious about their new playground, insects and birds roam about. The air smells fresh, like rain and sunshine at once. No other season makes the world come alive quite like springtime.

1. Does the beginning sentence give the specific idea of the paragraph? What is it?
2. Does the beginning sentence sound interesting? Do you want to read more?
3. Do the words in the beginning sentence create a picture in your mind?

Activity A

Only one sentence in each group is a good beginning sentence. Can you tell why?

GROUP 1

1. Brown bears can do somersaults.
2. Animals like to play just as much as human beings.
3. I like animals.

GROUP 2

1. Butterflies seemed to fill my stomach as I began to play my recital piece.
2. My recital piece was called "Dancing Leaves."
3. I put down my violin and took a bow.

Activity B

Write a beginning sentence for each paragraph.

1

The Pretzel Man

_______ . He stands at the corner near Wilson School with his delicious pretzels for sale. Just hand him a quarter, and he slips a warm pretzel into a bag for you. Even when we don't buy anything, his happy smile brightens our day.

2

Horseback Riding

_______ . My horse was trotting very fast when he tripped on a log and threw me off. That taught me to be more watchful. Now I look down more, and I don't always go so fast. I've become a much more careful rider.

Writer's Corner

▶ **Choose two of these ideas and write a beginning sentence for each. Read them to a partner and ask for suggestions.**

A. Saturday Fun
B. My First Time to . . .
C. A Special Trip
D. An Accident
E. A Pet Gets into Trouble
F. My Last Birthday
G. A Big Success
H. A Dream I've Had

LESSON 4

Writing Middle Sentences

The middle sentences give more information about the specific idea.

Middle sentences have a very important job—they add details to the paragraph. These details tell about the specific idea given in the beginning sentence.

In this paragraph, the beginning sentence gives the specific idea—my hamster is cute. Notice how each middle sentence adds a detail.

A Ball of Gold

My hamster is the cutest one in our neighborhood. Short yellow-brown fur covers her little, round body. Her stubby legs run on the wheel all night long. Alert brown eyes stare at you from her gentle face. I wouldn't want any other pet but Butterscotch.

In this paragraph, the middle sentences give three details. Can you name the details?

Activity A

Here are a beginning sentence and an ending sentence. Write three or four details that tell about the specific idea.

> To find my birthday present, I had to go on a treasure hunt. ______________________
>
> ____
>
> ____
>
> I had as much fun hunting for my present as I did opening it.

Here are another beginning sentence and an ending sentence. Write three or four details that tell about the specific idea.

> Balloon day is the best day of the whole year.
>
> ____
>
> ____
>
> This day seems to fly by, just like the balloons.

Activity B

Read this paragraph. Find the sentence that does *not* tell about the specific idea. Write a sentence to take the place of the misfit sentence.

Animal Chatter

Many animals love to talk. Birds, monkeys, and dolphins do the most chatting. They make sounds to call to their young. My mom rings a bell when it's time for me to come home. Sometimes they warn other members of their group that danger is near. If they are happy or sad, these animals talk about it. What fun it would be to understand them!

Writer's Corner

▶ **Here is a beginning sentence. Write at least three middle sentences that give information about the specific idea.**

Last Tuesday was one of the best days I have ever had.

Writing Ending Sentences

The ending sentence gives the last detail, asks a question, or tells how the writer feels.

An ending sentence can do different jobs. It can

- give the last detail.
- ask the reader a question.
- tell the writer's feelings about the specific idea.

Read this paragraph and the three possible ending sentences. Why would each sentence be a good ending sentence? Which one would you choose? Why?

Waffles Save the Day

Everybody loves ice-cream cones, but they didn't always exist. In 1904, an ice-cream stand ran out of dishes. A nearby waffle maker noticed the problem. He rolled up one of his waffles and placed a scoop of ice cream on top.

A. That first ice-cream cone was sold in a minute.
B. Wasn't that a clever idea?
C. Now I wouldn't want to eat my ice cream any other way.

Activity A

Which ending sentence do you like best? Why?

> **A Strange Clown**
>
> Yesterday my friends and I had a great time building a snowman. We rolled the soft, flaky snow into two big balls and one small one. Then we piled them one on top of the other. We added two stones for eyes and a carrot for a nose.

A. Is it any wonder that we welcome a snowstorm?
B. We were very proud of our jolly sculpture.
C. Then we perched a funny hat on his head.

Activity B

Read these paragraphs. Write an ending sentence for each one.

1

My Furry Friend

Tatters is a friendly stray dog that I found on the street. His sad eyes and droopy ears made me like him at once. His short stumpy tail kept wagging. He must have been happy. ________________ .

2

Native American Games

Native Americans played many games. Some played "snow snake," which is like shuffleboard. In this game, they slid darts across the ice to see which one went the farthest. Others played a game that used a ball and a basket just as we do in basketball. This game is also like soccer because they couldn't touch the ball with their hands! In the "hoop and pole" game, players tried to throw spears through a rolling hoop. ________________ .

Writer's Corner

▶ **Write a paragraph. Use the specific idea below to write a beginning sentence. Use the details in any order to write the best middle sentences you can. Then write an ending sentence.**

A Small Wonder

Specific Idea: Hummingbirds are among the smallest birds in the world.

Details:

- The nest is the size of a thimble.
- At birth, without feathers, the bird is about the size of a bumblebee.
- Four newly hatched birds can fit on a teaspoon.
- An adult bird weighs about the same as a penny.
- The smallest hummingbird is two inches long.
- The largest hummingbird is nine inches long.

LESSON 6

Giving the Paragraph a Title

A title is the name of a piece of writing.

Have you ever read a title that you really liked? Titles are important because they are the first thing you read.

A good title has sparkle. It should be short and give a clue about your paragraph.

Activity A

Read these titles. Which titles sound interesting? Why? Which titles do *not* sound interesting? Why not?

1. My First Plane Ride
2. Alone in the Woods
3. Talking Hands
4. Summertime
5. The Surprise Party
6. Wacky Weekend
7. Snow Sculpture
8. My Trip in Space

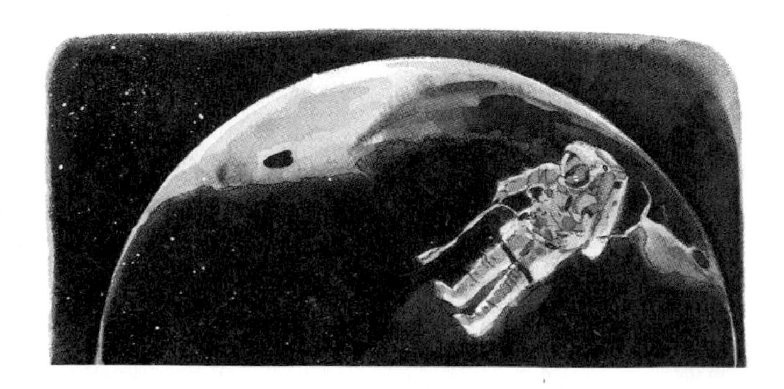

Activity B

Read the paragraph. Write an interesting title for it.

An invisible friend played with me last week. I was roller-skating outside on a windy afternoon. When I went up the street, the wind pushed against me and I had to skate very hard. When I came back down the street, the wind pushed me from behind and I rolled along with no effort at all. I really had a good time with that playful wind.

Writer's Corner

▶ **Here are some specific ideas. Think about details that could be included in a paragraph about each idea. Then create an interesting title for three of these ideas.**

A. You were on a TV show.
B. You returned from a trip on a space shuttle.
C. You rode in a bicycle race.
D. You carved an animal out of a bar of soap.
E. You received a special reward.
F. You received a gerbil for a pet.

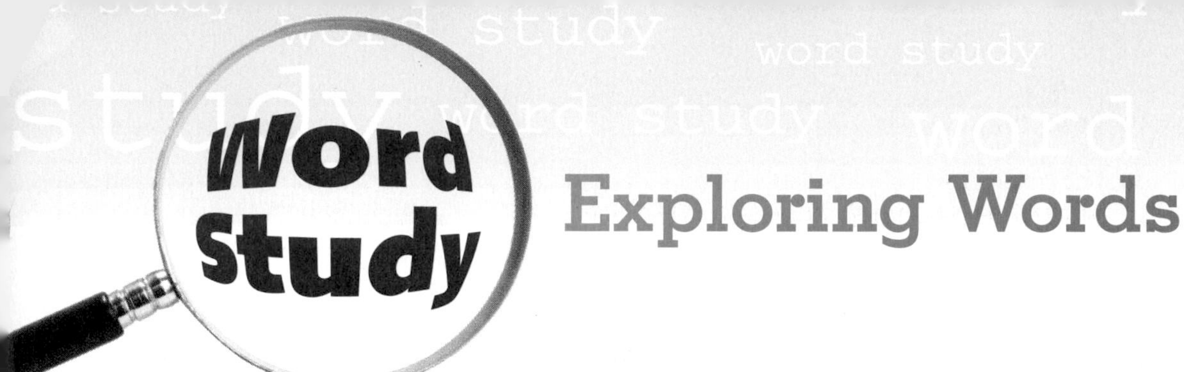

Exploring Words

Synonyms

Synonyms are words that have the same or almost the same meaning.

Here are pairs of synonyms. Do these pairs have

A. meanings that are almost the same?
or
B. meanings that are very different?

small—little   town—city   shiny—bright   rip—tear

These pairs of synonyms have meanings that are almost the same.

Activity A

Read these rhymes. Complete each rhyme with a correct synonym for the word in italics.

1. The *city* bus goes up and down,
   Then moves on quickly to the next _______ .
2. A *tear* in your paper you don't want to see.
   If you're not careful, a _______ there will be.
3. *Shiny* stars fill the sky at night.
   They glow in the dark and look so _______ .
4. My new baby brother is very *small.*
   His _______ fingers can't hold a ball.

Antonyms

Antonyms are words that are opposite in meaning. Antonyms are opposites.

Here are pairs of antonyms. Do these pairs have

A. meanings that are almost the same?

or

B. meanings that are very different?

good—bad   out—in   happy—sad   thick—thin

These pairs of antonyms have meanings that are opposite.

Activity B

Read these rhymes. Complete each rhyme with a correct antonym (opposite) of the word in italics.

1. When the weather's *good,* it isn't _______ .
When a clown is *happy,* she isn't _______ .

2. When the cat is *out,* he's never _______ .
When a pancake's *thick,* it's never _______ .

Activity C

Use an antonym in place of each word in italics.

1. The soup was so *thin* you could eat it with a fork.
2. I felt *good* when my friend went home.
3. A hummingbird flew *in* the window.
4. Five *sad* chicks followed the hen.
5. Megan writes *bad* mystery stories.

Homophones

Homophones are words that sound alike but are spelled differently and have different meanings.

Here are pairs of homophones.

know—no sea—see buy—by

Homophones sound alike. Say each pair of homophones. Homophones are spelled differently. Notice the spelling of each pair. Homophones have different meanings. Study these pairs of homophones.

Know and *No*

Which word is correct in each sentence?

A. The girls (know, no) the answer. (having knowledge)
B. (Know, No) pie was left on the plate. (not any)

Sea and *See*

Which word is correct in each sentence?

A. Many fish swim in the (sea, see). (ocean)
B. Can you (sea, see) the stars in the sky? (to look with your eyes)

Buy and *By*

Which word is correct in each sentence?

A. At the store, Gloria will (buy, by) a candy bar. (to pay a price for)
B. Kevin's house is (buy, by) the lake. (near, at thc side of)

Activity D

Use the homophones *know* and *no* correctly in these sentences.

1. _______ two snowflakes are alike.
2. Do you _______ how to square dance?
3. I _______ a secret code.
4. We had _______ bluejays at the feeder.
5. Newton wanted to _______ why apples fell down instead of up.

Activity E

Use the homophones *sea* and *see* correctly in these sentences.

1. Do you _______ the ladybugs on those leaves?
2. I want to _______ an eclipse of the moon.
3. A pelican bobbed up and down on the _______ .
4. The cat opened one eye to _______ the mice.
5. Columbus liked to sail the _______ .

Activity F

Use the homophones *buy* and *by* correctly in these sentences.

1. Did you _______ a baseball cap yet?
2. A spider sat _______ Miss Muffet.
3. Did Carly _______ a hot dog with onions?
4. The boys will _______ roses for their moms.
5. _______ the tent stood a brown bear.

Contractions

A contraction is a short way to write some words. A contraction always uses an apostrophe.

Here are two contractions.

I am—I'm let us—let's

I'm is the contraction or short way of writing *I am.*

What letter is missing in *I'm*?
What takes the place of this letter?

Let's is the contraction or short way of writing *let us.*

What letter is missing in *let's*?
What takes the place of this letter?

Activity G

Use the contraction *I'm* in place of *I am* and the contraction *let's* in place of *let us.*

1. *I am* going to the subway.
2. Every morning *I am* early for the bus.
3. *Let us* mark the spot with an X.
4. *I am* blowing up balloons for the contest.
5. After dinner, *let us* walk around the block.

Activity H

Imagine you are at the place described in each of these riddles. Answer each riddle. Use the contraction *I'm* in each answer.

1. You see clowns and acrobats. Where are you?
2. You smell home cooking. Where are you?
3. You hear the crowd yell, "Home run!" Where are you?
4. You see books, desks, and friends. Where are you?
5. You swim and build sand castles. Where are you?

Activity I

Answer each of these questions. Use the contraction *let's* in each answer.

1. Shall we go to the amusement park or to the zoo?
2. Shall we take the train or the bus?
3. Shall we meet at three o'clock or four o'clock?
4. Shall we bring our lunch or buy our lunch?
5. Shall we feed the ponies or feed the pigs?

WRITER'S WORKSHOP

A Day in Your Life

What do you know more about than anyone else? You, of course. Everyone's life is full of interesting experiences, and so is yours. Think of an important event in your life. Write about it. Bind everyone's paragraphs together to make a class *Who's Who* book.

Prewriting

Make a list of interesting things you have done. Then choose one event to write about. Ask yourself questions like these to help you get started.

- ❑ What is the funniest thing that ever happened to me?
- ❑ What is the scariest thing?
- ❑ What was my most embarrassing moment?
- ❑ What awards or prizes have I won?
- ❑ What have I done that most people in my class have not done?
- ❑ What famous people have I met?
- ❑ What interesting places have I visited?
- ❑ When did I use a special talent?

Choose a topic and write down everything you can remember about it. Use a word map to help you. After you finish your word map, number your ideas to show their order. Then you'll be ready to start writing.

Joanna, a third grader, made this word map.

Drafting

Your word map helped you sort out your ideas in your mind. Now it's time to put your ideas on paper. Start with a beginning sentence that makes your reader want to read more.

Here is Joanna's first sentence:

> Sometimes I can't wait to grow bigger, but one day I was glad to be small.

After you write your beginning sentence, write the middle sentences. Use the numbered details from your word map.

Write an ending. Here's what Joanna wrote:

> Mom hugged me and said, "You're my big girl, but I'm really glad you're still small right now."

Finally, write a title for your paragraph.

Guidelines for Writing Your Draft

1. Write your draft as soon as you finish your word map.
2. Keep your prewriting notes beside you.
3. Write quickly.
4. Don't stop to look up words or check your grammar.
5. Don't try to make your draft perfect.
6. Just try to get all your ideas written down.

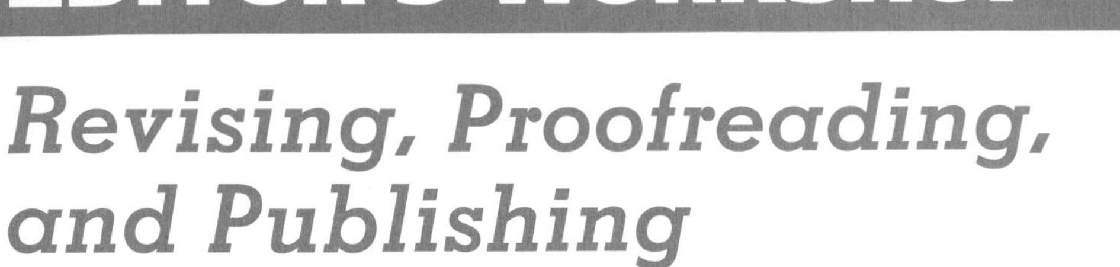

Revising, Proofreading, and Publishing

Revising

Time to Take Another Look

Revising means changing something to make it better. When you revise your paragraph, you reread it and think about it.

Ask yourself these questions to help you revise:

- ❑ Do I need to make my first sentence more interesting?
- ❑ Do I need to add any important details that I left out?
- ❑ Do I need to take out any extra details?
- ❑ Do I need to change the order of the details so my paragraph makes sense?
- ❑ Do I need to rewrite anything that is not clear?
- ❑ Do I need to choose more interesting words?
- ❑ Does my title tell what my paragraph is about?

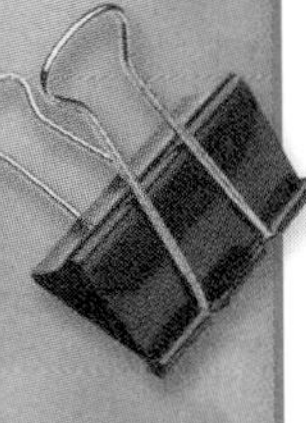

Use a colored pencil to make your changes. That will help make your changes stand out. Then talk about your changes with a partner or with your teacher.

Read Aloud
Read your draft to a partner. Ask if your partner understands your story.

Proofreading

Time to Look at Capitalization, Punctuation, and Spelling

Now your ideas are just the way you want them to be. But before you write your final copy, you'll need to check your capitalization, punctuation, spelling, and grammar. The checklist will help you.

- ❑ Did I indent the first word of my paragraph?
- ❑ Did I begin each sentence and proper noun with a capital letter?
- ❑ Did I use the correct mark of punctuation at the end of each sentence?
- ❑ Did I spell each word correctly?

Using a Computer
If you used a computer to write your paragraph, run the spell-checking program before you begin proofreading.

Publishing

Time to Share

Publishing is sharing your best work with others.

To publish, follow these steps:

1. Use your neatest handwriting to copy your revised draft.
2. After you finish, proofread your final copy one more time.
3. If possible, bring in a photo of yourself and attach it to your paragraph.

Make the class *Who's Who* book.

1. Collect everyone's final paragraph.
2. Make a cover for your book.
3. Write a title, such as *Who's Who.*
4. Bind the pages and the cover together with yarn or a stapler.
5. Add your book to the classroom library so everyone can enjoy reading it.

CHAPTER 3

Making the Paragraph Better

LESSON 1

Using Strong Verbs

Action verbs create pictures.

Read these two paragraphs.

1

Success at Last

I *wanted* to skateboard. I *asked* my brother to teach me. When I tried, I *fell* off the board as soon as I *got* on. Next I *went* into a tree. I was ready to give up when my mom said she would *show* me. I was *surprised* that she could skateboard. Soon I *skated* past my brother. He still wonders how I *got* to be such a terrific skateboarder.

2

Success at Last

I *couldn't wait* to skateboard. I *begged* my brother to teach me. When I tried, I *tumbled* off the board as soon as I *stepped* on. Next I *crashed* into a tree. I was ready to give up when my mom said she would *help* me. I was *shocked* that she could skateboard. Soon I *zoomed* past my brother. He still wonders how I *learned* to be such a terrific skateboarder.

About the Photograph

Writing, like skateboarding, takes practice to learn to do it better. Practice the tips in this chapter to help you become a better writer.

When you write sentences with strong verbs, your reader can see the action clearly. Did you notice that the second paragraph uses stronger action verbs? Name the stronger verbs. Does the second paragraph give you a clearer picture of the action?

Activity A

Read each set of sentences. Does the verb in each sentence create a different picture? Add two more sentences to each group. Use strong verbs to show other actions that dragons, winged horses, and dinosaurs might do.

A

- The dragon snorts.
- The dragon breathes.
- The dragon sneezes.

B

- The winged horse flies.
- The winged horse soars.
- The winged horse neighs.

C

- The dinosaur walks.
- The dinosaur trudges.
- The dinosaur plods.

Activity B

Use a new verb in place of the verb in italics in each sentence. Use strong verbs that paint clear pictures.

1. I *went* down the hill on my new sled.
2. I *put* my hand into the big bowl of candy.
3. The penguin *walked* toward me.
4. I *looked* at the rows of colorful sneakers in the window.
5. My puppy *likes* this dog chow.
6. Tina *laughed* when she saw me water the plastic plant.
7. My little brother *looked* everywhere for his sock.
8. We piled one block on top of the other until they *fell*.
9. The dish *broke* into many small pieces.
10. The class *picked* Collette as the winner.

Writer's Corner

▶ **Add strong action verbs to this paragraph.**

The fans _______ as the players ran onto the field. The cheerleaders _______ as they jumped up and down. The vendors _______ in and out of the seats, selling hot dogs and popcorn. Music _______ through the stadium. Everyone _______ when the game finally began.

LESSON 2

Using Colorful Adjectives

Adjectives add color to your writing.

Exact adjectives create pictures in the mind of the reader. When you use colorful adjectives, your reader can see, smell, hear, feel, and sometimes taste the thing you are writing about.

The *fierce* dragon blew *fiery* blasts of air.

The *graceful* winged horse flew over the *sparkling white* ground.

Activity A

Describe a park. Use two adjectives with each noun.

1. ________ ________ trees
2. ________ ________ pond
3. ________ ________ picnic tables
4. ________ ________ flowers
5. ________ ________ squirrels

Describe your classroom. Use two adjectives with each noun.

1. ________ ________ room
2. ________ ________ desks
3. ________ ________ windows
4. ________ ________ floor
5. ________ ________ lights

Activity B

Add a colorful adjective to describe each noun in italics.

1. *Balloons* floated in the *air.*
2. The *puppy* played with the *children.*
3. *Rain* poured from the *clouds.*
4. The *girl* picked a *bunch* of *flowers.*
5. We ate *brownies* for a *snack* after school.

Writer's Corner

▶ **Add adjectives to this paragraph. Use the list below the paragraph to help you. The way the room you describe looks, feels, and even smells will depend on which adjectives you choose.**

I walked slowly into the (1) _______ room. (2) _______ flowers sat on the (3) _______ , (4) _______ table in the corner. Next to the table was a (5) _______ chair. A (6) _______ book was lying by the chair on the (7) _______ floor.

(1)	stuffy	dark	bright
(2)	Colorful	Drooping	Fake
(3)	old	shaky	polished
(4)	broken	dusty	white
(5)	velvet	wooden	soft
(6)	torn	new	thick
(7)	spotless	dirty	sticky

LESSON 3

Combining Subjects

If two sentences have the same predicate, the subjects can be combined to make one sentence.

A good writer tries to use smooth, interesting sentences. Short, choppy sentences that repeat the same idea make a paragraph boring. Look at these sentences about David and Michael. Notice how they can be combined or joined into one sentence.

David dug for worms. Michael dug for worms.

These sentences repeat the same information—*dug for worms*—in the predicate. The subjects are different—*David, Michael.* You can make one smooth sentence by combining subjects with the word *and.*

David and Michael dug for worms.

Some sentences have different predicates, but the meaning of each predicate is almost the same. You can combine the subjects and then choose either predicate to complete the sentence. Try to choose the stronger predicate. Notice how these sentences about David and Michael are combined into one sentence.

David walked through the woods. Michael hiked through the woods.

David and Michael hiked through the woods.

Activity A

These pairs of sentences have the same predicate. Combine each pair to make one smooth sentence.

1. Joe played the piano. Miriam played the piano.
2. Puppies try to catch their tails. Lion cubs try to catch their tails.
3. Erica hit a home run. Katrina hit a home run.
4. Beth went to the store. Dad went to the store.
5. José washed the car. Rick washed the car.

Activity B

Combine each pair of sentences into one sentence.

1. The German shepherd ran down the street. The cocker spaniel raced down the street.
2. The president stepped out of the car. The secret service agents got out of the car.
3. Carlos read his report to the class. Marshall presented his report to the class.
4. Kim got the leaves. I raked the leaves.
5. Ms. Johnson spoke to my mom. The principal talked to my mom.

Writer's Corner

▶ **Combine the subjects of each pair of choppy sentences that share the same idea. From the ten sentences in this paragraph, try to create five smooth sentences.**

Company for Dinner

Marina helped set the table. Her brother, Antonio, helped set the table. Aunt Nora arrived about 6:30. Grandma and Grandpa came at 6:30. Mom was happy to see them. Dad was happy, too. The chicken was delicious. The apple pie tasted delicious. Aunt Nora thanked everyone before she went home. Grandma and Grandpa said thank you to everyone before they went home.

Lesson 4 Combining Predicates

If two sentences have the same subject, the predicates can be combined to make one sentence.

Sentences in a paragraph often give information about the same subject. When sentences have the same subject, you can combine the predicates to make one sentence. Look at these sentences. Notice how they can be combined or joined into one sentence.

> My tabby cat sits in the sun. My tabby cat purrs softly.

These sentences give information about the same subject—*My tabby cat.* The predicates are different—*sits in the sun, purrs softly.* You can make one smooth sentence by combining predicates with the word *and.*

> My tabby cat sits in the sun and purrs softly.

Activity A

Find the two predicate verbs in each sentence.

1. My dog, Sparky, rolled over and played dead.
2. After the party, I waved good-bye and left.
3. The hungry lion stalked through the forest and captured his prey.
4. An unusual bird swooped down and landed in our yard.
5. My uncle Bob wrote and illustrated a book.

Activity B

These pairs of sentences have the same subject. Combine each pair to make one smooth sentence.

1. The elephant walked into the circus ring. The elephant stood on the red ball.
2. My dad bought the hamburgers. My dad grilled the hamburgers.
3. I earned ten dollars. I spent most of it before I got home.
4. Rosa made the piñata. Rosa spun it around.
5. The monkey ate four bananas. The monkey threw the peels away.

Writer's Corner

▶ **Write two predicates for each subject. Use predicates that begin with the same letter as the subject. The first one is done as an example.**

SUBJECT	PREDICATE	PREDICATE
elephants	eat	exercise
trucks		
robots		
parrots		
fireworks		
dentists		

LESSON 5

Combining Sentences

Short sentences that tell about the same idea can be combined.

You can use the word *and* to combine subjects and predicates. You can also use the word *and* to combine two short sentences that give information about the same idea. Look at these sentences. Notice how they can be combined or joined into one sentence.

> Todd will be the leader. We will follow.
> Todd will be the leader, *and* we will follow.

A comma is used after the first sentence. The word *and* is used next. The second sentence does not begin with a capital letter unless the first word is a proper noun or the pronoun *I*.

Activity A

Combine each pair of short sentences with a comma and the word *and.*

1. I brought tacos. My friend made burritos.
2. Orange trees grow in California. Apple trees blossom in Washington.
3. The rainbow arched across the sky. I counted the colors in it.
4. Grandma takes her turn at bat. I run the bases for her.
5. The leader gave directions. The scouts pitched their tents.
6. The cat was lost. The dog looked for her.
7. Paula painted the pictures. Suzy hung them on the wall.
8. The guitar stood in the corner. The flute was on the chair.
9. Thanksgiving is almost here. My parents are planning the dinner.
10. Our park has an ice rink. We sometimes skate on it.

Activity B

Write your own idea after the word *and* in each sentence. Use a different subject and predicate. Be sure the ideas go together.

1. Alice draws the pictures, and _______ .
2. Mindy weeds the garden, and _______ .
3. I had the chicken pox, and _______ .
4. The owl hunts for food at night, and _______ .
5. Kelly put jelly on the bread, and _______ .

▶ **Rewrite this paragraph. Combine the sentences that tell about the same idea.**

The Fun Fair had finally begun. Everyone was excited. Kim worked at the popcorn booth. Mrs. Carter grilled hot dogs. Linda sold raffle tickets. Mr. Palmer organized a softball game. All the students had a chance to play. By the end of the day, we were tired. Everyone was ready to go home.

LESSON 6

Revising the Paragraph

When you revise a sentence or a paragraph, you change words and combine ideas to improve your writing.

You have learned how to make your sentences and paragraphs clear and how to create a picture in your reader's mind. You have learned

- to use strong verbs in place of weak ones.

  Fred *jogged* through the park.

- to use colorful adjectives.

  Fred jogged through the *busy* park.

- to combine subjects.

  Fred and *Fran* jogged through the park.

- to combine predicates.

  Fred *jogged through the park* and *puffed up the hill.*

- to combine short sentences.

  Fred jogged through the park, and *Fran waded in the pond.*

Activity A

Read these two paragraphs. Notice how the second paragraph is a revision of the first paragraph.

1

A Show

The third graders were having a show. Dale read a poem. Christa read a poem. Nancy played a song on the accordion. Ron played his clarinet. Eve sang a song. Eve danced at the same time. Kenny did gymnastics. Calvin jumped on the trampoline. When it was over, everyone clapped.

2

Talent Galore

The third graders presented their spring talent show. Dale and Christa read funny poems. Nancy played a lively song on the accordion, and Ron played his clarinet. Eve sang a popular song and danced at the same time. Kenny performed amazing gymnastics, and Calvin tumbled on the trampoline. When the exciting show was over, everyone clapped and cheered.

Find one or more places in the second paragraph where the writer did the following:

1. used adjectives to make a clearer picture.
2. used stronger verbs to make a clearer picture.
3. combined subjects.
4. combined predicates.
5. combined sentences.

Writer's Corner

▶ **Use the directions below to revise this paragraph about redwood trees.**

Tall Trees

[1]My family went on a trip to California. [2]I went on a trip to California, too. [3]We rode a train through a redwood forest. [4]We saw many trees. [5]Our guide told us about these trees. [6]Our guide said that some get to be three hundred feet tall. [7]Then he showed us a seed. [8]I could hardly believe that a little seed could become such a big tree.

1. Combine the subjects in sentences 1 and 2.
2. Use an adjective to describe *train* in sentence 3.
3. Use a stronger verb for *saw* in sentence 4.
4. Combine the predicates in sentences 5 and 6.
5. Use an adjective to describe *guide* in sentence 5.
6. Use an adjective to describe *trees* in sentence 5.
7. Use a stronger verb for *get* in sentence 6.
8. Use an adjective to describe *seed* in sentence 7.
9. Use a more colorful adjective than *big* to describe *tree* in sentence 8.
10. Write a more interesting title.

Exploring Words

Synonyms

Synonyms are words that have the same or almost the same meaning.

Here are synonyms you have learned.

small—little	shiny—bright
town—city	rip—tear

Here are new synonyms.

pal—friend	speak—talk
gift—present	bring—carry

Activity A

Complete each sentence with a new synonym. Do not use the same word twice.

1. _______ the sports magazine to me, please.
2. Vince is a _______ of mine.
3. Where did you hide my birthday _______ ?
4. Did you get a chance to _______ to the actor?
5. The telescope was too heavy for me to _______ .
6. The _______ was wrapped in purple paper.
7. Try to _______ in a loud, clear voice.
8. Terri and her _______ climbed into the tree house.

Activity B

Use a synonym in place of each word in italics.

1. I will buy a *present* for the new baby.
2. Did you know that some computers can *talk?*
3. Janet picked up the *bright,* new dime.
4. I had a *tear* in my old jeans.
5. Did you wrap my *gift?*
6. Please *carry* the salad to the table.
7. My *friend* Tom has a pet rabbit.
8. Did you see the umpire *speak* to the pitcher?

Antonyms

Antonyms are words that are opposite in meaning. Antonyms are opposites.

Here are antonyms you have learned.

good—bad out—in happy—sad thick—thin

Here are new antonyms.

first—last up—down fast—slow soft—hard

Activity C

Complete each sentence with the antonym of the word in italics. Use a new antonym.

1. December is the *last* month of the year. January is the _______ month.
2. After Mom put the curtains *up,* one fell _______ .
3. Some pretzels are *hard* and some are _______ .
4. The tortoise finished the race *first,* and the hare finished _______ .
5. The snail was too *slow,* but the worm wasn't very _______ either.

Activity D

Use an antonym from page 85 in place of each word in italics.

1. The trout swam *up* the stream.
2. Our team finished *last* in the relay race.
3. I am *happy* that you have my turtle.
4. Matt drew a *thick,* white line with the chalk.
5. The bear's bed was too *soft.*

Homophones

Homophones are words that sound alike but are spelled differently and have different meanings.

Here are homophones you have learned.

know—no sea—see buy—by

Here are new homophones.

deer—dear meet—meat ate—eight

Deer and *Dear*

Which word is correct in each sentence?

A. A (deer, dear) lives in a forest. (animal)
B. A baby is (deer, dear) to its parents. (much loved)

Meat and *Meet*

Which word is correct in each sentence?

A. I will (meet, meat) you at the corner. (come together)
B. For supper we had (meet, meat) and potatoes. (food from animals)

Ate and Eight

Which word is correct in each sentence?

A. There are (ate, eight) bikes outside. (number 8)
B. The boys (ate, eight) in the cafeteria. (chewed and swallowed)

Activity E

Use the homophones *deer* and *dear* correctly in these sentences.

1. Two _______ followed the cows into the barn.
2. _______ Peggy, please visit soon.
3. When Heidi left, her _______ grandfather missed her.
4. None of the _______ had antlers.
5. In her letter, she wrote, "_______ Jo."

Activity F

Use the homophones *meat* and *meet* correctly in these sentences.

1. _______ me at the merry-go-round.
2. Hamburgers are made from _______ .
3. I've always wanted to _______ Superman.
4. The computer club will _______ today.
5. Jimmy grilled the _______ over the fire.

Activity G

Use the homophones *ate* and *eight* correctly in these sentences.

1. _______ black crows sat on the scarecrow's arm.
2. My brother felt sick after he _______ the cake.
3. Jenny quickly _______ the salad.
4. Four times two equals _______ .
5. A dog _______ the flowers on Mrs. Purdy's hat.

Activity H

Complete each sentence with the correct homophone.

1. This package of (meat, meet) is heavy.
2. The donkey (eight, ate) the flowers in the field.
3. A (deer, dear) leaped over the stream.
4. When will I (see, sea) the North Star?
5. Sean left his bike (buy, by) the tree.

Contractions

A contraction is a short way to write some words. A contraction always uses an apostrophe.

Here are contractions you have learned.

I am—I'm	let us—let's

Here are new contractions.

I will—I'll	we will—we'll
she will—she'll	you will—you'll
he will—he'll	they will—they'll

What letters are missing in each contraction? What takes the place of these letters?

Activity I

Use the list on page 88 to help you give the contractions for these words.

1. she will ________
2. you will ________
3. we will ________

Use the list on page 88 to help you give the meaning of these contractions.

4. they'll ________
5. I'm ________
6. let's ________

Activity J

Use a contraction in place of the words in italics.

1. Next summer *I will* be going to the mountains.
2. *We will* stay in a cabin by the lake.
3. *I am* taking my camera.
4. If Dad can, *he will* take pictures of the deer.
5. *They will* look pretty when they are grazing.

WRITER'S WORKSHOP

Describing a Place

What is the best place you ever visited? Maybe you went on a family vacation to a faraway place. Or maybe your favorite vacation spot is right down the road. Write about a place you and your family visited. Then set up a class travel display.

Prewriting

Think of places you have visited with your family, and choose one place you really enjoyed. Close your eyes, and try to remember everything you can about the place.

Use your five senses: see, hear, feel, smell, and taste. Ask yourself questions like these to help you remember.

- What did I see there?
- Did the place look different from my own neighborhood?
- What sounds did I hear?
- Were nighttime sounds different from daytime sounds?
- Were the smells country smells or city smells?
- What did it feel like?
- Was it windy, cold, or hot?
- Did I taste anything special?

Make a chart for all five senses. List your ideas in the chart. Write the name of the place at the top.

The Seashore

(eye)	(ear)	(hand)	(nose)	(mouth)
bright, blue water	roaring waves	hot sand	sunscreen	salty water
colorful beach towels	happy laughter	cold water	smoke	roasted corn at barbecue
	crying seagulls	smooth rocks		

Drafting

Now you're ready to use your chart to write your draft. Remember, when you write a draft, put down your ideas as quickly as you can. Don't worry about spelling, punctuation, or grammar. You'll have a chance to check those things later.

Start with a beginning sentence to tell your readers where the place is. Choose details from your chart to write your middle sentences. Finish by writing an ending sentence and a title.

Read Kerry's first draft. Don't look for mistakes. Instead, try to imagine yourself at the seashore. Does Kerry's draft make you feel as if you are there?

A Day at the Seashore

I like to go to the seashore with my famly. We kno we're almost there when we hear the noise of the waves. Sometimes it can be hard to find a place to park the car. I never can wait to race across the hot sand and jump into the cold water. After playing in the water, it feels good to lie on my towel and dry off. I close my eyes and listen to seagulls crying and people laughing When I smell smoke from the bonfire, I open my eyes. Soon well be eatin tasty, roasted corn as we watch the fiery red sun sink into the osean.

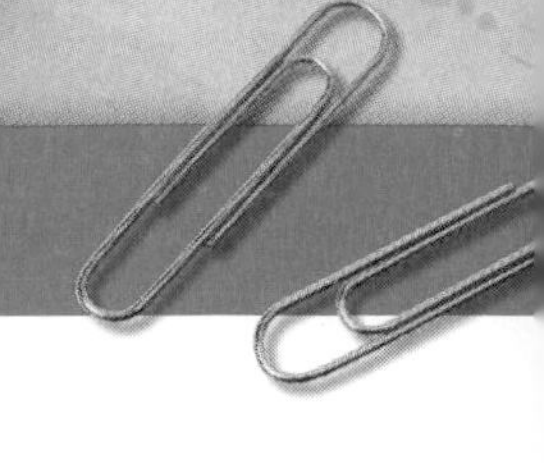

Revising, Proofreading, and Publishing

Revising

Time to Take Another Look

When you revise your paragraph, you think of ways to make it better. Imagine that you've never been to the place you wrote about. Would your paragraph make readers who have never been there feel that they know just what the place is like?

Ask yourself these questions to help you revise.

- ❑ Does my first sentence tell my reader what place I am writing about?
- ❑ Do I need to add any details to make the place seem more real?
- ❑ Do I need to take out any details that don't help to describe the place?
- ❑ Do I need to rewrite anything that is hard to understand?
- ❑ Do I need to choose more interesting sensory words?
- ❑ Does my title let readers know what my paragraph is about?

Make the changes you think will make your paragraph better. Then find a partner who has never been to the place you described. Read your paragraph aloud to your partner.

Be an Editor

Listen carefully as your partner reads aloud. Don't just say, "That's good." Be specific about something you like. You might say, "*Cry* is a good word for the sound seagulls make." Don't be afraid to mention something that doesn't seem to work, such as, "I don't think the sentence about parking the car really describes the seashore."

Pay special attention to the words you chose. The words "race across the hot sand" tell more than "go across the sand." What words would be better than "*hot* sand" and "*cold* water"?

Proofreading

Time to Look at Capitalization, Punctuation, and Spelling

Once your ideas sound just right, you can check your punctuation, capitalization, spelling, and grammar. This checklist will help you.

- ❑ Did I indent the first word of my descriptive paragraph?
- ❑ Did I begin each sentence, proper noun, and the word *I* with a capital letter?
- ❑ Did I use the correct mark of punctuation at the end of each sentence?
- ❑ Did I spell each word correctly?

Capitalizing the Name of a Place
Remember that the name of a common noun, such as *seashore,* is not capitalized. The name of a particular place, such as *Cape Cod National Seashore,* is capitalized.

Publishing

Time to Share

Publish your work by making a travel poster.

To publish, follow these steps:

1. Use your neatest handwriting to copy your revised draft.
2. Proofread your final copy one more time.
3. Glue your final copy in the middle of a poster board.
4. Decorate the poster with photos, drawings, or souvenirs.

Make the class travel display.

1. Collect everyone's poster.
2. Arrange the posters on a wall or bulletin board.
3. Visit the travel display whenever you feel like taking a short vacation.

CHAPTER 4

Writing a Report

LESSON 1

Choosing an Idea and Finding Facts

A report gives facts about a specific idea.

When you write a paragraph that gives facts about a specific idea, you are writing a report. Before you begin to write a report, you must do two things:

1. Choose a specific idea that interests you.

2. Find facts about your idea.

You should write a report about something that interests you. Do you like animals? Information about an animal would make an interesting report.

Once you have chosen an animal, you have to find facts about the animal. You can find facts in many sources.

A source is any book, magazine, or encyclopedia in which you can find information for your report.

About the Photograph

This friendly, wooly animal is being fed a special treat. Do you know what kind of animal this is? Where could you find more facts about the animal?

Your source will tell you many things:

- how the animal looks
- where it lives
- what it eats
- what it does

Marcy wanted to learn about hermit crabs. She decided to write about where they live. She read about hermit crabs in the encyclopedia and in a book. Marcy wrote down the encyclopedia name and volume number. She wrote down the author and title of the book.

World Book Encyclopedia, Vol. 8

Eastman, Katherine. Facts About Sea Animals

Then Marcy made a word map to help her remember what she read. She wrote the specific idea in the middle of the word map and put an oval around it. She put the details that gave information in ovals around the specific idea.

Here is a list of animals. Can you recognize their names? Which animals would you like to know more about?

aardvark	jaguar	quail
beaver	koala	raccoon
camel	lion	sea lion
dolphin	llama	tarantula
eagle	moose	turtle
frog	newt	vulture
gnu	octopus	weasel
hamster	ostrich	yak
iguana	polar bear	zebra

Activity A

Choose an animal from the above list. Use a source to find four facts that describe how the animal looks. Make a word map. Name your source.

Activity B

Choose another animal from the list. Use a source to find four facts that tell where the animal lives. Make a word map. Name your source.

Writer's Corner

- Choose another animal from the list. Then choose one of the specific ideas listed below. Use a source to find facts about this idea. Make a word map. Be sure to name your source.

A. how the animal looks
B. where it lives
C. what it eats
D. what it does

LESSON 2

Planning the Report

A good report follows a definite plan.

The word map helped Marcy "see" a picture of all her facts. She studied her word map carefully.

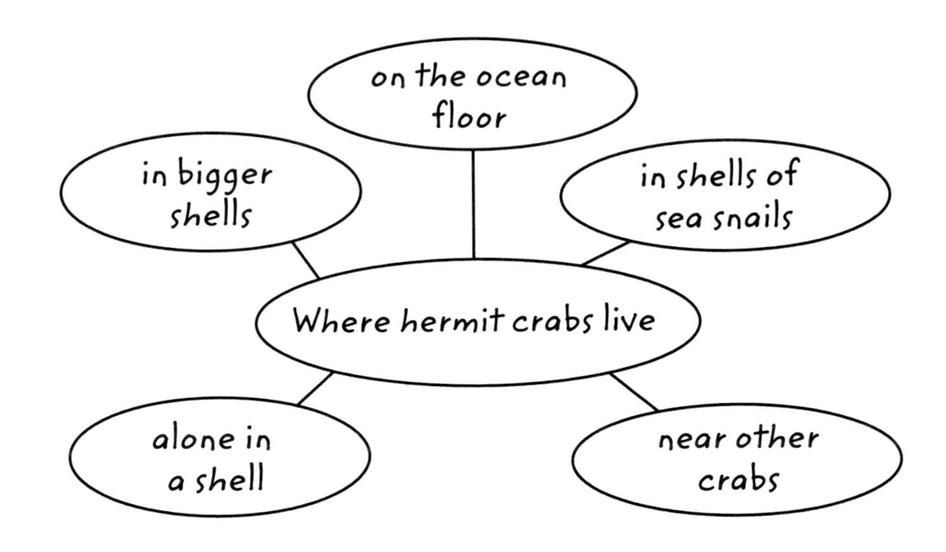

She was now ready to plan her report. She knew her plan would have these three parts.

BEGINNING SENTENCE	Gives the specific idea of the report
MIDDLE SENTENCES	Give details about the specific idea
ENDING SENTENCE	Gives the last details, or tells how the writer feels about the specific idea

Marcy's plan for a report on hermit crabs looked like this.

BEGINNING SENTENCE	Hermit crabs live in funny places.
MIDDLE SENTENCES	**1.** They live on the ocean floor. **2.** They live inside the shells of sea snails. **3.** When they get bigger, they find bigger shells. **4.** They live alone. **5.** They live near other hermit crabs.
ENDING SENTENCE	The name "hermit crab" is perfect for this animal.

Activity A

This word map gives facts about what goldfish need to stay healthy. Use the word map to plan a report. The beginning and ending sentences are given. Write the details for the middle sentences.

BEGINNING SENTENCE	Goldfish do not need much to stay healthy.
ENDING SENTENCE	Taking care of goldfish is fun and easy.

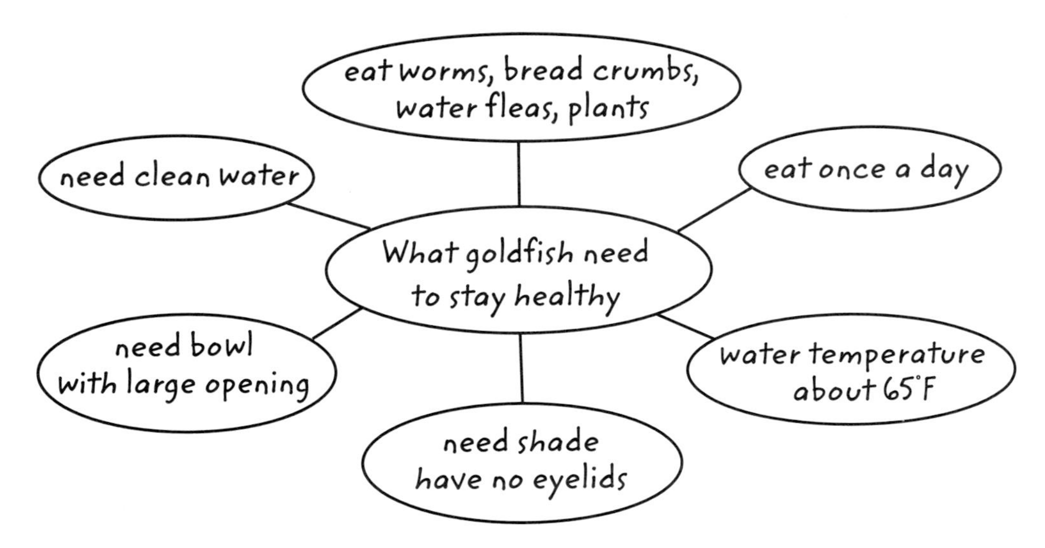

Turner, Joseph. Healthy Fish

The Pet Digest, Spring 19__

Activity B

Here is a word map that gives facts on how alligators look. Make a plan for a report. Decide what information you will put in the beginning sentence, in the middle sentences, and in the ending sentence.

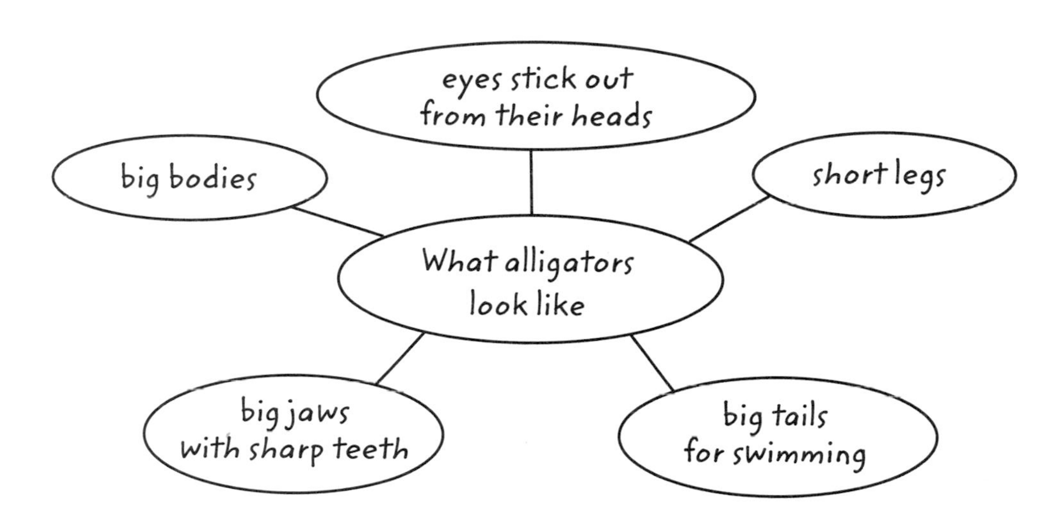

World Book Encyclopedia, Vol. 1

Perez, Luis. Alligator Almanac

Writer's Corner

▶ **Use one of the word maps you made about an animal you chose in Lesson 1. Use this word map to make a plan for a report.**

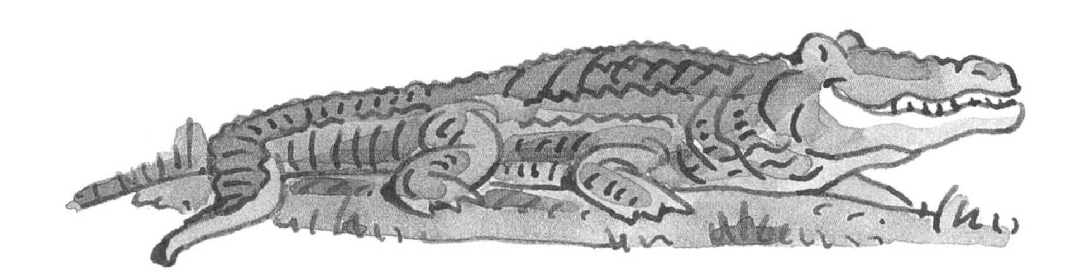

LESSON 3

Writing the Report

A report has a beginning sentence, middle sentences, and an ending sentence.

You have learned that every paragraph has a beginning sentence, middle sentences, and an ending sentence. Each kind of sentence has a special job in a paragraph.

- The beginning sentence gives the specific idea and catches the reader's attention.
- Middle sentences give details about the specific idea.
- The ending sentence gives the last fact or detail. It may tell how the writer feels about the specific idea.

Marcy began to write her report on where hermit crabs live. She used the plan that she made from the word map. She put the facts into sentences. Then Marcy put the sentences into a paragraph.

Plan

BEGINNING SENTENCE	Hermit crabs live in funny places.
MIDDLE SENTENCES	**1.** They live on the ocean floor. **2.** They live inside the shells of sea snails. **3.** When they get bigger, they find bigger shells. **4.** They live alone. **5.** They live near other hermit crabs.
ENDING SENTENCE	The name "hermit crab" is perfect for this animal.

The first time Marcy wrote her report it looked like this:

Where Hermit Crabs Live

Hermit crabs live in funny places. They live on the ocean floor. They live inside the shells of sea snails. When they get bigger, they find bigger shells. They live alone. They live near other hermit crabs. The name "hermit crab" is perfect for this animal.

Activity A

Here is a plan for a report on what goldfish need to stay healthy. Write a sentence for each fact. Write the sentences as a paragraph.

BEGINNING SENTENCE	Goldfish do not need much to stay healthy.
MIDDLE SENTENCES	**1.** They need water that is clean. **2.** They need a bowl with a large opening for air. **3.** The water temperature should be about 65° F. **4.** They eat once a day. **5.** They eat worms, bread crumbs, water fleas, and plants. **6.** They need shade. **7.** They have no eyelids.
ENDING SENTENCE	Taking care of goldfish is fun and easy.

Activity B

Here is a plan for a report on how alligators look. Write a sentence for each fact. Write the sentences as a paragraph.

BEGINNING SENTENCE	Alligators are interesting animals.
MIDDLE SENTENCES	1. They have big bodies. 2. They have big jaws with sharp teeth. 3. They have short legs. 4. They have big tails that help them swim. 5. Their eyes stick out from their heads.
ENDING SENTENCE	Alligators make most people nervous.

Writer's Corner

▶ **Use the plan you made in Lesson 2. Write a report. Write on every other line so you can make any changes easily.**

Revising the Report

Revising means to change words or combine ideas.

You have already learned several ways to revise a paragraph.

- Use strong verbs in place of weak verbs.
- Use colorful adjectives.
- Combine subjects and predicates.
- Combine short sentences.

Marcy's report needed revision. This is what she did.

Where Hermit Crabs Live

Hermit crabs ~~live in funny places.~~ have very unusual homes. They live on the ocean floor. ~~They live~~ inside the shells of sea snails. When they ~~get~~ grow bigger, they ~~find bigger~~ search for larger shells. They live alone, but ~~They~~ they ~~live~~ are near other hermit crabs. I think The name "hermit crab" is perfect for this ~~animal.~~ tiny creature.

A report needs a title. A title should attract the reader's attention and give a hint about the topic.

To think of a title, Marcy brainstormed for ideas. Here are some of her ideas:

The Hermit Crab	A Shell House
Alone in a Shell	Home Sweet Home
At Home in a Shell	An Unusual Home

Here is Marcy's finished report.

Home Sweet Home

Hermit crabs have very unusual homes. They live on the ocean floor inside the shells of sea snails. When they grow bigger, they search for larger shells. They live alone, but they are near other hermit crabs. I think the name "hermit crab" is perfect for this tiny creature.

Activity A

Revise this report on what goldfish need to stay healthy. Then rewrite the report and give it a title.

Goldfish do not need much to stay healthy. They need clean water. They should be in a bowl with a big opening for air. The water should be about 65 degrees F. Goldfish eat once a day. They eat worms, bread crumbs, water fleas, and plants. Goldfish need some shade. They have no eyelids. Taking care of goldfish is fun and easy.

Activity B

Revise this report on how alligators look. Then rewrite the report and give it a title.

Alligators are interesting animals. They have big bodies. They have big jaws and sharp teeth. They have short legs and big tails that help them swim. Their eyes stick out from their heads. Alligators make most people nervous.

Writer's Corner

▶ **Revise and rewrite the report you wrote in Lesson 3. Give it an interesting title. At the end of your report, name your source.**

Exploring Words

Synonyms

Synonyms are words that have the same or almost the same meaning.

Here are synonyms you have already learned.

pal—friend	gift—present
speak—talk	bring—carry

Here are new synonyms.

store—shop	kind—friendly
select—choose	hunt—search

Activity A

Use a synonym in place of each word in italics.

1. The *kind* waitress asked us if we wanted a sundae.
2. Did you *choose* a book about the planets?
3. My parents *search* every morning for the car keys.
4. My *friend* Stefan won the three-legged race.
5. Aunt Rosita *talks* in Spanish with her friends.

6. Wanda bought a chess set at a new *store* on Elm Street.
7. Did you *carry* the garden tools into the house?
8. I will *select* three people to be on my team.
9. There was a little *present* inside the bag.
10. Casey asked the *friendly* gentleman for directions.

Antonyms

Antonyms are words that are opposite in meaning. Antonyms are opposites.

Here are antonyms you have already learned.

first—last	fast—slow
up—down	soft—hard

Here are new antonyms.

careful—careless	strong—weak
open—close	top—bottom

Activity B

Use a new antonym in place of each word in italics. Refer to the list on page 111.

1. The tea is too *weak* for me to drink.
2. She was *careful* and let the kite string go.
3. Sheila tried to *open* the box.
4. The basement is at the *top* of the house.
5. The *weak* swimmer swam across the lake.
6. Did you *close* the box of crackers?
7. *Careless* people don't litter.
8. The attic is at the *bottom* of the house.
9. Mary was too *strong* to lift the weights.
10. Don't *close* the package until Christmas.

Activity C

Choose the antonym that best fits the meaning of each sentence.

1. Carl chipped his tooth on the (soft, hard) roll.
2. The puppy (opened, closed) its eyes and went to sleep.
3. Cats catch (careful, careless) mice.
4. The (slow, fast) snail reached the finish line in an hour.
5. Everyone clapped when Liang won (first, last) prize.

word study word study word study wor

Homophones

Homophones are words that sound alike but are spelled differently and have different meanings.

Here are homophones you have already learned.

deer—dear meet—meat ate—eight

Here are new homophones.

be—bee our—hour here—hear

Be and *Bee*

Which word is correct in each sentence?

A. I'll (be, bee) home at four o'clock. (form of *is*)

B. The (be, bee) was black and yellow. (insect)

Our and *Hour*

Which word is correct in each sentence?

A. We waited one (our, hour). (sixty minutes)

B. (Our, Hour) dog's name is Trixie. (owned by us)

Here and *Hear*

Which word is correct in each sentence?

A. They (here, hear) the song. (listen with your ears)

B. The subway will stop (here, hear). (in this place)

Activity D

Complete each sentence with the correct homophone.

1. The salad with the onions is over (hear, here).
2. Baby (deer, dear) are called fawns.
3. It takes an (our, hour) to walk through the park.
4. A (be, bee) makes honey from nectar.
5. Can you (here, hear) the sound of the train?
6. Pete solved (ate, eight) math problems.
7. Alice will (bee, be) playing softball next year.
8. A tiny mouse can (here, hear) a big cat's footsteps.
9. May Josh play at (hour, our) house?
10. Mr. Gray has a recipe for bear (meet, meat).

Contractions

A contraction is a short way to write some words. A contraction always uses an apostrophe.

Here are contractions you have already learned.

I will—I'll	we will—we'll
she will—she'll	you will—you'll
he will—he'll	they will—they'll

Here are new contractions.

is not—isn't	was not—wasn't
are not—aren't	were not—weren't

What letter is missing in each contraction?
What takes the place of this letter?

Activity E

Give the contractions for these words.

1. is not _______
2. was not _______
3. are not _______
4. they will _______
5. were not _______

Activity F

Give the meanings of these contractions.

1. I'll _______
2. aren't _______
3. weren't _______
4. isn't _______
5. wasn't _______

Activity G

Use a contraction in place of the words in italics.

1. *Is not* Harry the captain of the track team?
2. *Are not* the fishermen hauling in oysters?
3. *Were not* the stones nice and smooth?
4. *Was not* the boat rocking on the waves?
5. *Is not* the team electing a new captain?
6. *You will* see more stars on a clear night.
7. The hikers *are not* camping out.
8. These kittens *were not* playing with the string.
9. Tomorrow *I will* make a special breakfast.
10. This jar *is not* big enough to hold the beetles.

WRITER'S WORKSHOP

Reporting the Facts

What do you think is the most important invention? A complicated computer? A simple zipper? Research an invention and use the facts you find to write a report. Share your research by presenting your report to the class.

Prewriting

Before you begin writing, you'll need to do two things. First, choose your topic. Second, research sources such as books, magazines, or encyclopedias to find facts for your report.

Ask yourself questions like these to help you get started:

- ❑ What do I already know about inventions or inventors?
- ❑ What inventions would be interesting to find out more about?
- ❑ What sources are most likely to have the facts I need?
- ❑ Where can I find those sources?
- ❑ Can I do my research at school?
- ❑ Will I need to ask a family member to take me to the library after school?

If you take notes, it will be easy to organize your ideas for your draft. As you read about your topic, write each fact on a separate note card. Under each note, write the name of the source and the author.

Tran, a third grader, took these notes.

> Garrett Morgan invented the three-way traffic signal.
> Extraordinary Black Americans,
> Susan Altman

> Invented it in 1923
> Garrett Morgan, Inventor,
> Garnet Nelson Jackson

Drafting

Your note cards will make it easy to write the middle part of your draft. Just put the cards in order. Rearrange them until they are in the order you like. Take out cards with facts you decide not to use.

Write an interesting beginning sentence about the invention. Tell an interesting fact. Or tell what life would be like if the invention had not been invented.

Use your note cards to write the middle part of your paragraph. Don't just copy the words of your source. Tell what you learned in your own words.

Write an ending sentence. Tell how you feel about the invention.

Remember to add a title.

WRITER'S WORKSHOP

Guidelines for Using Your Own Words
1. Use different words that mean the same thing as the words in your source. automobiles = cars
2. If you had to look up a word in your source, use an easier word in your report. excursion = trip
3. If you can't pronounce a word, replace it with a word you use often. pedestrians = walkers
4. Read your report aloud. Does it sound as if you are talking to a friend?

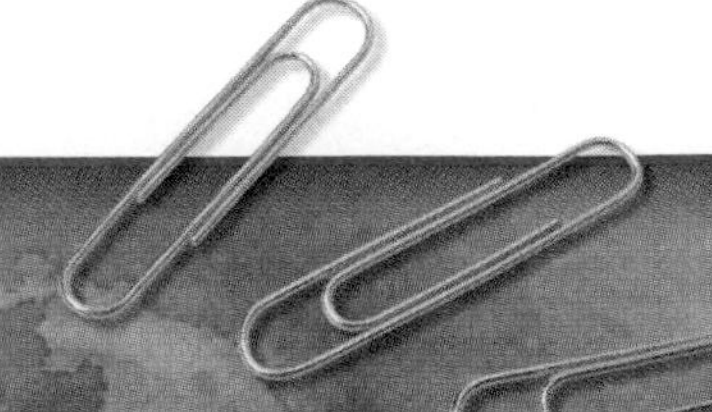

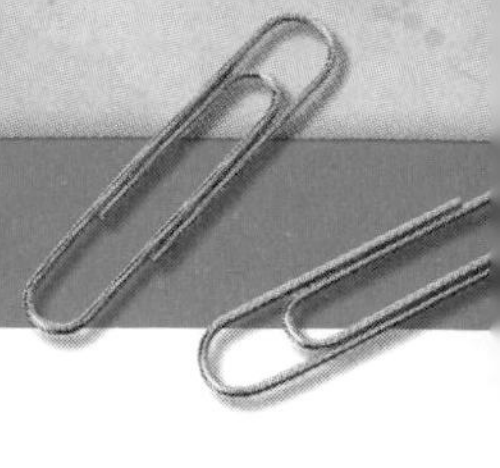

EDITOR'S WORKSHOP

Revising, Proofreading, and Publishing

Revising

Time to Take Another Look

Reread your report to make sure it makes sense and sounds interesting. Look for ways to revise it to make it better.

Ask yourself these questions to help you revise:

- ❑ Do I need to rewrite my first sentence to get the reader's attention?
- ❑ Do I need to add any facts to make my ideas clear?
- ❑ Do I need to remove any details that don't tell more about the main idea?
- ❑ Do I need to change the order of any of the details?
- ❑ Does my report use my own words, not the words of my source?
- ❑ Does my report show why the invention is important?
- ❑ Does my title tell what my paragraph is about?

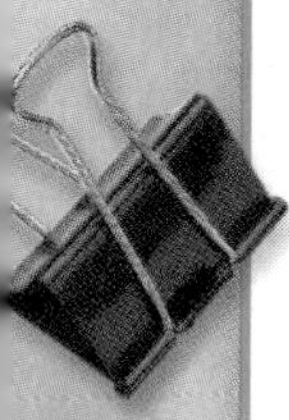

Use a colored pencil to revise your draft. Then read your report aloud to see how it will sound when you present it to the class.

Use a Tape Recorder

Read your draft into a tape recorder. Then listen to your report without looking at what you wrote. Pretend you are hearing the report for the first time.

Read your note cards once more. Try to find an interesting fact or story about the inventor to add.

> *Garrett Morgan could only go to school for six years, but he was always curious. After he got a job, he hired a tutor to help him learn what he had missed.*

Proofreading

Time to Look at Capitalization, Punctuation, and Spelling

After your report sounds just the way you want it to, check your capitalization, punctuation, spelling, and grammar. The checklist will help you.

- ❑ Did I indent the first word of my paragraph?
- ❑ Did I use capital letters for every name?
- ❑ Did I use the correct mark of punctuation at the end of each sentence?
- ❑ Did I spell all the words correctly?

Starting Backwards
Start at the last word of your report. Read backwards, one word at a time, to check for spelling mistakes.

Publishing

Time to Share

Share the interesting facts you found out about your invention by presenting your report aloud.

To publish, follow these steps:

1. Use your neatest handwriting to copy your revised draft.
2. After you finish, proofread your final copy one more time.
3. If the invention is an everyday object, bring in an example. If not, find or draw a picture to show.

Present your report.

1. Practice reading your report aloud. Make sure you can pronounce all the words.
2. Read your report aloud. Read slowly, clearly, and with expression.
3. Look up often to make eye contact with your listeners.
4. Show an example or a picture of the invention.
5. Be ready to answer questions from the audience.

CHAPTER 5

More to Explore About Writing

LESSON 1

Writing a News Story

A news story tells the facts about an event.

You can find news stories in the newspaper. A news story is full of facts. Facts are pieces of information that are true. Why do you think people read news stories?

A news story has a headline. The headline is the title. The news story tells five very important facts. It tells *who* is in the event, *what* happened in the event, *when* the event took place, *where* the event took place, and *why* it took place.

About the Photograph

People want to know about the world and those who live in it. Newspapers must include facts that are interesting and useful to the reader. Do you like to read the newspaper?

Read this news story and then answer the questions.

Main Entrance Closed

From September 13 to 17, visitors were not able to use the main entrance to Dixon Elementary School. Workers were building a ramp. This ramp helps people who cannot use the stairs to enter the school easily. The Home and School Association helped pay for this improvement.

1. *Who* is in the event?
2. *What* happened?
3. *When* did the event happen?
4. *Where* did the event happen?
5. *Why* did it happen?
6. What is the headline?

Activity A

Every spring your school has a fair. You have been assigned to write a news story about the event. Give the information for each of the questions. Then write your news story. Be sure to give your story a headline.

1. *Who* is in the event?
2. *What* happened?
3. *When* did it happen?
4. *Where* did it happen?
5. *Why* did it happen?

Writer's Corner

▶ **Choose one of these events and write a news story. Make sure you give information about *who, what, when, where,* and *why*.**

A. Your principal's special award
B. A new stoplight being installed
C. A monkey getting loose at the zoo
D. A family of skunks living behind the playground

LESSON 2

Writing a How-To Paragraph

A how-to paragraph tells how to do something. It gives directions step-by-step.

You have probably read how-to paragraphs many times—how to cook something, how to set up a science experiment, how to do a magic trick, or how to plant seeds. When you write a how-to paragraph, all the steps must be in order.

For example, here are the steps to follow to soft boil an egg:

1. Take an egg from the refrigerator.
2. Put the egg under warm running water.
3. Get a small pot.
4. Put enough water in the pot to cover the egg.
5. Put the pot on the stove. (Ask for help to turn on the burner.)
6. When the water bubbles, count to sixty slowly three times (or set a timer for three minutes).
7. Turn off the burner.
8. Hold the pot handle with a pot holder.
9. Use a large spoon to take out the egg.

Read this paragraph on how to soft boil an egg.

Perfect Every Time

Some morning, surprise your mom and make her an "egg-cellent" breakfast. *First,* carefully take an egg from the refrigerator and hold it under warm running water for a minute. *Next,* take a small pot, place the egg in it, and put in enough water to cover the egg. *Then,* with the help of someone older, put the pot on the stove and turn on the burner. When the water bubbles, count to sixty slowly three times and then turn off the burner. *Finally,* take hold of the pot with a pot holder and use a big spoon to lift out the egg. Present the surprise and watch your mom smile at this "egg-cellent" breakfast!

Notice the words in italics. These words help to put the directions in order. They are called order words. They are clues that tell what comes next in a how-to paragraph.

Here are some order words you can use when you write a how-to paragraph.

after that	later
before	next
finally	second
first	then

Activity A

Think of something you know how to do. Write the steps to follow. Make sure the steps are in the correct order.

Here are some suggestions.

A. How to make chocolate milk
B. How to make a bed
C. How to wrap a present
D. How to plant a seed
E. How to climb a tree
F. How to study spelling
G. How to throw a football
H. How to jump rope

Activity B

Look back at the steps you wrote in Activity A. Now use the steps to write a how-to paragraph. Use order words in your directions to tell what comes next.

Writer's Corner

- **Draw three pictures for any three steps in your how-to paragraph. Put these three pictures at the end of your paragraph.**

LESSON 3

Writing About Yourself

Some of the most enjoyable stories are stories about yourself.

There is one topic you know a great deal about—yourself! Many famous people, such as A. A. Milne, Benjamin Franklin, and Booker T. Washington, have written about themselves. You, too, are a special person. You have things to share about your life.

Have you ever

- had an accident?
- had a frightening experience?
- had a funny thing happen to you?
- won an award for something?
- gotten lost?
- taken a helicopter ride?
- lost or found something important?

Matt remembered that when he was in first grade, he had an accident on his bike. Matt made a word map so he wouldn't forget any details. He wrote the specific idea in the center, and then put the details of the accident around it.

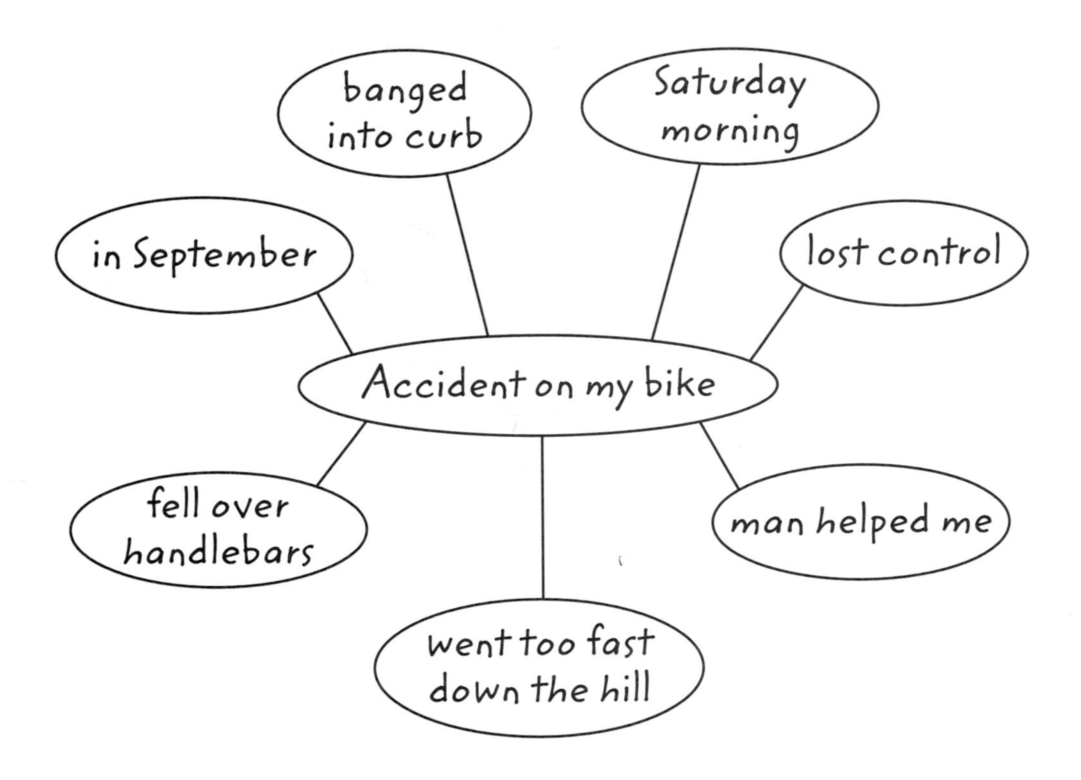

When he finished his word map, Matt thought about the rules for writing a good paragraph. He wrote a beginning sentence. This sentence gave the specific idea of the paragraph. Then he wrote middle sentences. These were the details he had in his word map. He made sure these details were in the order in which they happened. Finally, he wrote an ending sentence. After revising and proofreading, Matt gave his paragraph a title.

Head First

I'll never forget the day of my accident. One Saturday in September I went for a ride on my new bike. I was having a good time until I reached the top of a hill. Zoom! I flew down the hill! I tried to steer, but I was traveling too fast. I hit the curb with a jolt and tumbled over the handlebars head first. A man ran to help me. He picked me up. I never went near that hill again.

Activity A

Think of something special or interesting that has happened to you. Make a word map so you can remember all the details. Share your ideas with the class.

Activity B

Use your word map to write a paragraph telling your special story. You don't have to tell every detail you remember. You must decide which are the most important and the most interesting details for your reader.

Writer's Corner

▶ **Write a paragraph about another event in your life. If you already wrote about something that happened at home, think about something that happened at school.**

LESSON 4

Writing a Book Report

A book report is a way to share information about a book you have read.

Books are like magic carpets. They can take you anywhere you want to go. Books can make years go backward or forward! You can visit the lands of long ago or imaginary places. There is so much to explore in the world of books.

Writing a book report is one way to share what you have read. Book reports should not tell the ending or the whole story. They should give just enough information to make someone else want to read the book and discover what happens.

In a book report, you should include

- the title.
- the author.
- what the book is about.
- your opinion of the book.

Activity A

Read this book report on *Crow Boy* and then answer the questions.

Title: Crow Boy
Author: Taro Yashima

In the book Crow Boy by Taro Yashima, I enjoyed meeting Chibi, a shy, young boy. His teacher, Mr. Isobe, discovers Chibi's special talent. This discovery changes Chibi and his classmates. You will enjoy reading this book, especially if you've ever felt shy.

1. What is the title of the book?
2. Who is the author?
3. What is the story about?
4. What is the opinion of the person who read it?

Activity B

Write a book report about a book you've read. Give the name of the book and the author. Then tell just enough about the story to interest your reader. Tell how you feel about the story. Share your report.

Writer's Corner

- **To make your book report a little different, try writing one as if you were an object in the story. Here is a beginning:**

I am very important and yet I don't even have a name. I am the amazing web in *Charlotte's Web* by E. B. White.

LESSON 5

Writing About a Book Character

A character in a story is a person or an animal who is important to the action of the story.

A character should not be just a name in a book but someone who seems real to you. You should be able to close your eyes, see the character, and hear the voice.

To help others see and hear a character in a story you have enjoyed, you can write a report called a character sketch. When you write a character sketch, you paint a picture with words.

A character sketch should include

- the title of the book.
- the author of the book.
- who the character is.
- what the character does.
- your opinion of the character.

You should not tell everything about the character. Just tell the most important things—the things that make that character seem real to you.

Activity A

Read this character sketch about Ralph S. Mouse and then answer the questions.

Title: The Mouse and the Motorcycle
Author: Beverly Cleary

You'll enjoy meeting Ralph S. Mouse in the story The Mouse and the Motorcycle by Beverly Cleary. Ralph lives like a mouse but thinks, feels, and acts like a human being. He gets into trouble because he does more than he should. Ralph rides motorcycles with lots of speed and teases the dog terribly. He escapes danger and even risks his life to save a friend. I like Ralph. He makes you laugh and sometimes makes you angry, but you always want to forgive him.

1. Does the report name the character, the book, and the author?
2. Do you know all that happens in the story?
3. Does the report tell about one character?
4. Does the author of the report like Ralph?
5. Does the report make you want to read about Ralph S. Mouse?

Writer's Corner

▶ **In books such as *Peter Pan, The Wind in the Willows, Winnie-the-Pooh,* and *The Wizard of Oz,* there are many fascinating characters about whom you can write. Choose a character from one of these stories or from another story. Write a character sketch. Tell**

- the title of the book.
- the author of the book.
- who the character is.
- what the character does.
- your opinion of the character.

▶ **Now draw a picture of your character. Make sure the character is doing one of the actions you wrote about in your character sketch.**

Exploring Words

Synonyms

Synonyms are words that have the same or almost the same meaning.

Here are synonyms you have already learned.

store—shop	kind—friendly
select—choose	hunt—search

Here are new synonyms.

see—watch	glad—happy
begin—start	shout—yell

Activity A

Use a new synonym in place of each word in italics.

1. Turn off the oven before the pies *start* to burn.
2. Did you *watch* our new goldfish?
3. The coach *shouted,* "Get ready!"
4. Andrea is *glad* you are going to the party.
5. Our math class *begins* at two o'clock.

Activity B

Match the words in column A with their synonyms in column B. Refer to the list on page 136.

COLUMN A		COLUMN B
1. choose	________	**a.** happy
2. store	________	**b.** kind
3. glad	________	**c.** begin
4. shout	________	**d.** shop
5. friendly	________	**e.** yell
6. start	________	**f.** select

Antonyms

Antonyms are words that are opposite in meaning. Antonyms are opposites.

Here are antonyms you have already learned.

careful—careless	strong—weak
open—close	top—bottom

Here are new antonyms.

come—go	new—old
empty—full	right—wrong

Activity C

Use a new antonym in place of each word in italics.

1. My stomach is *empty* from the apple pie.
2. The *old* shoes hurt Nina's feet.
3. The *right* directions caused us to get lost.
4. Do not *come* into the dark tunnel.
5. The *new* teddy bear was torn and dirty.

Activity D

Choose the antonym that best fits each sentence. Refer to the list on page 137.

1. Be (careful, careless) when you cross Main Street.
2. The (new, old) car has rusty bumpers.
3. "(Come, Go) join me for a game of checkers," Billy said.
4. Jack ate the snacks until he was (empty, full).
5. Only a (strong, weak) person could carry the heavy boxes.
6. I found a penny at the (top, bottom) of the glass.
7. Please (open, close) a can of cat food for Boots.
8. Theo was worried that he had made the (right, wrong) choice.
9. The stiff (new, old) shoes squeaked.
10. Because she is sick, Tara is very (strong, weak).

Homophones

Homophones are words that sound alike but are spelled differently and have different meanings.

Here are homophones you have already learned.

be—bee   our—hour   here—hear

Here are new homophones.

red—read   mail—male   rode—road

Red and Read

Which word is correct in each sentence?

A. Mrs. Miller wore a (red, read) hat. (color)

B. Leo (red, read) a story about an inventor. (past of *read*)

Mail and *Male*

Which word is correct in each sentence?

A. A (mail, male) sheep is called a ram. (man)

B. A letter from Nicole came in the (mail, male). (delivered letters)

Rode and *Road*

Which word is correct in each sentence?

A. This is the (rode, road) to Dodge City. (path or street)

B. We (rode, road) in a horse-driven carriage. (past of *ride*)

Activity E

Complete each sentence with the correct homophone.

1. My brother and I (red, read) aloud to each other on the train.
2. Turn right onto the narrow (rode, road).
3. A (male, mail) duck is called a drake.
4. (Be, Bee) careful and (bee, be) quick!
5. Helen (rode, road) a donkey in Greece.
6. Mr. Green will (mail, male) the valentine to his wife.
7. These T-shirts have (our, hour) team's name on them.
8. The (red, read) bus could be seen for miles.
9. Am I on the right (road, rode) to Pleasant Lake?
10. Can you (here, hear) the hummingbird?

Contractions

A contraction is a short way to write two words. A contraction always uses an apostrophe.

Here are contractions you have already learned.

is not—isn't	was not—wasn't
are not—aren't	were not—weren't

Here are new contractions.

can not—can't	will not—won't

Can't is the contraction or short way of writing *can not.*

What letters are missing in *can't?*
What takes the place of these letters?

Won't is the contraction or short way of writing *will not.*

What letters are missing in *won't?*
What new letter is added?
What takes the place of the missing letters?

Activity F

Answer these pairs of riddles. Use the contractions *can't* or *won't*. Use the second riddle as a clue to the first answer. Use the first riddle as a clue to the second answer. The first one is done for you.

1. Who *can not* fly? A horse *can't* fly.
   Who *can not* gallop? A bird *can't* gallop.
2. Who *can not* hop?
   Who *can not* walk with a shell on its back?
3. Who *will not* squirt water with its trunk?
   Who *will not* squeeze through small holes and squeak?
4. Who *will not* eat leaves from a treetop?
   Who *will not* drink milk from a saucer?
5. Who *can not* live in the ice and snow?
   Who *can not* travel through the desert?

Activity G

Use a contraction in place of the words in italics.

1. Carlos said, "I *can not* find my tennis shoes."
2. Ships *can not* sail in shallow water.
3. Missy *will not* dive from the high dive.
4. The stagecoach drivers *can not* see in the fog.
5. The book I want *is not* in the library.
6. Butterflies *will not* fly when it's very cold.
7. *Were not* the eggs colorful?
8. My little brother *can not* tell time.
9. The panda *will not* move.
10. My gloves *are not* warm enough.

WRITER'S WORKSHOP

A Book About Books

How do you choose a good book to read? The best way is to ask friends to tell you about books they like. And the best way to help your friends is to write a report for them to read. Practice by writing a book report about your favorite fairy tale. Put your report in a class Readers' Reference book.

Prewriting

Think about fairy tales you have read, viewed, or listened to. List their names. What do you remember about each fairy tale? Which story on the list is your favorite? Ask yourself questions like these to help you get started:

- What is the title of the fairy tale?
- If the story is in a book, does it have an author? What is the author's name?
- Who are the characters in the fairy tale?
- What is the story about?
- Did you learn a lesson from the fairy tale? If so, what is it?
- What is your opinion of the story?

Choose your favorite fairy tale. Use an idea frame like the one below to write notes about everything you remember.

Title?

Author?

Who are the characters?

What happens?

What did I learn?

What is my opinion of the story?

Drafting

Your fairy tale report draft will have four parts:

- the title.
- the author (if you know who the author is).
- what the story is about.
- your opinion of the fairy tale.

Use the notes you made, but don't tell everything about the book. Just tell enough of the story to help your reader decide whether he or she would like to read it.

Look at Keeshia's report below. Use the same form for your report. Start by writing the title. Write the author's name next. Some fairy tales were written so long ago that no one knows who the author was. If you don't know the name of the author, leave it out. Use your notes to write about the story. End the report by writing your opinion.

Keeshia's Book Report

Title: The Ugly Duckling

Author: Hans Christian Andersen

The Ugly Duckling starts out to be a sad story. One little duck looks different from all the rest. The ducklings tease the little duck and call it "the ugly duckling." If this sounds like a sad story, it doesn't turn out to be. When the ugly duckling grows up, the other ducks get a big surprise. You'll like the book because everybody feels like an "ugly duckling" sometimes. This story will make you feel better.

WRITER'S WORKSHOP

EDITOR'S WORKSHOP

Revising, Proofreading, and Publishing

Revising

Time to Take Another Look

Reread your book report and look for ways to revise it to make it better. Ask yourself these questions to help you revise:

- ☐ Do I need to add information to make the story sound more interesting?
- ☐ Do I need to take out any details that give away too much of the story?
- ☐ Do I need to change the order of the details so my paragraph makes sense?
- ☐ Do I need to rewrite anything that is not clear?
- ☐ Does my report clearly state my opinion of the book?
- ☐ Do I need to choose more interesting words?

Revise your report, using a colored pencil. Then read it again to make sure it's just the way you want it to be.

Try a New Point of View

One way to make your book report more interesting is to pretend you are one of the characters. Tell how you feel about the story. Use the pronoun *I*.

Proofreading

Time to Look at Capitalization, Punctuation, and Spelling

You've revised your book report, and you're sure that you've given your reader the right amount of information. Now use the checklist to check your capitalization, punctuation, spelling, and grammar.

- ❑ Did I indent the first word of my paragraph?
- ❑ Did I begin each sentence and proper noun with a capital letter?
- ❑ Did I use the correct mark of punctuation at the end of each sentence?
- ❑ Did I underline the book's title?
- ❑ Did I spell each word correctly?

Checking Commas and Periods
Read your report aloud. Pause each time you see a comma. Stop for each period.

Publishing

Time to Share

Publishing your report will help your friends find good books to read.

To publish, follow these steps:

1. Use your neatest handwriting to copy your revised draft.
2. After you finish, proofread your final copy one more time.
3. If you use a computer to publish, you can *italicize* your book's title instead of underlining it.

Make the Readers' Reference book for your class.

1. Collect everyone's final report.
2. Arrange the reports so the titles are in alphabetical order.
3. Place the pages in a three-ring notebook.
4. Add a new report to the notebook whenever you read a good book.
5. Place the book in the classroom library.

CHAPTER 6

Writing Letters

LESSON 1

A Friendly Letter

A friendly letter is a written message to someone you know. A friendly letter has five parts.

Have you ever written a letter to a friend? It is fun to write letters. It is also fun to receive letters. When you write a friendly letter, you can "talk" to a friend or a relative who lives far away. When you go on vacation, you can send a letter to a friend at home. Letters are even fun to write to someone who lives close by.

In a letter, you can share ideas or news about what you are doing. You can keep the letters you receive and reread them any time.

A friendly letter has five parts:

- Heading
- Greeting
- Body
- Closing
- Signature

About the Photograph

The arrival of the letter carrier is a special moment when he or she has mail for you. From whom would you like to get a letter? To whom would you like to write?

Look at this letter. Notice how the different parts of a friendly letter are written.

HEADING	July 24, 1999
GREETING	Dear Grandma,
BODY	You won't believe how much fun I'm having at this cottage. We've been swimming, water skiing, and boating every day. Tonight we are having a big cookout, and I'm going to make my special s'mores. I hope you and Grandpa are well. I miss seeing you both. When we come home, I'll show you the pictures I took. Some of them are very funny. I especially like the one of Dad falling into the lake!
CLOSING	Your loving granddaughter,
SIGNATURE	*Stephanie*

When you write a friendly letter, it is important to use the correct punctuation and capitalization. Look at the following rules and find each part in the sample letter.

The Heading

The heading of a letter gives the date.

Begin the month with a capital letter. Put a comma between the day and the year.

July 20, 19__ March 31, 19__

Write the heading at the top of the paper. Start the heading at the center of the first line.

The Greeting

The greeting gives the name of the person to whom you are writing. The greeting helps you say hello.

Begin the greeting and the person's name with a capital letter. Put a comma after the person's name.

Dear Eric, Hello Katie,

The greeting begins at the left side of the paper.

The Body

The body is where you write your message.

Indent the first word of each paragraph in the body. Begin the rest of the body at the left-hand margin. Begin the first word of each paragraph with a capital letter.

The Closing

The closing comes at the end of the letter and helps you say good-bye.

Begin the first word of the closing with a capital letter. Put a comma at the end of the closing.

Your friend,   *Sincerely yours,*

The closing begins two lines below the last sentence. It starts at the center of the line just like the heading.

The Signature

The signature is your name. You should write your name—do not print it.

Always begin your name with a capital letter.

Kristina *Jeffrey*

The signature is written under the first word of the closing.

Activity A

Look back at the letter on page 148. Answer these questions about Stephanie's letter to her grandmother.

1. When was the letter written?
   How is the date written?
2. To whom is the letter written?
   How is the greeting written?
3. What message does Stephanie give her grandmother?
   How many paragraphs are in the body of the letter?
4. What closing does Stephanie use?
   How is the closing written?
5. What is the written name of the person writing the letter called?
   Where are the closing and signature written?

Activity B

First tell what part of a friendly letter each of these items is. Then write each one correctly.

1. dear tamara,
2. may 8, 1988
3. your friend,
4. katie miller
5. dear uncle bob
6. april 1, 1994
7. sincerely yours
8. carolyn
9. dear mr. collins,
10. december 29, 1967
11. your grateful niece,
12. j. t. jones

Activity C

Here is all the information you need for a friendly letter. However, it is not written in the correct order or form. First, name each part of the letter. Then rewrite the letter in the correct form.

Margo Williams

Your friend,

September 1, 19__

Dear Saskia,

I miss seeing you every day. Have you started school in Germany yet? We won't start until September 8. I bet it will be different hearing only German again.

Please write to me when you have time.

Writer's Corner

▶ **Follow these directions to write your own friendly letter.**

1. Think of a person to whom you would like to write a letter.
2. Think of what you would like to say.
3. Write your letter. Make sure you use the five parts of a friendly letter.
4. Remember to use commas and capital letters where needed.
5. Revise and proofread your letter carefully.

LESSON 2

Letters of Invitation and Acceptance

A Letter of Invitation

A letter of invitation asks a person to join you in an activity.

When you want to ask your friends to come to your birthday party or a special event, you can send a letter of invitation.

An invitation must give this information:

- *What kind* of event it is. If it is a party, tell what kind of party.
- *When* the event will take place. Give the date and the time.
- *Where* the event is taking place. Give the address.

A letter of invitation has the same five parts as a friendly letter. You should use the same rules for punctuation and capital letters.

Look at this letter of invitation.

March 8, 19__

Dear Julia,

Please come to my birthday party. It will be from one to four o'clock on Saturday, March 25. Wear old, fancy clothes because we are going to pretend this is an old-time, dress-up party. The party will be at my house at 603 Pine Street.

Please let me know if you can come.

Your friend,

Molly Simon

1. What kind of party is Molly having?
2. What date is the party?
3. What time is the party?
4. Where is Molly's party?
5. What does Molly say at the end of the invitation?

Activity A

Add the information that is missing from this letter of invitation. Invite your friend to a birthday party. Sign your name at the end.

January 4, 19__

Dear ________,

I am having a ________ party on ________ from ________ to ________. The party will be at ________. We will play fun games and give prizes to the winners.

Please let me know if you can come.

Your friend,

____

Activity B

Here are three events to which you might invite a friend or relative. Can you name four other events?

scout activity school play valentine party

The following invitations will never have to be written, but they are fun to think about. Now, you create three more ideas for fun invitations.

1. Invite a flower to grow in your yard.
2. Invite the snow to fall just in your school yard.
3. Invite a seal to live in your bathtub.
4. Invite a hermit crab to live in your old shoe.
5. ______________________________.
6. ______________________________.
7. ______________________________.

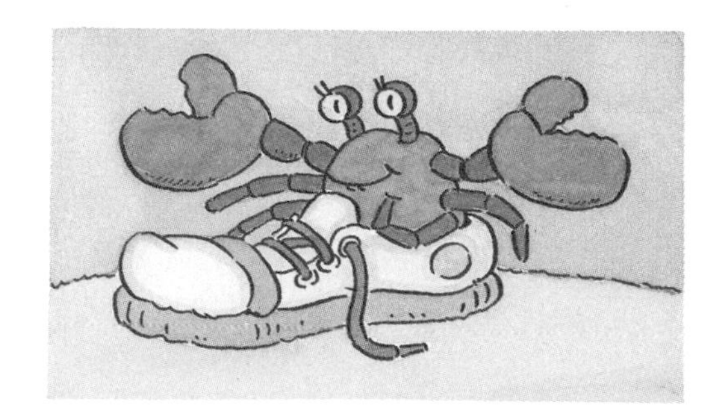

A Letter of Acceptance

A letter of acceptance is an answer to an invitation.

When you receive an invitation, you can answer with a letter of acceptance. The person who invites you would like to know if you can come. You should answer the letter as soon as possible.

When you write a letter of acceptance,

- thank the person for the invitation.
- say that you are coming.

Look at this letter of acceptance.

March 15, 19__

Dear Molly,

Thank you for inviting me to your birthday party. I can't wait to come to a fancy dress-up party! I will see you on Saturday.

Your friend,

Julia

Activity C

Write a letter to accept the invitation you completed in Activity A, on page 156.

Writer's Corner

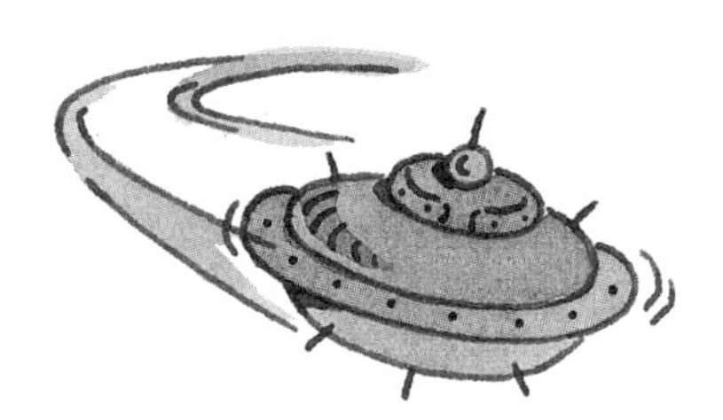

▶ **Think of an imaginary event to which you would invite a friend. Write a letter of invitation. Don't forget to include information about what kind of event, when the event is, and where the event is.**

Use one of these ideas or think of your own.

A. You have been elected President of the United States. Invite a friend to a special party.

B. You are the first person to swim across Lake Feathertop. Invite a friend to a celebration in your honor.

C. You have just returned from Mars. You have a guest from this planet at your home. Invite a friend to come to meet the visitor.

LESSON 3 A Thank-You Letter

When someone gives you a gift or does something especially nice for you, you should write a thank-you letter.

A thank-you letter is also a friendly letter and has five parts. When you write a thank-you letter,

- say thank you.
- name the gift or the favor.
- tell why you like the gift or why the favor made you happy.

Look at this thank-you letter.

September 25, 19__

Dear Aunt Laura and Uncle Vince,

Thank you for the scarf and gloves that you sent me for my birthday. They are so warm and fuzzy! They match my coat perfectly. On cold days, I will look great and feel wonderfully warm.

Your niece,

Kit

1. Did Kit say thank you?
2. Did her letter say what the gift was?
3. Did she tell why she liked the gift?

Activity A

Fill in the missing information in this thank-you letter.

January 16, 19__

Dear ______,

The ______ you gave me for ______ is ______. I will ______. Thank you for being so ______.

______

______

Writer's Corner

▶ **Choose one of these situations. Answer with a letter to accept the invitation or to say thank you.**

A. You receive a computer from your grandparents.

B. Your teacher spent an hour after school helping you with a lesson that you missed when you were sick.

C. You are invited to spend a holiday with a friend who has moved to a new town.

D. You are invited to live with one of your favorite storybook characters.

Addressing the Envelope

You should write a mailing address and a return address on the envelope.

After you write a letter, the next step is to send it. You need to put your letter into an envelope and address the envelope before you mail it.

Look at this envelope.

Molly Simon RETURN ADDRESS
603 Pine Street
Cleveland, Ohio 44413

MAILING ADDRESS Julia Perez
1809 Oak Lane
Cleveland, Ohio 44420

You should write the return address in the top left corner of the envelope. The return address has three lines.

On line 1, write your first and last name.

On line 2, write your house number and street name.

On line 3, write your city, state, and ZIP code.

You should write the mailing address in the middle of the envelope. The mailing address also has three lines.

On line 1, write the first and last name of the person to whom you are writing.

On line 2, write the person's house number and street name.

On line 3, write their city, state, and ZIP code.

Activity A

This return address and mailing address are not in the correct order. Draw an envelope on a sheet of paper and write each address in the correct place.

RETURN ADDRESS	MAILING ADDRESS
Buffalo, New York 14216	Ann Anderson
Bert Havlis	Buffalo, New York 14211
18 Center Street	367 Flower Lane

Activity B

Draw an envelope on a sheet of paper. Write your own address as the return address. Write a friend's or relative's address as the mailing address. Check that you have this information in the correct order:

- first and last name.
- house number and street name.
- city, state, and ZIP code.

Writer's Corner

▶ **Bring these three things to school:**

- a sheet of writing paper.
- an envelope.
- a stamp.

Has someone in your family done a special favor for you recently? Write a thank-you letter to a family member. When you finish the letter, address the envelope. Write your school address as the return address. Write your home address as the mailing address. Put the stamp on the envelope and seal it. Now you are ready to mail your letter.

Filling Out Forms

A form is an easy way to give information.

There are many different kinds of forms. You might have to fill out a form to apply for a library card, to order a book, or to enter a contest.

A form has blank spaces for information. When you fill out a form, you should remember three things.

- Read the entire form first.
- Fill in all the blanks.
- Check over the form when you have finished.

Activity A

Here is a form for a library card. Copy it onto a piece of paper. Then fill in the correct information.

Library Card Form

(Please print)

Name ______________________________________
First Last

Address ____________________________________
House number Street name

____
City State ZIP code

Age __________ Signature ____________________

Activity B

You would like to give your friend a magazine subscription to *Pets on Parade.* Copy this form onto a sheet of paper. Then fill in the correct information.

Order Form

(please print)

Send subscription to

Name ______________________

Address ______________________

City __________ State __________ ZIP Code ______

Gift sent by

Name ______________________

Address ______________________

City __________ State __________ ZIP Code ______

On the gift card, please write this message:

____

Writer's Corner

▶ **Sometimes a form has blocks instead of lines. You should write one letter or one number in each block. Copy this form onto a sheet of paper. Then complete the form with information about *you.***

Last Name	First Name		
Address			
City	State	ZIP Code	
Telephone Number ___ - ___ - ____	Birth Date: Mo. Day Year	Female	Male

Exploring Words

Synonyms

Synonyms are words that have the same or almost the same meaning.

Here are synonyms you have already learned.

see—watch	glad—happy
shout—yell	begin—start

Here are new synonyms.

end—stop	path—road
late—tardy	fast—quick

Activity A

Complete each sentence with a new synonym from the list above. Do not use the same word twice.

1. Some _______ trains travel over one hundred miles an hour.
2. Recess will _______ when the bell rings.
3. That is the _______ to Mr. Potter's farm.
4. Jack was _______ for band practice.
5. The _______ rabbit outran the dog.
6. Does the ballet _______ when the curtain goes down?
7. The bus to Springfield is never _______ .
8. Does this _______ lead to the cottage?

Activity B

Match the words in column A with their synonyms in column B.

COLUMN A		COLUMN B
1. end	___	**a.** happy
2. shout	___	**b.** tardy
3. see	___	**c.** start
4. path	___	**d.** quick
5. late	___	**e.** stop
6. glad	___	**f.** yell
7. fast	___	**g.** road
8. begin	___	**h.** watch

Antonyms

Antonyms are words that are opposite in meaning. Antonyms are opposites.

Here are antonyms you have already learned.

come—go new—old
right—wrong empty—full

Here are new antonyms.

near—far short—long
on—off rise—fall

Activity C

Complete each sentence with the correct pair of antonyms. Use the new antonyms listed on page 171.

1. If Patty's hair is _______ , it can't be _______ .
2. If the lights are _______ , they can't be _______ .
3. If the balloons _______ , they won't _______ .
4. If my school is _______ , it can't be _______ .

Activity D

Use an antonym in place of each word in italics.

1. Gina gave the *wrong* answer in science class.
2. The actor was supposed to be *on* the stage.
3. Aunt Laura's *old* straw hat has yellow roses on it.
4. The bread will *rise* if you open the oven door.
5. In summer, the nights are *long*.
6. The fire alarm was turned *off*.
7. The planet Mercury isn't very *near*.
8. It's time for the visitors to *come*.
9. The night sky was *empty* of stars.
10. The *new* table was sanded and painted.

Homophones

Homophones are words that sound alike but are spelled differently and have different meanings.

Here are homophones you have already learned.

red—read mail—male rode—road

Here are new homophones.

beet—beat sent—cent hole—whole

Beet and *Beat*

Which word is correct in each sentence?

The (beet, beat) grows under the ground. (vegetable)
Bob (beet, beat) the drum. (hit again and again)

Sent and *Cent*

Which word is correct in each sentence?

Tommy didn't have a (sent, cent) in his pocket. (money)
The package was (sent, cent) to my grandparents. (past of *send*)

Hole and *Whole*

Which word is correct in each sentence?

There is a (hole, whole) in my shoe. (opening)
I can't believe I ate the (hole, whole) pie! (entire)

Activity E

Complete each sentence with the correct homophone.

1. The farmers were in the (beet, beat) fields.
2. My toe wiggled through the (hole, whole) in my sock.
3. He painted his car fire engine (read, red).
4. Patricia was (sent, cent) to the wrong classroom.
5. I'm expecting a letter in the (mail, male).
6. The (whole, hole) mountain was covered with pine trees.
7. Not a (sent, cent) was to be spent.
8. (Beet, Beat) the whites of the eggs.
9. We (road, rode) in a buggy pulled by a horse.
10. Doug's quarter fell through the (hole, whole) in the grate.

Contractions

A contraction is a short way to write some words. A contraction always uses an apostrophe.

Here are contractions you have already learned.

can not—can't	will not—won't

Here are new contractions.

have not—haven't	does not—doesn't
has not—hasn't	do not—don't
did not—didn't	

What letter is missing in each contraction?

What takes the place of this letter?

Activity F

Answer each of these questions. Use the new contractions listed on page 174 in your answers.

1. Have you ever visited Paris?
2. Does the earth stand still?
3. Did the trees fall during the storm?
4. Has the whale learned to walk?
5. Do you fly to school?
6. Has the iceberg melted?
7. Does the monkey want to shake hands with you?
8. Have the books been left out in the rain?
9. Did the archaeologist find a dinosaur bone?
10. Do you wish you were older?

Activity G

Match the words in column A with the correct contractions in column B.

COLUMN A		COLUMN B
1. do not	___	**a.** isn't
2. can not	___	**b.** didn't
3. does not	___	**c.** haven't
4. did not	___	**d.** won't
5. I am	___	**e.** hasn't
6. will not	___	**f.** we'll
7. have not	___	**g.** can't
8. is not	___	**h.** don't
9. we will	___	**i.** doesn't
10. has not	___	**j.** I'm

WRITER'S WORKSHOP

A Letter to a Friend

A friendly letter is a message you write to someone you know. You can use friendly letters to keep in touch with a friend in another city, to thank a family member for a gift, or to cheer up a sick classmate. Write a friendly letter. Don't forget to mail it!

Prewriting

Decide to whom you will send your friendly letter. Then think of things that you could write that will be interesting to that person.

Ask yourself questions like these to help you get started:

- ❑ What funny, exciting, or unusual things have happened to me?
- ❑ What news do I have about people we both know?
- ❑ Do I need to thank the person for a gift?
- ❑ Do I want to comment about something from a letter the person sent to me?
- ❑ What questions can I ask my reader?

All friendly letters follow the same pattern. They all have five parts.

Five Parts of a Friendly Letter

Heading: *February 28, 2001*

Write the date. Begin the name of the month with a capital letter. Put a comma between the day and the year.

Greeting: *Dear Grandma,*

Say hello by writing the name of the person who will receive your letter. Begin each word with a capital letter. Put a comma after the name.

Body: *your message*

Indent the first word of each paragraph.

Closing: *Your friend,*

Say good-bye with a friendly phrase. Put a comma at the end of the closing.

Signature: *Mei*

Write your name under the closing.

Drafting

Before writing your draft, review your notes. Choose news that will be most interesting to your reader. For example, your grandmother will be interested in news about your activities, and a friend who has moved away will be interested in news about his or her old friends.

You might comment on or question something from the person's last letter to you. Remember to include all five parts of a friendly letter in your draft. The letter below that Molly wrote to cheer up her absent friend shows you where the parts belong.

April 3, 1999

Dear Eric,

Everyone is sorry to hear that you broke your leg. We miss you. I hope you can come back soon.

Lots of things have been happening here at school. We played soccer against the fourth-grade team. Guess what? We won! In science class, we planted seeds, and I planted some for you. They should be starting to grow soon.

We'll all be glad when you're well enough to come back.

Your pal,

Molly

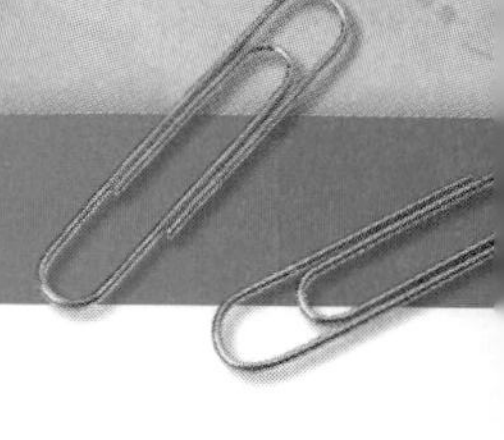

Revising, Proofreading, and Publishing

Revising

Time to Take Another Look

Reread your draft to revise it. Imagine that you are the person who will receive the letter. Ask yourself if you would find your letter interesting.

Use these questions to help you revise your draft:

- ❑ Does my letter tell news that will be interesting to the person who receives it?
- ❑ Do I need to take out news that will not be interesting?
- ❑ Does my letter include everything I want to say?
- ❑ Does my letter say something about the person who is receiving it?
- ❑ Do I want to add a question for my reader to answer?
- ❑ Do I need to rewrite anything that is not clear?
- ❑ Do I need to choose more interesting words?

Make your changes with a colored pencil. You may want to read it aloud to a friend.

Addressing an Envelope

Make sure you have all the information you need to send the letter. Get the address from a telephone book or an address book. Write your name and address in the top left corner of the envelope. Write the address of the person who will receive the letter in the middle of the envelope.

Molly Miller
501 Franklin St.
Smithtown, OH 44000

Eric Jones
1927 Stevens Ave.
Smithtown, OH 44000

Proofreading

Time to Look at Capitalization, Punctuation, and Spelling

When you've decided what to say, check your capitalization, punctuation, spelling, and grammar so your letter will be easy to read. This checklist will help you.

- ❑ Did I capitalize each part of my letter correctly?
- ❑ Did I indent each paragraph?
- ❑ Did I use the correct mark of punctuation at the end of each part of my letter?
- ❑ Did I spell all the words correctly?

Proofreading Your Envelope

Proofreading your envelope is just as important as proofreading your letter. If the address is not right, your letter won't get there! Remember to use the correct ZIP code.

Publishing

Time to Share

Publishing is sharing your best work with others.

To publish, follow these steps:

1. Use your neatest handwriting to copy your revised draft.
2. After you finish, proofread your letter once more.
3. Send along a photograph or a newspaper clipping if you wish.

Mail your letter.

1. Use your best handwriting to address your envelope.
2. Double-check the address.
3. Add a stamp with the correct amount of postage in the upper right corner.
4. Drop your letter in the mailbox.
5. Sit back and wait for an answer!

CHAPTER 7

Speaking and Listening Skills

LESSON 1

Oral Presentations

An oral presentation is a way to tell others about things you know and things you like to do.

An oral presentation is different from an ordinary conversation. You must prepare and practice an oral presentation before you give it to your class.

Which of these talks do you think would be an oral presentation?

A. You talk to your cousin on the phone.
B. A police officer gives you directions.
C. The weather forecaster from the local TV station comes to talk to all the students in your school.
D. One of your classmates gives an oral book report.
E. At lunch, you tell your friends about a movie you saw on Saturday.

You are right if you said that C and D are oral presentations. The weather forecaster and your classmate had to prepare and practice before they gave their talks.

About the Photograph

This boy is giving an oral presentation to his class. He is using the large map as a visual aid. Have you ever given an oral presentation?

What kinds of ideas do you talk about with your friends and family? Some of these same ideas could be given as oral presentations.

Have you ever visited an interesting place? Have you read, heard, or seen something that you would like to share with your classmates? Have you learned anything on your own in science or social studies? Do you have any special hobbies or projects? Any of these ideas could be used for an oral presentation.

In two weeks, Lynn will have to give an oral presentation. She knew it was time to prepare.

- She thought of an idea—her dance classes.
- She thought about what she does in her dance classes.
- She wrote down some key words on note cards to help her remember.
- She looked for pictures that would help explain her dance classes.
- She studied her notes carefully.

After she prepared her presentation, Lynn practiced.

- She asked her mother and a friend to listen to her talk.
- She followed their suggestions for improvement. They told her to speak louder and not to say the word *um.*

Here are some things Lynn did when she gave her presentation.

- She looked quickly at her note cards when she needed to.
- She looked at her audience when she spoke.
- She spoke loudly, clearly, and slowly.

Activity A

Choose one of these ideas. As you think about your idea, write down some key words on note cards. Look for pictures to help explain your presentation.

A. _______ is a very exciting sport.

B. There are many unusual toys today.

C. Summer vacations should be longer.

D. The people of _______ have some customs different from ours.

E. One of the most surprising things I learned in science is _______ .

F. If I could be another person for one day, I'd choose to be _______ .

Activity B

Practice your presentation. Ask a member of your family or a classmate to give you suggestions for improvement. Give your presentation to the class.

Writer's Corner

▶ **Listen to a classmate's presentation. Write down key words and phrases that you notice. Share these with your classmate to check that the right ideas were stressed in the presentation.**

LESSON 2

Choral Speaking

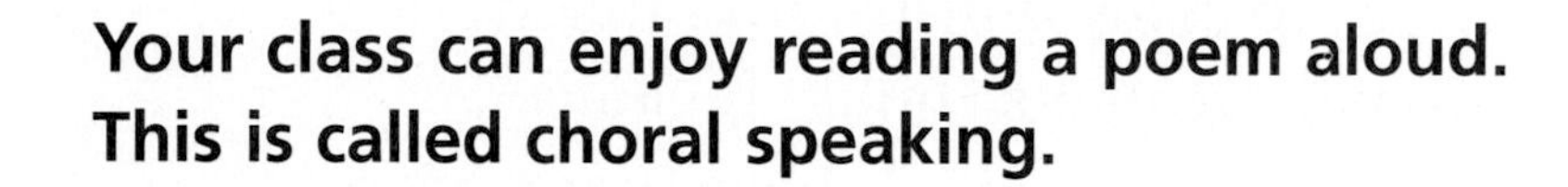

Your class can enjoy reading a poem aloud. This is called choral speaking.

The lines of a poem can be read aloud in different ways. For some lines, your voice will rise or fall. Some lines are meant to be read with a loud or a soft voice. Finally, every poem has a special beat, or rhythm. In choral speaking, readers are divided into groups to read different lines. Sometimes only one person will read a part. This is called a solo. When everyone reads together, it is called unison.

What would a band sound like if the trumpets or the drums played a little slower or faster than the other instruments? The sound would probably make you want to cover your ears! In choral speaking, you must listen to your own voice and to the voices of your classmates.

In choral speaking, try to

- speak together and pause together.
- speak with rhythm to help show the meaning of the words.
- say each word clearly.

Tuning-Up Exercises

Imagine that your voice is like a musical instrument. You can tune up your voice with a few simple exercises. Some exercises help you breathe slowly and evenly. Others help you say words clearly.

Breathing

Try these three exercises.

1. Breathe in deeply.
   Then let the air out through your nose.

2. Breathe in and hold your breath for eight counts.
   Let the air out slowly in puffs as if you are blowing out candles one by one.

3. Breathe in deeply as if you are smelling a flower and hold your breath for ten counts.
   Let the air out with the sound of *puff, puff, puff.*

Enunciation

Try these exercises to help you *enunciate*—to say the vowels and consonants clearly.

1. Say *a* as in *tag*.
   Now say *rap, pad, hat, patch, tap.*
2. Say *e* as in *pet.*
   Now say *red, bed, pen, ten, hen.*
3. Say *i* as in *sit.*
   Now say *fit, mit, itch, chin, grin.*
4. Say *o* as in *fog.*
   Now say *log, hog, bog, smog, dog.*
5. Say *u* as in *tug.*
   Now say *rug, under, mug, ugly, up.*
6. Practice the sound of thc *e* and the *l* in *tell* by saying this sentence: *Tell Nell to sell the bell.*

Activity A

What kind of sound does a trumpet make? Read this poem about Lewis and his trumpet and find out.

Lewis Has a Trumpet

SOLO 1: A trumpet
SOLO 2: A trumpet

UNISON:
Lewis has a trumpet
A bright one that's yellow
A loud proud horn.

LIGHT VOICES:
He blows it in the evening
When the moon is newly rising
He blows it when it's raining
In the cold and misty morn

DEEP VOICES:
It honks and it whistles
It roars like a lion
It rumbles like a lion
With a wheezing huffing hum

LIGHT VOICES:
His parents say it's awful
Oh really simply awful

SOLO 3: But

UNISON:
Lewis says he loves it
It's such a handsome trumpet
And when he's through
with trumpets
He's going to buy a drum.

Karla Kuskin

Activity B

Imagine that you're walking down a street in your town. Suddenly, rain starts falling. Colorful umbrellas pop up everywhere. Read this poem. Can you feel the rhythm of umbrellas popping up quickly? Try to use the sound of your voice to show this rhythm.

Sudden Storm

DEEP VOICES: The rain comes in sheets.
Sweeping the streets;

LIGHT VOICES: Here, here, and here
Umbrellas appear.

UNISON: Red, blue, yellow, and green,
They tilt and they lean

LIGHT VOICES: Like mushrooms, like flowers

UNISON: That grow when it showers.

Elizabeth Coatsworth

Activity C

This poem has different speakers: a narrator, the parent grasshoppers, and the young grasshoppers. Can you show the hopping rhythm as you read?

The Grasshoppers

SOLO 1:

High
Up
Over the top
Of feathery grasses the
Grasshoppers hop.
They won't eat their suppers;
They will not obey
Their grasshopper mothers
And fathers, who say:

DEEP VOICES:

'Listen, my children,
This must be stopped—
Now is the time your last
Hop should be hopped;
So come eat your suppers
And go to your beds—'

SOLO 2:	But the little green grasshoppers Shake their green heads.
LIGHT VOICES:	'No No—'
SOLO 3:	The naughty ones say,
LIGHT VOICES:	'All we have time to do Now is to play. If we want supper we'll Nip at a fly Or nibble a blueberry As we go by; If we feel sleepy we'll Close our eyes tight And snooze away in a Harebell all night. But not Now. Now we must hop. And nobody, NOBODY, Can make us stop.'

Dorothy Aldis

Activity D

Do you like bugs? Experiment with this short poem. Use light voices and deep voices. Then try soft voices and loud voices to read this poem in a different way.

Hey, Bug!

LIGHT VOICES:
Hey, bug, stay!
Don't run away.
I know a game that we can play.
I'll hold my finger very still
and you can climb a finger-hill.

DEEP VOICES:
No, no.
Don't go.
Here's a wall—a tower, too,
A tiny bug town, just for you.
I've a cookie. You have some.
Take this oatmeal cookie crumb.

LIGHT VOICES: Hey, bug, stay!

DEEP VOICES: Hey, bug!

UNISON: Hey!

Lilian Moore

Activity E

Which parts of this poem do you think should be read with loud voices? Which parts should be read with soft voices?

Tiptoe

Yesterday I skipped all day,
The day before I ran,
Today I'm going to tiptoe
Everywhere I can.
I'll tiptoe down the stairway.
I'll tiptoe through the door.
I'll tiptoe to the living room
And give an awful roar
And my father, who is reading,
Will jump up from his chair
And mumble something silly like
"I didn't see you there."
I'll tiptoe to my mother
And give a little cough
And when she spins to see me
Why, I'll softly tiptoe off.
I'll tiptoe through the meadows,
Over hills and yellow sands
And when my toes get tired
Then I'll tiptoe on my hands.

Karla Kuskin

Writer's Corner

▶ **Think of a sound that is very loud and noticeable. Using ideas you have from reading the poems in this lesson, write a poem about this noise.**

LESSON 3

Listening for Sequence

Sequence is the order in which actions happen.

When you do something, you usually follow a sequence, or specific order. For example, before you tie your shoes, you put them on your feet. Following a sequence makes things easier to do.

Activity A

The actions in a story happen in sequence. Listen to the short stories that your teacher will read. Name the first and last action of each student to fill in this chart.

	FIRST ACTION	LAST ACTION
Marissa	________	________
Becky	________	________
Chen	________	________
Pedro	________	________

Activity B

Would you like to be a reporter? Here is your chance. Listen to the stories that your teacher will read. Take notes and tell what happens in the correct sequence.

Writer's Corner

▶ With a partner think of something you both know how to do or make. You may think of making a peanut butter and jelly sandwich or tying your shoes. Now write down all the steps needed to complete your task and number them in the correct sequence.

LESSON 4

Listening to Directions

Directions tell you how to do something.

Directions tell you how to do something in the quickest and easiest way. Imagine what it would be like to try to do these things without directions.

bake a cake	build a car
play soccer	work a computer

School is a place where you will hear many directions. What would happen in these situations if you did *not* listen carefully?

A. The secretary gives directions for finding Mr. Barnes, the eighth-grade teacher.
B. The principal announces the directions for a fire drill.
C. Your teacher gives directions for taking a test.

Listening to directions is important for people in many jobs. Why do you think it is important for these people to listen carefully to the directions on their jobs?

an airline pilot	a car mechanic
a nurse	a taxi driver

Activity A

You will need a large sheet of paper and a pencil. Listen to the directions that your teacher will read. Carefully complete each step that you hear. What have you drawn?

Activity B

Play the Direction Game. Ten students should form a line. The first student in line should take an object in the classroom, such as an eraser. This student should give a direction and then follow it. The next student in line should follow the first direction and then give and follow a new direction. The third person follows the first two directions and adds a third. Whoever does not do all the directions sits down and a new person takes the last place in line. The first person to do all ten directions wins!

Activity C

Try to think of a word for every letter of the word DIRECTIONS. The words should be ones you hear in school when someone gives directions.

Writer's Corner

- Write directions from your school to your home. Exchange directions with a partner to see if they make sense.

Listening to Poetry

A poet uses the sounds of words to create feelings and pictures in the mind of the listener.

Close your eyes and listen to the sounds around you. What do you hear? If you listen closely to the words a poet uses, you will be able to see and hear many things. A poet also uses words to create feelings.

Read these four lines of poetry aloud. What does the poet feel when she walks barefoot in the grass?

> In the morning, very early,
> That's the time I love to go
> Barefoot where the fern grows curly
> And grass is cool between each toe.
>
> *Rachel Field*

Answer these questions about the poem.

1. Does the poet like to walk barefoot?
2. Do you feel the poet is walking slowly or running? Why?
3. Why do you think the poet said "between each toe" instead of "on my toes"?
4. Where do you think this place is?

Listen to the rhyme and rhythm of this poem as your teacher reads it. It almost sounds like a song.

Alligator Pie

Alligator pie, alligator pie,
If I don't get some I think I'm gonna die.
Give away the green grass, give away the sky,
But don't give away my alligator pie.

Alligator stew, alligator stew,
If I don't get some I don't know what I'll do.
Give away my furry hat, give away my shoe,
But don't give away my alligator stew.

Alligator soup, alligator soup,
If I don't get some I think I'm gonna droop.
Give away my hockey-stick, give away my hoop,
But don't give away my alligator soup.

Dennis Lee

Activity A

Listen to this poem as your teacher reads it. What color do you imagine when you listen to this poem? How does this poem make you feel?

The Sound of Water

The sound of water is:
Rain,
Lap,
Fold,
Slap,
Gurgle,
Splash,
Chum,
Crash,
Murmur,
Pour,
Ripple,
Roar,
Plunge,
Drip,
Spout,
Slip,
Sprinkle,
Flow,
Ice,
Snow.

Mary L. O'Neill

Activity B

Listen to this poem as your teacher reads it. What sounds do you hear repeated? What kind of feeling does this sound create? How does this poem make you feel?

Poemsicle

If you add sicle to your pop,
Would he become a Popsicle?
Would a mop become a mopsicle?
Would a cop become a copsicle?
Would a chop become a chopsicle?
Would a drop become a dropsicle?
Would a hop become a hopsicle?
I guess it's time to stopsicle,
Or is it timesicle to stopsicle?
Heysicle, I can't stopsicle.
Ohsicle mysicle willsicle Isicle
Havesicle tosicle talksicle
likesicle thissicle foreversicle—
Huhsicle?

Shel Silverstein

Activity C

Poems paint pictures. Listen to this poem as your teacher reads it. What things do you see? Do you agree with the poet?

Flowers Are a Silly Bunch

Flowers are a silly bunch
While trees are sort of bossy.
Lakes are shy
The earth is calm
And rivers do seem saucy.
Hills are good
But mountains mean
While weeds all ask for pity.
I guess the country can be nice
But I live in the city.

Arnold Spilka

Activity D

Now listen to this poem. How is the feeling of this poem different from the poem on page 200?

Rudolph Is Tired of the City

These buildings are too close to me.
I'd like to PUSH away.
I'd like to live in the country,
And spread my arms all day.

I'd like to spread my breath out, too—
As farmers' sons and daughters do.

I'd tend the cows and chickens.
I'd do the other chores.
Then, all the hours left I'd go
A-SPREADING out-of-doors.

Gwendolyn Brooks

Writer's Corner

▶ Choose three of the six poems in this lesson and draw a picture for each poem. Draw what you see in your mind as you listen to the poem. Next to each picture write a short explanation of why you drew it. Exchange with a partner and compare drawings.

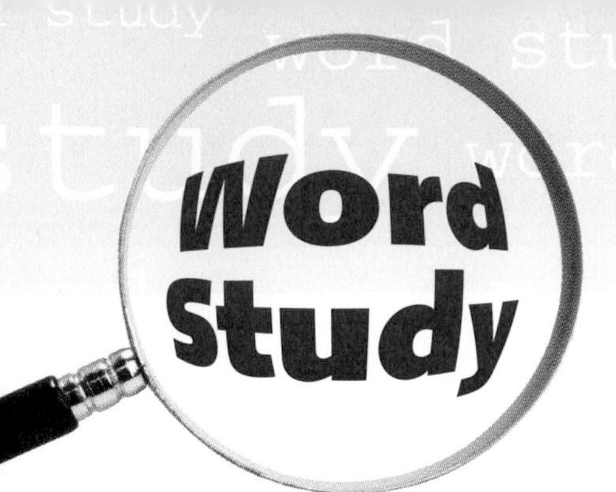

Exploring Words

Synonyms

Synonyms are words that have the same or almost the same meaning.

Here are synonyms you have already learned.

end—stop	path—road
late—tardy	fast—quick

Here are new synonyms.

place—put	peal—ring
large—big	help—aid

Activity A

Use a new synonym from the list above in place of each word in italics.

1. Please *place* the chart on the wall.
2. We should *aid* the younger child.
3. My Uncle Fred caught a *large* fish at Silver Creek.
4. The bells in the clock tower *peal* at six o'clock.
5. Did Oscar *put* the cereal box on the shelf?
6. The Coast Guard will *help* the boats at sea.
7. Why did all the bells in the town *ring* just now?
8. Forty people rode on the *big* bus.
9. *Place* the food up high so the bears can't reach it.
10. *Aid* is on the way!

Antonyms

Antonyms are words that are opposite in meaning. Antonyms are opposites.

Here are antonyms you have already learned.

near—far	short—long
on—off	rise—fall

Here are new antonyms.

tiny—giant	back—front
hot—cold	leave—stay

Activity B

Use a new antonym from the list above in place of each word in italics.

1. John will *leave* for two hours.
2. There is a scratch on the *front* of the chair.
3. Be careful! The pan is very *cold.*
4. A *giant* spider made a web on the tree.
5. Please sew a button on the *back* of this shirt.
6. Rick cannot *stay* because he has chores to do.
7. Did you add *hot* water to the iced tea?
8. The bride's bouquet was tied with a *tiny* bow.
9. The goat is walking in *front* of you.
10. Don't *leave.* Your mom will be waiting.

Activity C

Choose the antonym that best fits each sentence.

1. Twelve miles is a (short, long) way to walk.
2. The pilot sits in the (front, back) of the plane.
3. China and the United States are (near to, far from) each other.
4. In the morning, the sun will (rise, fall).
5. Whales are (tiny, giant) mammals.

Homophones

Homophones are words that sound alike but are spelled differently and have different meanings.

Here are homophones you have already learned.

beet—beat　　sent—cent　　hole—whole

Here are new homophones.

your—you're　　for—four　　pair—pear

Your and *You're*

Which word is correct in each sentence?

A. (Your, You're) trophy is in the trophy case. (belonging to you)

B. If (your, you're) ready, let's go. (contraction of *you are*)

For and *Four*

Which word is correct in each sentence?

A. (For, Four) puppies scurried across the floor. (number 4)
B. This gold chain is (for, four) you. (belonging to)

Pair and *Pear*

Which word is correct in each sentence?

A. Ellen bought a new (pair, pear) of gloves. (two of a kind)
B. An apple and (pair, pear) were on the table. (fruit)

Activity D

Complete each sentence with the correct homophone.

1. Next to the road was a (pair, pear) orchard.
2. (For, Four) sparrows sat on the telephone wire.
3. (Your, You're) dental appointment is tomorrow.
4. A (hole, whole) bag of cookies is missing.
5. Steve looked through my (pair, pear) of binoculars.
6. Do you think (your, you're) ready for the party?
7. He (beet, beat) the small fire with a rug.
8. Jacqueline won a prize (for, four) her drawing.
9. Somebody (cent, sent) me a small alligator pin as a gift.
10. Do (your, you're) glasses have your initials on them?

Contractions

A contraction is a short way to write some words. A contraction always uses an apostrophe.

Here are contractions you have already learned.

have not—haven't
has not—hasn't
does not—doesn't
do not—don't
did not—didn't

Here are new contractions.

he is—he's
she is—she's
it is—it's
I have—I've
we are—we're
you are—you're
they are—they're

What letter or letters are missing in each contraction?

What takes the place of these letters?

Activity E

Answer each of these riddles. Use a contraction for the words in italics in your answer.

1. *He is* tall and eats the leaves from the trees. What is he?
2. *She is* able to jump and carry her baby in a pouch. What is she?
3. *They are* long and crawl on the ground. What are they?
4. *We are* funny and can swing by our tails. What are we?

5. *She is* white and furry and lives in a cold climate. What is she?
6. *You are* able to talk and fly. What are you?
7. *He is* the king of the jungle. What is he?
8. *They are* friendly and do tricks in the water. What are they?
9. *He is* huge with big ears and a long nose. What is he?
10. *We are* desert animals with big humps on our backs. What are we?

Activity F

Write the two words that make up each contraction. Then write a short paragraph using all five contractions.

1. I've ________
2. he's ________
3. they're ________
4. don't ________
5. it's ________

WRITER'S WORKSHOP

A Nature Poem

What is your favorite poem? Did the poet write a poem that rhymes or a poem whose words just sound good together? Poets use the sounds of words to create special feelings in the mind of the listener. You can be a poet, too. Write a poem about nature. Add your poem to a class book of nature poetry.

Prewriting

Whether you live in the country or in the city, nature is all around. Write a list of things you have noticed about nature. Ask yourself questions like these to help you find a topic for your nature poem:

- What is my favorite season?
- What natural things do I see during my favorite season?
- What are some nature sounds I hear around me?
- Where do I find natural things around my own home?
- What are they?
- What things about nature cheer me up when I'm sad?
- What natural things can be scary?

Choose your topic and write its name in the middle of a word map. Then write all the different words and ideas you can think of for that topic.

Timothy, a third grader, made this word map for his topic, Trees.

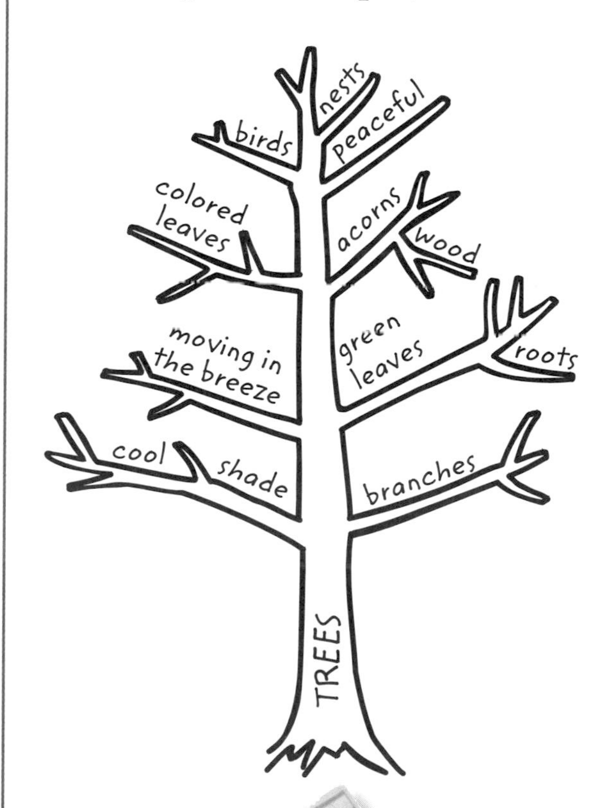

Drafting

Choose words and ideas from your word map to use in your poem.

You might enjoy writing a poem with rhyming words.

If you want to write a poem that doesn't rhyme, try writing a sentence about your topic. Then write parts of the sentence on different lines so your sentence looks like a poem.

Don't worry about getting everything just the way you want it the first time. Try different poems about the same idea. Try writing different kinds of poems. Leave a space between each line as you write. You'll probably want to make many changes.

When you've finished experimenting, choose your favorite poem. Write a title for it.

WRITER'S WORKSHOP

Poems Don't Have to Rhyme

Some poems have rhyming words. Others just express an idea in a different way.

Thank a Tree

A home for birds,

Some shade for me,

Crisp, colored leaves,

Thank you, kind tree.

—Timothy

A Tree in Summer

Deep in green leaves

baby birds

are sheltered

from the burning sun,

and in my tree house

so am I.

—Timothy

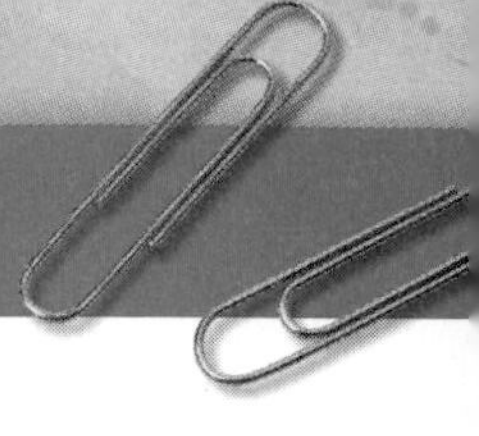

EDITOR'S WORKSHOP

Revising, Proofreading, and Publishing

Revising

Time to Take Another Look

Now revise your poem. Make sure it sends the message you want to tell. Because your poem will be short, the words you choose are very important. Think about each word. Make sure you've chosen the best one.

Ask yourself these questions to help you revise:

- ❑ Do I need to rewrite anything to make my idea clear?
- ❑ Do I need to add details to help my reader feel a special feeling?
- ❑ Do I need to take out any details that do not help send my message?
- ❑ Do I need to choose more interesting words?
- ❑ Do I need to change the order of the words to make my poem sound better?
- ❑ Do I need to make my title more interesting?

Use a colored pencil to write your changes in the spaces between the lines. If your poem gets too cluttered, copy your draft again, and then make more changes.

Finding Synonyms

If your poem still doesn't sound quite right, look in a dictionary or thesaurus to find synonyms for some of the words.

Reread your prewriting notes. Look for words and ideas you can use as you revise.

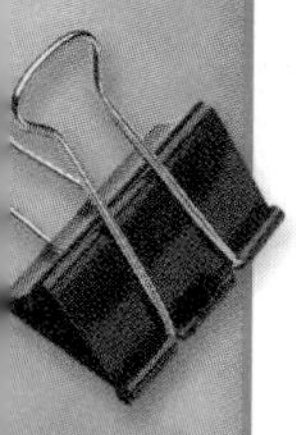

Proofreading

Time to Look at Capitalization, Punctuation, and Spelling

Poems do not always follow the normal rules for capitalization, punctuation, and spelling. But the meaning of your poem must still be clear to your reader. Use the checklist to help you proofread your poem.

- ❑ Did I use capital letters correctly in the title?
- ❑ Did I arrange the lines of the poem to make them easy to read?
- ❑ Did I use marks of punctuation to show my reader where to pause?
- ❑ Did I spell each word correctly?

Listen to Your Poem

Ask a partner to read your poem aloud. Close your eyes and listen. Listen to make sure you did not leave out any words. Listen to make sure your punctuation marks show your reader where to pause.

Publishing

Time to Share

Publishing is sharing your best work with others.

To publish, follow these steps:

1. Use your neatest handwriting to copy your revised draft.
2. After you finish, proofread your final copy one more time.
3. Draw a picture to illustrate your poem.

Make a class nature poetry book.

1. Collect everyone's final poem.
2. Make a cover for your book.
3. Write a title, such as *Poems About Earth, Air, and Sky.*
4. Bind the pages and the cover together with yarn or a stapler.
5. Take the book to the classroom library and read the poems aloud with a partner.

CHAPTER

8

Dictionary and Library Skills

LESSON 1

Dictionary Skills—Alphabetical Order

A dictionary is a book of words in alphabetical order.

You read that a scientist found a fossil. You want to find out what a fossil is. You see the word *aardvark* in a book about animals. You want to know how to say this word. A dictionary gives this information.

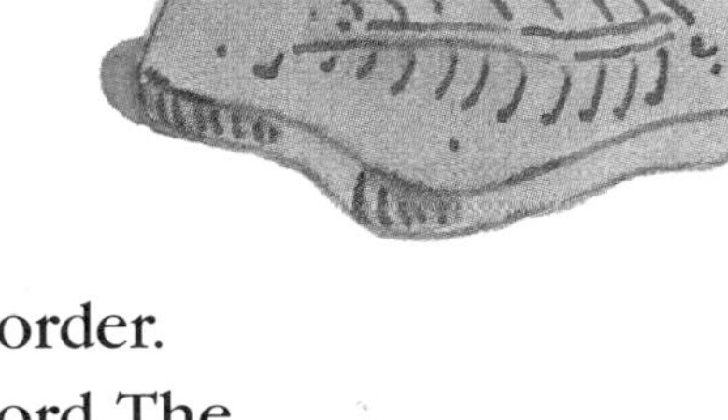

In a dictionary, you can find
- the correct spellings of words.
- the way words are pronounced.
- the meanings of words.

The words in a dictionary are in alphabetical order. Each word listed in a dictionary is an entry word. The entry word is followed by the pronunciation and the meaning of the word. It is easy to use the dictionary because it is divided into three alphabetical sections: the beginning, the middle, and the end. In these sections, the letters of the alphabet are grouped like this:

BEGINNING	MIDDLE	END
a b c d e f g h i	j k l m n o p q	r s t u v w x y z

About the Photograph

Do you have a question? Do you need more information? Look it up! Dictionaries, atlases, and libraries are standing by, ready to give us the answers.

Activity A

Put each group of letters in alphabetical order.

1. s, v, y, t
2. k, h, i, j
3. r, t, e, o
4. n, l, g, q
5. f, k, d, b
6. m, c, h, i
7. w, m, q, r
8. j, t, h, k

Activity B

Put each list of words in alphabetical order.

1	2	3	4
space	Saturn	Earth	weightless
planets	Jupiter	Venus	asteroids
astronaut	Mars	Uranus	shuttle
moon	Pluto	Neptune	rotate

Activity C

Rewrite the scrambled letters in alphabetical order. Each group of letters will make a word.

1. tosc
2. enbt
3. somt
4. yocp
5. mfil
6. gesg
7. wlfo
8. pmo
9. rof
10. nya
11. tac
12. ojy
13. ria
14. icyt
15. ristf
16. micph
17. yocphp
18. rolfo
19. edep
20. stol

Activity D

Write the number 1 if the word is at the beginning of the dictionary, 2 if the word is in the middle of the dictionary, and 3 if the word is at the end of the dictionary. Use the list on page 213 to help you.

1. astronaut
2. moonscape
3. orbit
4. command
5. energy
6. travel
7. reentry
8. discover
9. scientists
10. capsule
11. unknown
12. oxygen
13. spacecraft
14. target
15. launch

Writer's Corner

▶ **Write down ten words that begin with ten different letters. Then rewrite them in alphabetical order.**

LESSON 2

Dictionary Skills—Guide Words

Guide words tell the first and last word found on a dictionary page. The guide words are located at the top corner of the page.

When you look for a word in the dictionary, you should follow these steps.

1. Decide whether the word can be found at the beginning, middle, or end of the dictionary.
2. Look at the guide words at the top of the pages.
3. Decide if you would find the word between the two guide words.
4. If so, look for the word on that page.

Activity A

Write *before* if you would find the word before the word *planet.* Write *after* if you would find the word after the word *planet.*

1. paddle
2. prairie
3. peace
4. polite
5. pencil
6. product
7. phone
8. pyramid
9. pneumonia
10. piano
11. prance
12. push-up

Activity B

Find the five words that come between the guide words *fill—fingerprint.*

film filter final
filing freeze flagpole
fast fin file
feast finish find

Activity C

Tell whether each word comes before, after, or between each pair of guide words.

	WORD	GUIDE WORDS
1.	double	door—dove
2.	rug	ruby—rule
3.	kitchen	knife—koala
4.	spruce	sponge—square
5.	power	practice—praise
6.	watch	wallet—warmth
7.	gravel	grasp—gull
8.	normal	nomad—noon
9.	movie	multiply—mumps
10.	electric	elbow—empty

Writer's Corner

▶ **For each of the following pairs of guide words, write a word that comes between them.**

1. land—life
2. shallow—sky
3. background—balance
4. crawl—crusade
5. pack—penny
6. train—trout

LESSON 3

Dictionary Skills—Word Meaning

A dictionary gives the meaning or meanings of a word.

Each word listed in a dictionary is called an entry word. The entry word is in dark print. It is usually divided into syllables. Each entry word is followed by one or more meanings. If the word has more than one meaning, each different meaning is given a number. Learning different meanings for words can be fun and interesting.

Activity A

Look carefully at the different meanings for the entry word *break.* Decide which meaning matches the meaning of the word *break* in each sentence.

break (brāk), **1** come apart or make come apart. **2** crack the bone of. **3** fail to keep. **4** escape. **5** change suddenly. **6** dawn, appear. **7** a short interruption in work or practice.

1. She *breaks* her toys quickly.
2. Soon day will *break.*
3. I won't *break* our promise.
4. How did he *break* his arm?
5. We hope the hot weather will *break* soon.
6. The lion tried to *break* away from its trainer.
7. Let's take a *break.*

Activity B

Some words have more than one meaning. Use your dictionary to find two correct meanings for each word.

1. sharp
- a. having a point
- b. cutting with a razor
- c. having a quick mind

2. back
- a. to go hiking or camping
- b. in return
- c. part of a person's body

3. mark
- a. line, dot, or stain
- b. grade on a test paper
- c. food store

4. bark
- a. outside covering of a tree
- b. type of musical instrument
- c. sharp sound a dog makes

5. crane
- a. large box for shipping furniture
- b. machine for lifting heavy objects
- c. large bird with long legs

Activity C

Find these words in your dictionary. Tell how many meanings your dictionary gives for each word.

1. cymbal
2. laser
3. mission
4. cot
5. note
6. universe
7. menu
8. slide
9. kick

Writer's Corner

▶ **Write a definition for each of the following words. If you think a word may have more than one meaning, write each meaning. Check your definitions with a dictionary. Then use each word in a sentence of your own.**

1. cast
2. peace
3. soap
4. twist
5. tear

Library Skills—Cover, Spine, Title Page

A book has a cover, a spine, and a title page.

Many years ago it took a great deal of time to make a book. Now thousands of books are printed each day about many different subjects.

You can discover a lot about a book by looking at its cover, title page, and spine.

The cover of a book gives
the title
and usually the author's name.

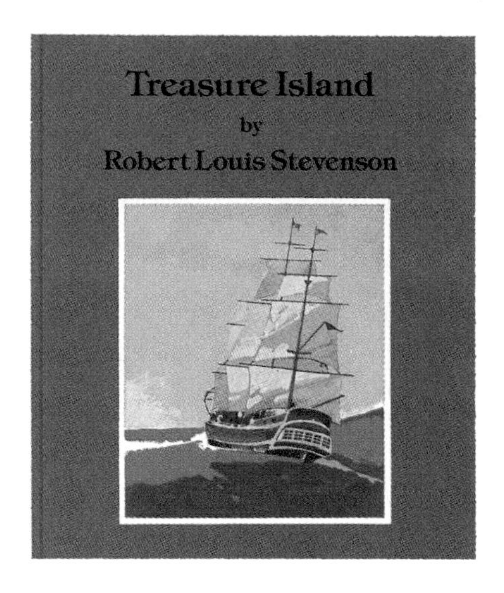

The title page gives
the title of the book,
the author's name,
and sometimes the illustrator's name.

The spine of a book gives
the title
and usually the author's last name.

Activity A

Choose a book that you would like to read. Look at it carefully. Give the following information about your book.

1. title
2. author's name
3. illustrator's name
4. number of pages

Activity B

Use the word bank to answer these questions.

WORD BANK	
cover	title
title page	spine
author	illustrator

1. In what three places can you find the title of a book?
2. What do you call the name of a book?
3. Where can you find the name of the illustrator?
4. What do you call the writer of a book?
5. What protects the pages of a book?

Writer's Corner

▶ **What is your favorite movie or story? Draw a book cover for it. Tell why you chose to draw that picture for your book cover.**

Library Skills—Table of Contents, Index, Glossary

The table of contents and index help you locate information in a book. The glossary helps you pronounce and understand words.

Table of Contents

The table of contents is a page that tells the name of each chapter and the page on which the chapter begins.

The table of contents is found at the beginning of a book. The names of the chapters give you an idea of what is included in the book.

Activity A

Use this sample table of contents from a book on Mars to answer the questions.

TABLE OF CONTENTS

Chapter		Page
1	The Red Planet	1
2	Life on Mars	15
3	Temperature	26
4	Flights to Mars	32
5	Surface	39
6	Satellites	43
Index		47

1. How many chapters are in this book?
2. On what pages would you find information about the temperature on Mars?
3. On what page does the index begin?
4. On what page would you find another name for the planet Mars?
5. What chapter tells you about space flights to Mars?
6. On what page does chapter 6 begin?
7. What is the title of chapter 4?

Index

An index lists, in alphabetical order, all or most of the persons, places, things, and events mentioned in a book. It gives the page numbers where specific information can be found.

Most nonfiction books have an index in the back of the book. The page numbers are beside the subject. The dash (-) between numbers tells you to continue reading from the first page number up to the second page number: "8–11" means "read from page 8 to page 11."

Activity B

Use this sample index to answer the questions.

INDEX

magnetic field, 8–11
Milky Way, 10–13
moons, 43
orbit, 13–16
planets, 2-6
plant life, 17–21
satellites, 43–46
space travel, 32–38
surface, 39–42
temperature, 26–31
US *Mariner 6* (spacecraft), 35–36

1. On what pages would you find information about how hot it is on Mars?
2. What subject would you learn about on pages 39–42?

3. Which pages would you read to learn about space travel to Mars?
4. Which pages contain information on how long it takes Mars to orbit the sun?
5. On what page would you discover how many moons Mars has?
6. What subject would you learn about on pages 8–11?
7. What is the name of a U.S. spacecraft? On what pages would you find information about this spacecraft?
8. On what pages would you find information about the Milky Way?

Glossary

A glossary shows you how to pronounce special words in a book and also gives their meanings.

A glossary is like a small dictionary. The words in a glossary are printed in alphabetical order and are usually found at the end of a book.

Activity C

Use this sample glossary to answer the questions.

GLOSSARY

gal ax y (gal´ ək sē)	a group of billions of stars forming one system
Mil ky Way	a broad band of faint light that stretches across the sky at night
or bit (ôr´ bit)	the path of the Earth or any one of the planets around the sun
ro ta tion (rō tā´ shən)	a turning around a center; turning in a circle
sat el lite (sat´ əl īt)	a heavenly body that revolves around a planet or other larger heavenly body
Sat urn (sat´ ərn)	the second-largest planet; Saturn has rings around it.

1. What is the word for a heavenly body that revolves around Jupiter?
2. Which is the second-largest planet?
3. Which term does not have the pronunciation given?
4. Write the pronunciation for the word *galaxy.*
5. What is the definition of the word *orbit?*

Writer's Corner

▶ **Write a paragraph that explains the differences between a table of contents, an index, and a glossary.**

LESSON 6

Library Skills—Reference Books: The Encyclopedia and the Atlas

Reference books contain useful facts and information. The encyclopedia is a set of reference books that contains facts about persons, places, things, and events. An atlas is a book of maps.

You have learned that the dictionary is a reference book that helps you spell, pronounce, and know the meaning or meanings of words. Another important reference work is the encyclopedia. In the encyclopedia, you can find articles about many different topics. Each book in a set is called a volume. On the spine of each volume are a number and letters that tell which part of the alphabet is covered in that volume.

For some reports, you may have to find where a country, city, or state is located. An atlas will help you find this information.

Both the encyclopedia and the atlas contain an index that will help you find information quickly.

Activity A

Look at the numbers and letters on this encyclopedia set, and then answer the questions below.

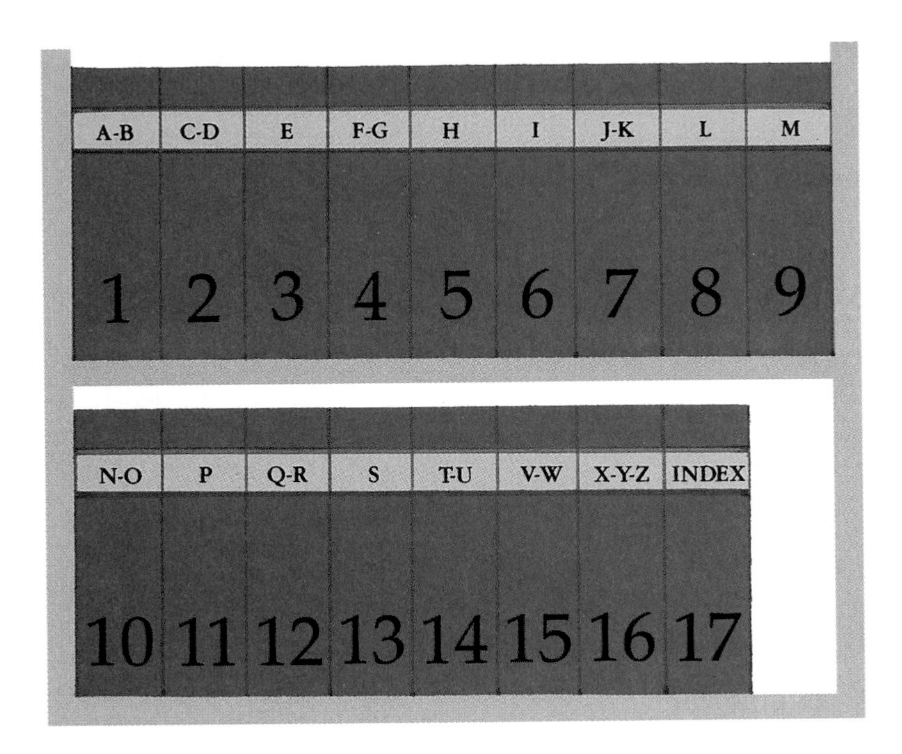

1. How many volumes are in this set?
2. In which volume would you find information about elephants?
3. Many elephants live in India. Which volume would you use to find information about this country?
4. In Volume 1, you would find information about another country where elephants live. Which country is it? China Africa Japan
5. Which of these topics would *not* be in Volume 10? newspapers ocean leopards
6. In which volume would you find the index?

Activity B

Tell whether you would find each type of information in a dictionary, an encyclopedia, or an atlas.

1. the meaning of the word *tusks*
2. things that are made from ivory
3. a map of India
4. the meaning of the word *pachyderm*
5. how people train elephants

Activity C

To find what you want in the encyclopedia, you sometimes have to look under a general topic. For example, if you want to learn about the brontosaurus, you may have to look under *dinosaurs.*

Match the word in column A with the encyclopedia topic in column B.

COLUMN A		COLUMN B
1. peanut butter	___	**a.** astronaut
2. space suit	___	**b.** snakes
3. folk songs	___	**c.** music
4. cobra	___	**d.** oceans
5. Atlantic	___	**e.** peanuts

Writer's Corner

▶ **Use an atlas to find four bodies of water. Then use an encyclopedia to find and write an interesting fact about each body of water. Share what you find with your class.**

LESSON 7

Library Skills—Kinds of Books

There are three kinds of books in the library—fiction, nonfiction, and reference books.

A library is filled with different kinds of books.

Fiction books tell stories about imaginary people, places, things, and events. A book about little green people on the moon is a fiction book.

Nonfiction books contain facts and true statements. A book that explains the surface of the moon is a nonfiction book.

Reference books help you find information about different persons, places, things, and events. A dictionary, an encyclopedia, and an atlas are types of reference books.

Activity A

Tell whether you would find these books in the fiction or nonfiction sections of the library.

1. A book about elves and leprechauns
2. A book about a young prince and his dragon
3. A book about the life cycle of a whale
4. A book about the solar system
5. A book about different kinds of sports
6. A book about dinosaurs

Activity B

Find the fiction, nonfiction, and reference sections of your library. Look carefully through each section, and then answer these questions.

1. Which section do you use the most?
2. In which section would you find a book of fairy tales?
3. How many sets of encyclopedias do you have in your library?
4. Where would you find an atlas of the world?
5. Where would you find a book about trees?
6. Would a book about famous inventions be found in the fiction section?
7. Would you find a mystery story in the reference section?

Activity C

Tell whether each book is a fiction, a nonfiction, or a reference book.

1. *The Planets* by Roy Gallant
2. *World Book Encyclopedia*
3. *Prehistoric Animals* by Peter Zallinger
4. *The Mousewife* by Rumer Godden
5. *Compton's Encyclopedia*

Writer's Corner

▶ **Go to the library with a partner, and find**
- **three fiction books.**
- **three nonfiction books.**
- **three reference books.**

Write down all nine titles.

LESSON 8

Library Skills—The Card Catalog

The card catalog helps you find books in the library.

You may have noticed that librarians know where every book belongs in the library. They know that fiction books are placed on the shelves in alphabetical order according to the author's last name.

The librarian looks on the spine of each book to help put the books in order. On the spine of each fiction book is the letter *F*. This tells the librarian what type of book it is. Underneath the *F* are the first three letters of the author's last name. This information is called the book's call number. Each book in the library has a call number. It is like the book's home address on the shelf.

Activity A

Write the author's last name, first name, and the call number of each of these books from the fiction section.

1. Beverly Cleary
2. Maurice Sendak
3. Evaline Ness

4. Marcia Brown
5. Leo Lionni
6. Muriel Feelings
7. Brian Wildsmith
8. Paula Hogan
9. Tony Johnson
10. Roy Gallant

Activity B

Put the authors' names in Activity A in alphabetical order. Remember to put the last names first.

Activity C

Help the librarian reshelve these fiction books. Rewrite the list in alphabetical order by the author's last name.

Homer Price by Robert McCloskey
Harriet the Spy by Louise Fitzhugh
The Black Stallion by Walter Farley
Out of the Silent Planet by C. S. Lewis
Ordinary Jack by Helen Cresswell

Writer's Corner

▶ **Think of three fiction books you have read, or choose three fiction books from a library. Write the titles, authors' names, and call numbers. Then write one sentence for each book that tells what the book is about.**

WRITER'S WORKSHOP

A Friend from a Book

Story characters are people or animals who are important to the action of the story. As you read a book, you may begin to feel as if you really know one of the characters. You can introduce the character to other readers by writing a character sketch and adding it to a favorite-character scrapbook.

Prewriting

Think about books you enjoyed reading. Choose a character you think would make a good friend. Then make notes about what the character is like.

Ask yourself questions like these to help you get started:

- ❑ Why would I like to have this character for a friend?
- ❑ What words could I use to describe him or her?
- ❑ What are some of the things the character did in the story?
- ❑ What do I especially like about the character?

Organize your ideas about the character with a chart like the one below. Write words that describe the character on the left. Beside each word, write an event from the story that shows why the word describes the character.

Julia, a third grader, made these prewriting notes.

Book Title: Best Buddies

Author: Lynn Lott

Character's Name: Nikki

Character Description	Proof from the story
brave	stands up to bully
creative	makes up game
funny	tells jokes that make her friends laugh

Drafting

Your character sketch will begin the same way a book report does. First, write the book's title. Then, write the author's name.

Introduce the character in your first sentence. Here's how Julia introduces the character Nikki.

> As soon as you start reading Best Buddies, Nikki will become one of your best buddies, too.

Use your notes to write about what the character is like and what he or she does. End by telling how you feel about the character. Here is Julia's ending.

> Nikki is a brave girl with a good imagination. She would be a great friend.

When you write a character sketch, don't tell everything you know about the character. Just give enough information to help your reader enjoy the character, too.

Guidelines for Writing a Character Sketch

You probably know that a sketch is a drawing. A character sketch is a word drawing. A character sketch helps readers know an important character in a book.

1. Begin your character sketch with the title of the book. Underline the title.
2. Tell the name of the book's author.
3. Tell who the character is.
4. Tell what the character is like.
5. Tell what the character does.
6. End with your opinion of the character.

EDITOR'S WORKSHOP

Revising, Proofreading, and Publishing

Revising

Time to Take Another Look

Before you make your final copy, reread your draft. Look for ways to help your reader know your character better.

Ask yourself these questions to help you revise your character sketch:

- ❑ Does my character seem like a person who would make a good friend?
- ❑ Do I need to add information to show why I like the character?
- ❑ Do I need to take out any details that don't really tell about the character?
- ❑ Do I need to take out any details that give away the story's ending?
- ❑ Do I need to rewrite anything that is not clear?
- ❑ Do I need to choose more interesting words?

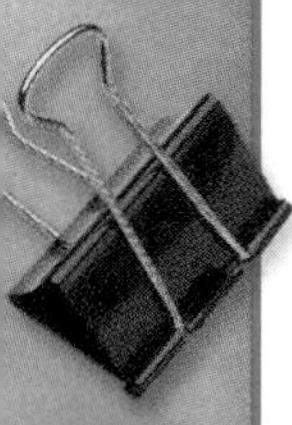

Now you're ready to revise. Use a colored pencil to make your changes stand out.

Add a Quotation
A quotation is a character's exact words. It is enclosed in quotation marks. Instead of telling your reader about the character, use a quotation from the book to let the reader find out for himself or herself about the character.

Check your book for a quotation that shows what the character is like. Julia used this quotation in her character sketch to show that the character Nikki is fun to be around.

Life with Nikki is never dull. She's always saying, "Bored people are boring people. Let's make up a new game."

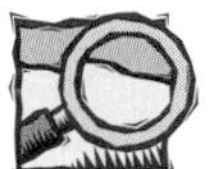

Proofreading

Time to Look at Capitalization, Punctuation, and Spelling

When you think your character sketch is ready, check your capitalization, punctuation, spelling, and grammar. Use the checklist to remind yourself what to look for.

- ❑ Did I indent the first word of my paragraph?
- ❑ Did I include the title of the book and the name of the author?
- ❑ Did I use the correct mark of punctuation at the end of each sentence?
- ❑ Did I spell each word correctly?

Checking Quotation Marks

To make sure you've put your quotation marks in the right place, read the words in the quotation marks aloud. Do the words make sense? Did you include any extra words, such as *said*? Look up the quotation again if you need to.

Publishing

Time to Share

To introduce your favorite character to the rest of the class, publish your character sketch.

To publish, follow these steps:

1. Use your neatest handwriting to copy your revised draft.
2. After you finish, proofread your final copy one more time.
3. Draw a picture of the character.

Make the class favorite-character scrapbook.

1. Collect everyone's final character sketch and illustration.
2. Make a cover for your book.
3. Write a title, such as *Book Buddies.*
4. Bind the pages and the cover together with yarn or staples.
5. Add your book to the classroom library.

PART 2

Grammar, Usage, and Mechanics

SENTENCES
NOUNS
PRONOUNS
VERBS
ADJECTIVES
ADVERBS
PUNCTUATION/
CAPITALIZATION

CHAPTER 9 SENTENCES

What Is a Sentence?

A sentence is a group of words that expresses a complete thought.

Which of these word groups sounds complete?

A. Two hard salty pretzels
B. I ate two pretzels

You are right if you noticed that

A. *Two hard salty pretzels* does NOT express a complete thought.
B. *I ate two pretzels* expresses a complete thought.

Which of these word groups expresses a complete thought?

A. Walk fast
B. The tall apple trees
C. The apple tastes good
D. Much later in the day
E. Don won the game

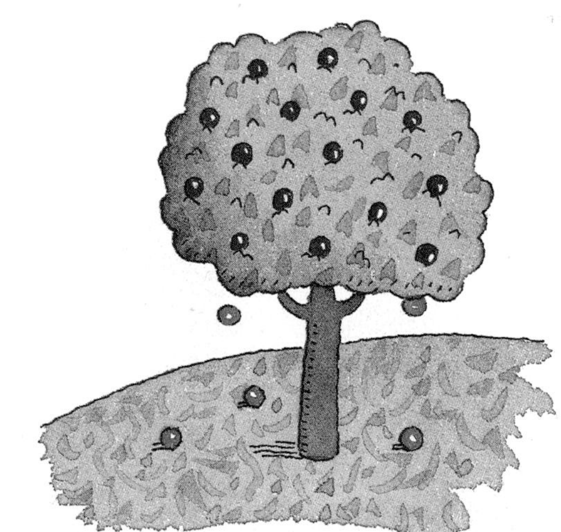

About the Photograph

Books are made up of many sentences that express complete thoughts. Reading opens our minds to these ideas. Do you enjoy reading as much as these boys do?

You are right if you noticed that A, C, and E are complete thoughts. They are sentences.

A. *Walk fast* is a sentence.
C. *The apple tastes good* is a sentence.
E. *Don won the game* is a sentence.

Word groups B and D are NOT complete thoughts.

B. *The tall apple trees* is NOT a sentence.
D. *Much later in the day* is NOT a sentence.

Remember . . .
A sentence is a group of words that expresses a complete thought.

Exercise 1

Tell which of these word groups are sentences because they express complete thoughts. Tell which are not sentences.

1. Caterpillars change into butterflies
2. A huge pile of shoes
3. On the side of the hill
4. Cotton is soft and fluffy
5. We couldn't count the leopard's spots
6. The giraffe's long legs
7. A duckling is a young duck
8. Two kites flew over the skyscrapers
9. Come quickly
10. Call me after school

Exercise 2

Here are two lists of incomplete thoughts. Match a group of words from column A with a group of words from column B to form a complete thought.

COLUMN A	COLUMN B
1. At the circus, clowns	**a.** went to Virginia
2. For our vacation, we	**b.** are small, gentle animals
3. Our nation is called	**c.** sold in supermarkets
4. White rabbits	**d.** make us laugh
5. Breakfast cereals are	**e.** the United States

Practice Power

▶ **Choose three of these ideas. Write one sentence about each idea. Write sentences that are different from the ones above.**

A. our nation
B. breakfast cereals
C. a vacation
D. white rabbits
E. a circus

LESSON 2

Telling and Asking Sentences

Some sentences tell thoughts. Telling sentences are called statements. Telling sentences end with a period.

Here are three statements, or telling sentences.

Flowers need rain.
Your skateboard looks new.
Kim likes to watch the fish in the pond.

Some sentences ask. Asking sentences are called questions. Asking sentences end with a question mark.

Here are three questions, or asking sentences.

Do flowers need rain?
Is your skateboard new?
Does Kim like to watch the fish in the pond?

These sentences are missing end punctuation marks. Which are statements, or telling sentences? Which are questions, or asking sentences?

A. Did Jack lose his pencil
B. Jack lost his pencil
C. Yesterday Sue bicycled to school
D. Has Sue left for school
E. Did Bill finish his homework
F. Bill could not complete his math work
G. Did Sue help Bill with his math

You are right if you noticed that B, C, and F are statements.

B. *Jack lost his pencil* is a telling sentence.
C. *Yesterday Sue bicycled to school* is a telling sentence.
F. *Bill could not complete his math work* is a telling sentence.

You are right if you noticed that A, D, E, and G are questions.

A. *Did Jack lose his pencil* is an asking sentence.
D. *Has Sue left for school* is an asking sentence.
E. *Did Bill finish his homework* is an asking sentence.
G. *Did Sue help Bill with his math* is an asking sentence.

Remember . . .

A telling sentence is a statement.
A telling sentence ends with a period.
A telling sentence begins with a capital letter.

Remember . . .

An asking sentence asks a question.
An asking sentence ends with a question mark (?).
An asking sentence begins with a capital letter.

Exercise 1

Tell which sentences need a period because they are statements, or telling sentences. Tell which sentences need a question mark because they are questions, or asking sentences.

1. Did you hear the roosters crowing
2. This dog is too lazy to chase cats
3. Where was Liz born
4. She has an aunt in Chicago
5. The spy hurried to the airport
6. Do bears really like honey
7. How many stars are there in our flag
8. Have you had the measles
9. The boys ran to hide in their tree house
10. Are those Kip's goldfish
11. We picked oranges from the tree
12. Is that a book about puppets
13. How many uses are there for peanuts
14. The spider's web was very sticky
15. A firefly glows in the dark

Exercise 2

Write an answer statement for each of these questions. Be sure that your answer is a complete thought. Begin with the word given and place a period at the end of each answer statement.

Example: Do you like corn on the cob? I
I like corn on the cob.

1.	Do you like pizza?	I
2.	How old are you?	I
3.	Do you have any brothers or sisters?	I
4.	What is your favorite sport or activity?	My
5.	What is your favorite ice cream?	My
6.	What is your first name?	My
7.	What story have you read lately?	I
8.	Do you watch TV?	I
9.	What color are your eyes?	My
10.	When is your birthday?	My
11.	What color is your hair?	My
12.	On what street do you live?	I
13.	What is your favorite holiday?	My
14.	Do you have any pets?	I
15.	On what street is your school?	My

Exercise 3

Write a question for each of these telling sentences. Begin with the words given and place a question mark at the end of each sentence.

Example: Apple pie is my favorite.
What kind of . . .
What kind of pie is your favorite?

1.	My sister wears big, fuzzy slippers.	What kind of . . .
2.	I like toasted marshmallows.	Do you . . .
3.	Dave grills hamburgers at camp.	Who grills . . .
4.	Ellen put a collar on the cat.	Who put . . .
5.	The president lives in Washington, D.C.	Where does . . .
6.	Lincoln School has a new gym.	Which school . . .
7.	There are sixteen ounces in a pound.	How many . . .
8.	The children like their new jungle gym very much.	How much . . .
9.	My cousins live on a farm.	Where do . . .
10.	Blue paint dripped on the floor.	What color paint . . .

Practice Power

▶ **Here are some words that begin asking sentences. Choose three words. Use each word to begin a question.**

A. Who	**D.** Which	**G.** Did
B. What	**E.** How	**H.** Am
C. Where	**F.** Do	**I.** Why

Commanding Sentences

Some sentences command. They tell you what to do. They are called commanding sentences.

Commanding sentences tell you what to do. Game directions are an example of commanding sentences.

Select a card.
Roll the dice.
Skip a turn.
Go to the next green block.

These are commanding sentences.

Many commanding sentences begin with a verb. They sound more courteous when a person's name or the word *please* is used.

Do your homework, Katy.
Clean your room, Josh.
Mow the lawn, please.
Hold the door, Billy.
Order the cake, please.

Which of these sentences are commanding sentences? Remember, commanding sentences give you directions or tell you what to do.

A. Have some ice cream.
B. He finished his homework.
C. Unwrap your gift.
D. Turn on the light, please.
E. Are you going with Ed?
F. Our cat looks guilty.
G. Go in the living room.

You are right if you noticed that sentences A, C, D, and G tell you what to do.

A. Have some ice cream.
C. Unwrap your gift.
D. Turn on the light, please.
G. Go in the living room.

These are commanding sentences.

Sentences B, E, and F are NOT commanding sentences.

B. *He finished his homework* is a telling sentence, or statement.
E. *Are you going with Ed* is an asking sentence, or question.
F. *Our cat looks guilty* is a telling sentence, or statement.

Remember . . .

A commanding sentence tells you what to do.

A commanding sentence usually ends with a period.

A commanding sentence begins with a capital letter.

Exercise 1

Tell which of these sentences command. Put a period at the end of each commanding sentence. If the sentence is not a commanding sentence, put the correct mark of punctuation at the end.

1. Listen to the whistle
2. Sprinkle sugar on your strawberries
3. Mario, can you hear the crickets
4. Rewind the yo-yo
5. Cut the grass, please
6. Close your lunch boxes, class
7. Yesterday it snowed three inches
8. Line up here, swimmers
9. Leave the piglet outside, Sue
10. Come home early
11. Do you like to swim
12. My mom told me to clean my room
13. Wash the dishes
14. Fold the towels
15. My brother plays baseball

Exercise 2

Look at these four pictures. What are the people doing? Write a commanding sentence for each picture.

Exercise 3

Think of a game you like to play. Give four directions for this game. Use commanding sentences to give your directions.

Practice Power

▶ **Give two commanding sentences for each of these scenes. Begin each sentence with a verb. Remember, a commanding sentence begins with a verb and tells someone what to do. Check your answers.**

1. You are the owner of a pet store, telling a customer how to care for a pet.
2. You are an announcer for an ice-cream commercial.
3. You are an art teacher showing the class how to draw a house.
4. You are a parent saying good-bye to your children as they go to school.
5. You are a crossing guard helping children across the street.

Exclaiming Sentences

Some sentences exclaim. They express strong or sudden feelings. They are called exclaiming sentences.

Exclaiming sentences express strong feelings like wonder, respect, surprise, happiness, worry, or fear.

> What a huge spacecraft!
> How different the passengers look!
> A beautiful light glows around them!

Exclaiming sentences end with an exclamation point (!).

Which of these sentences are exclaiming sentences? Remember, exclaiming sentences need an exclamation point because they express strong feelings.

A. Who was our first president
B. George Washington was our first president
C. What a great leader he was
D. How much courage he showed
E. Name another president

You are right if you said that sentences C and D express strong feelings.

C. *What a great leader he was* is an exclaiming sentence.
D. *How much courage he showed* is an exclaiming sentence.

Sentences A, B, and E are NOT exclaiming sentences.

A. *Who was our first president* is an asking sentence.
B. *George Washington was our first president* is a telling sentence.
E. *Name another president* is a commanding sentence.

Remember . . .

An exclaiming sentence expresses a strong or sudden feeling.

An exclaiming sentence ends with an exclamation point (!).

An exclaiming sentence begins with a capital letter.

Exercise 1

Tell which sentences need an exclamation point because they express strong or sudden feelings. If the sentence is not an exclaiming sentence, give the correct mark of punctuation.

1. What a huge banana split this is
2. You're playing my favorite song, Jean
3. What a long snake that is
4. Alaska and Hawaii are states
5. I'm so happy to see you
6. Oh, you frightened me
7. Will you be home today
8. This chili is so hot
9. The water in this pool is ice cold
10. We just saw a beautiful rainbow

Exercise 2

Some exclaiming sentences can express two different feelings. When actors are in a play, stage directions often tell them what feelings to express. Pretend you are an actor. Below are stage directions that will tell you how to read sentences from Exercise 1.

STAGE DIRECTIONS:

A. Imagine you are very hungry. Read sentence 1.
Imagine you have just finished a big meal. Read sentence 1.

B. You are a person who likes hot, peppery food. Read sentence 8.
You are a person who does not like hot, peppery food. Read sentence 8.

C. You are alone at night in your dining room, and suddenly your sister taps you on the shoulder. Read sentence 6.
Your mother tells you that your brother is waiting in your room so he can scare you. You walk into your room. Read sentence 6.

D. You are walking through the woods. Suddenly you see something moving near your foot. Read sentence 3.
You are at the zoo. You are watching a reptile move about in its own environment. Read sentence 3.

Practice Power

▶ **Many exclaiming sentences begin with the word *how.* Write an exclaiming sentence for each of these ideas. Begin each sentence with the word *how.* The first two are done for you.**

1. Ed lost his puppy. *How worried Ed was!*
2. In a few hours, he found her asleep under his bed. *How happy Ed was!*
3. Luís couldn't wait for his birthday to arrive.
4. Luís ate too much birthday cake.
5. With this much snow, we won't have school.
6. With this much snow, our class trip is canceled.
7. Noelle thought she failed the math test.
8. When she got her paper back, she saw she had passed.
9. Joe longed for a dog of his own.
10. On Saturday morning, he awoke to his new dog licking his face.

LESSON 5

The Four Kinds of Sentences

A chart helps you organize ideas. Here is a chart to help you remember the four kinds of sentences.

KIND OF SENTENCE	WHAT IT DOES	END MARK
Telling	States a fact	Period (.)
Asking	Asks a question	Question mark (?)
Commanding	Tells what to do Gives a direction	Period (.)
Exclaiming	Expresses a feeling	Exclamation point (!)

Exercise 1

These sentences are on a sign outside a small restaurant. The sign maker forgot to punctuate them. Use the chart to tell the sign maker which kind of sentence it is and which mark of punctuation to place at the end of each sentence.

Hello, Meal Planners!

1. Have you tried our new minicheeseburgers
2. Try one now
3. What a delicious treat they are
4. They are three for a dollar
5. Take a bag home
6. Your family will enjoy them

Exercise 2

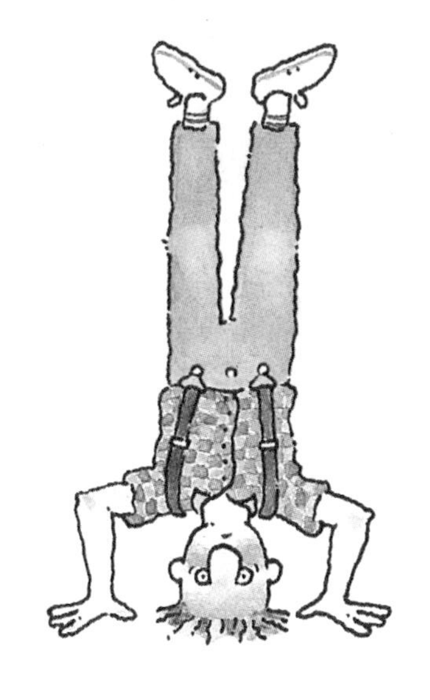

Tell whether each sentence is a telling, an asking, a commanding, or an exclaiming sentence.

1. Two cats meowed all night.
2. How does an octopus protect itself?
3. How beautiful the quilt is!
4. Stand on your head.
5. Can you play the banjo?
6. We're going to Yellowstone National Park.
7. What ocean is east of the United States?
8. What a spicy sauce Arnie made!
9. Make your bed.
10. Why did the chicken cross the road?
11. Do you have a favorite fable?
12. What a huge spider web this is!

Exercise 3

Tell which mark of punctuation is needed at the end of each sentence. Explain why.

1. Name an animal that hunts at night
2. Don't step in that wet cement
3. Have you ever eaten cauliflower
4. How quickly the taxi got here
5. Let the sheep out of the barn
6. The whistling contest will be on Friday
7. What a great birthday party that was
8. Tell me a story about knights and dragons
9. How are raisins made
10. Say the alphabet backwards
11. Dana spread peanut butter on the banana
12. Will you teach me to skateboard

Practice Power

- For picture 1—Write an asking and a telling sentence.
- For picture 2—Write a commanding and an exclaiming sentence.
- For picture 3—Write an asking and a commanding sentence.
- For picture 4—Write an exclaiming and a telling sentence.

Lesson 6 Subject Nouns and Predicate Verbs

The subject noun and predicate verb are the most important words in a sentence.

Read these sentences.

Dogs bark.	Horses gallop.
Birds fly.	Flowers grow.
Children play.	Rocks roll.
Snakes slither.	Fish swim.

In these sentences, the action words are predicate verbs. Which word in each sentence shows action?

You are right if you said

bark	gallop	
fly	grow	These are predicate verbs.
play	roll	
slither	swim	

Asking *who* or *what* before each predicate verb tells you the subject noun. Who or what swims? Who or what flies? In these sentences, what are the subject nouns?

You are right if you said

Dogs	Horses	
Birds	Flowers	These are subject nouns.
Children	Rocks	
Snakes	Fish	

Even if there are many other words in the sentence, the predicate verbs and the subject nouns are the most important words. Find the predicate verbs, or action words, in these sentences.

A. Swimmers splashed in the shallow water.
B. Many small boats sailed on the lake.
C. Rowers pushed the other boats with their long oars.
D. People snapped pictures from the shore.
E. The sunlight bounced on the water.
F. Children built a sand castle on the beach.

Did you choose these predicate verbs (action words)?

A. splashed
B. sailed
C. pushed
D. snapped
E. bounced
F. built

To find the subject noun, ask *who* or *what* before each predicate verb. Who or what splashed? Who or what sailed? Find the subject nouns in the sentences above.

Did you choose these subject nouns?

A. Swimmers
B. boats
C. Rowers
D. People
E. sunlight
F. Children

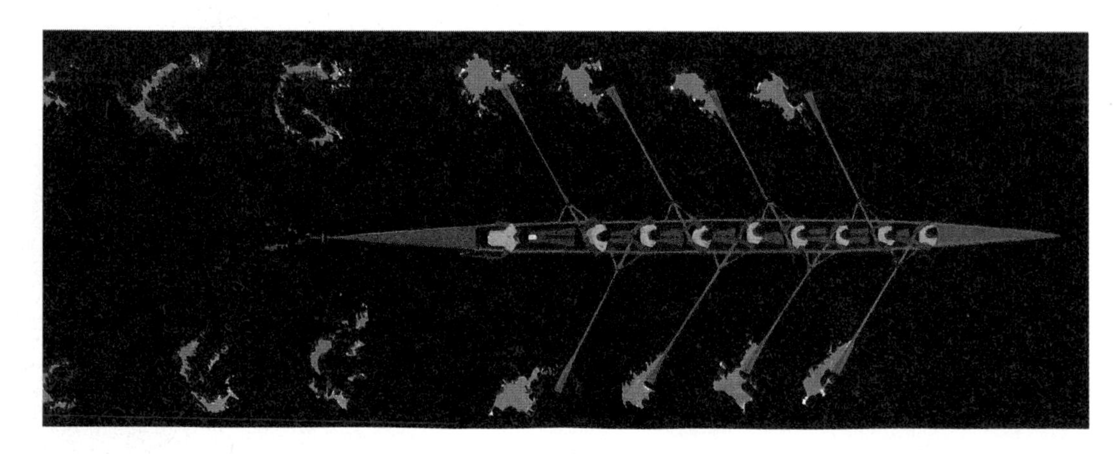

Exercise 1

The predicate verb is in italics in each sentence. Ask the question *who* or *what* before each predicate verb to find the subject noun.

1. The young robin *flew* out of the nest.
2. Two brown rabbits *hopped* along the path.
3. The wind *whistled* through the trees.
4. In the springtime, tulips *grow.*
5. Soft snow *fell* on the ground.
6. Near the pier, the boat *rocked* gently.
7. Last summer, the children *biked* in the woods.
8. At the circus, the clowns *juggled* balls.
9. The airplane *landed* safely.
10. Brad *washed* his bicycle.

Exercise 2

Match these subject nouns with a predicate verb that fits. Write them as sentences. Use *Many* to begin your sentences. The first one is done for you.

SUBJECT NOUNS	PREDICATE VERBS
canaries	chase cats
cats	eat bananas
dogs	sing songs
cows	play with string
monkeys	lay eggs
hens	give milk

Many canaries sing songs.

Exercise 3

Find the predicate verb in each sentence. Then find the subject noun.

1. The bee flew onto the flower.
2. I enjoyed this movie.
3. Steven rode his bike.
4. Pedro went to the library.
5. A carpenter fixed the wooden doll.
6. The children gathered around the piñata.
7. We saw a flock of geese.
8. Janet ran to the park.
9. Balloons blew into the trees.
10. A frog perched on the lily pad.

Putting It All Together

With a partner, make up a long sentence. Write each word in the sentence on a separate card. Remember to make a card for the end mark. Then make three more cards and put each of the other kinds of end marks on a card.

Repeat the process to make a second sentence. Then put all the cards in a hat or box. Give it to another pair. Challenge your classmates in the other pair to reconstruct the sentences as you wrote them.

Chapter Challenge

These sentences tell a story. Read each sentence carefully, and then answer the questions.

1. The day for the Clearfield skateboard contest was here.
2. How hard and long Louis had practiced!
3. His parents had told him, "Do your best. That's all."
4. Would all his practice pay off?
5. Among the other skaters at the starting line, Louis leaned forward.
6. The whistle blew loudly.
7. The skateboarders raced down the hill.
8. Louis crossed the finish line first.
9. What a happy day it was for him!
10. Did the judge treat all the skaters to pizza?

SENTENCE NUMBER	QUESTION
1.	Is this a telling or an asking sentence?
2.	Is this a commanding or an exclaiming sentence?
3.	Is "Do your best" a commanding or an asking sentence?
4.	What kind of sentence is sentence 4?
5.	What is the predicate verb?
6.	Name the predicate verb that goes with the noun *whistle.*
7.	What is the predicate verb and subject noun?
8.	What kind of sentence is sentence 8?
9.	What kind of sentence is sentence 9?
10.	Make up an answer to the question in sentence 10. Use a telling sentence to write your answer. Then write an exclaiming sentence to describe how the skaters felt.

Creative Space

Size-wise
Elephants
make
footprints
in the mud
and so
do
I.

Pencil Pal
My
pencil
wrote a poem
just
for
me!

Letting Go
Two leaves
cling to a branch
afraid
to
fall.

Explore the Poem . . .

You can be a poet! Creative sentences, like those you have seen and written in this chapter, can be made into poems. It's fun to think of ideas and then write your words on the page in a special way. A poet doesn't just write a sentence. A poet separates words into lines to make ideas stand out.

If these three poems were written as sentences, they would look like this:

Elephants make footprints in the mud and so do I.

My pencil wrote a poem just for me!

Two leaves cling to a branch afraid to fall.

Here is a sentence. Put one word on each line to make a poem.

A daisy bowed its head and said "good-bye."

______ ______ ______

______ ______

______ ______

______

Write the same sentence in a different way. Now the poem should have a new look. What words stand out?

Picture something in your mind. Now describe it in words. Write a sentence and then rewrite it as a poem. Give your poem a title.

CHAPTER 10 NOUNS

Identifying Nouns

A noun names a person, place, or thing.

If you go to a circus, you might see

PERSONS	PLACES	THINGS
friends	center ring	souvenirs
acrobats	restaurants	peanuts
clowns	stores	hoops

These are words that name persons, places, or things. They are called nouns. Can you add other nouns to the circus lists?

About the Photograph

The word *friends* is a noun. These friends are pretending to be clowns. Who do you and your friends like to pretend to be?

Remember . . .

A noun names a person, place, or thing.

Exercise 1

Use these nouns to complete the sentences.

canary Matthew doctor coconut

1. _______ is Alice's brother.
2. Dip the banana in chocolate and roll it in _______ .
3. The _______ looked at my broken toe.
4. A green _______ sang by itself.

Use these nouns to complete the sentences.

New York ribbon tent Spain

5. Columbus sailed from _______ .
6. The _______ was full of fireflies.
7. _______ is a large city.
8. Millie tied a pink _______ around the cow's neck.

Use these nouns to complete the sentences.

daisy players drum popcorn

9. Would you like butter on your _______ ?
10. One _______ grew in the middle of the field.
11. Toby plays a _______ in the band.
12. The _______ passed the football.

Exercise 2

It's fun to make up your own noun riddles. First, choose a word that names a person, place, or thing. Then, think of some clues to make a riddle. Here are some noun riddles.

1. I'm the name of a thing. I keep time in hours, minutes, and seconds. I often hang on a wall. What am I?
2. I am the name of a popular food. I am often served with cheese, ketchup, and mustard. Many people like to eat me with french fries. What am I?
3. I'm the name of a person. My job is to fly airplanes, both large and small. Who am I?

Exercise 3

Make three columns on a piece of paper. Print PERSONS at the top of the first column, PLACES at the top of the second, and THINGS at the top of the third. Decide if each of these words names a person, place, or thing. Write each word in the correct column.

sister
farmer
Iowa
spoon
moon

camera
bubbles
school
zoo
park

beach
teacher
magician
carrots
uncle

Practice Power

▶ **How many persons, places, and things can you see in this picture? Name them. Now write one sentence each for one person, one place, and one thing. Try to write sentences that tell a story about the picture.**

LESSON 2

Proper and Common Nouns

A proper noun names a particular person, place, or thing.

A common noun names any of a group of persons, places, or things.

Study these two lists of nouns. How are the two lists different?

COMMON NOUNS	PROPER NOUNS
president	George Washington
street	Maple Avenue
day	Tuesday
book	*Goodnight Moon*
holiday	Fourth of July
town	Chicago
teacher	Mr. Mudron

The nouns in the first column name any person, place, or thing. These nouns are common nouns. Can you add other common nouns to this list?

The nouns in the second column name a particular person, place, or thing. These nouns are proper nouns. Proper nouns begin with a capital letter. Can you add other proper nouns to this list? Begin your list with your own name.

Exercise 1

Tell if each noun is a proper noun or a common noun.

1. Bronx Zoo
2. planet
3. Sunday
4. Ohio River
5. lion
6. Lake Michigan
7. Long Beach
8. ocean
9. fudge
10. banjo
11. Disneyland
12. Bambi
13. grandmother
14. lizard
15. Jimmy
16. apartment
17. Aunt Liza
18. crayon

Exercise 2

Name the nouns in each sentence. Tell whether they are proper nouns or common nouns.

1. Benji is a famous dog in the movies.
2. Anita hit the baseball.
3. Sharks leaped from the ocean.
4. Hummingbirds can fly sideways and backward.
5. Some people in Oregon think they saw Bigfoot.
6. Ernie skips stones on the pond.
7. A seismologist is a person who studies earthquakes.
8. Jody painted the wagon red and blue.

Practice Power

▶ **Write sentences about a place, a person, and a thing. Follow the directions below to help you write your sentences.**

1. Name your city or town. Tell one important fact about it.
2. Name a famous person. Tell one special thing this person has done.
3. Name your favorite holiday. Tell why you like it.

Singular and Plural Nouns

Singular nouns name only one person, place, or thing. Plural nouns name more than one person, place, or thing.

Study the difference in spelling of the two nouns in the boxes.

I wished on one bright star.

There were many stars in the sky.

The noun which names only one is spelled s-t-a-r. The noun which names more than one is spelled s-t-a-r-s.

Study these nouns in italics.

six *telescopes*	two *boxes*	the *trumpet*
one *museum*	five *newspapers*	an *apricot*

Which three nouns are singular nouns?
Which three nouns are plural nouns?

You are right if you noticed that

- the singular nouns are *museum, trumpet, apricot.*
- the plural nouns are *telescopes, boxes, newspapers.*

Remember . . .
Nouns which name only one are called singular nouns.
Nouns which name more than one are called plural nouns.

Forming Plural Nouns

Many nouns form the plural by adding *s* or *es* to the singular.

SINGULAR NOUNS	PLURAL NOUNS
one day	fifty days
an ocean	four oceans
one hand	six hands
the book	ten books

Nouns ending in *s, sh, x, ch,* and *z* form the plural by adding *es* to the singular.

SINGULAR NOUNS	PLURAL NOUNS
one guess	two guesses
one bush	three bushes
one ax	four axes
one couch	five couches
one buzz	six buzzes

Exercise 1

Tell if each noun is singular or plural.

1. owl
2. monsters
3. shoes
4. street
5. rug
6. boxes
7. nurse
8. carpenters
9. marbles
10. colors
11. bushes
12. mouse
13. cars
14. whale
15. penguin
16. shells
17. island
18. peaches
19. horses
20. plums

Exercise 2

Give the plural of each noun.

1. wish
2. book
3. map
4. inch
5. kitten
6. toy
7. box
8. torch
9. race
10. clown
11. mix
12. glove
13. pool
14. cone
15. match

Exercise 3

Tell if each noun in italics is singular or plural.

1. The *rose* is in bloom.
2. Name your favorite green *vegetable.*
3. We heard the *firecrackers.*
4. That *boy* can walk on his hands.
5. *Bells* rang through the fog.
6. The *finches* flocked to the tree.
7. The *street* is full of clowns.
8. I piled the *boxes* as high as I could.
9. The bird found a golf *ball* in its nest.
10. They play basketball in their *wheelchairs.*
11. My sister will knit red *mittens.*
12. Colored shells dotted the *beaches.*
13. The dog chased the *kittens* around the kitchen.
14. The girls took *towels* to the beach.
15. Jim ate two *cheeseburgers* for dinner.

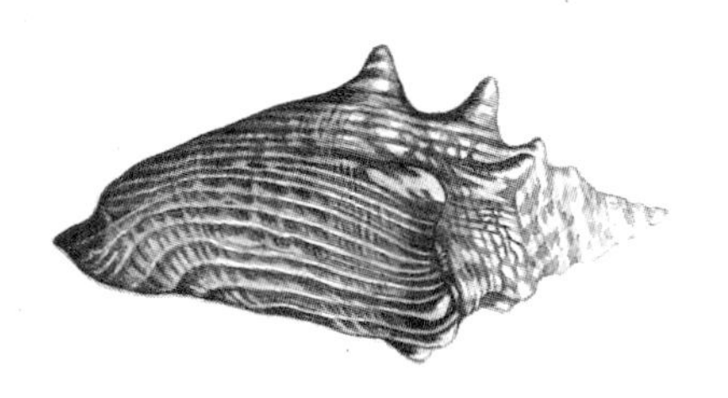

Practice Power

▶ **Pretend you are visiting your great-grandmother's house. In the attic you find an old dusty trunk. Make a list of the things you find in the old trunk. Then tell if each noun you name is singular or plural.**

Irregular Plurals

A few nouns form their plurals in a different way. They are called irregular plurals.

Look at this chart.

SINGULAR NOUNS	PLURAL NOUNS
one tooth	two teeth
one foot	two feet
one man	two men
one woman	two women
one child	two children
one ox	two oxen
one mouse	two mice
one goose	two geese

How does *tooth* become *teeth?*

Some nouns form their plural by changing letters within the word. What other nouns on the chart follow this rule?

How does *child* become *children?*

Some nouns form their plural by adding a syllable. Name another noun on the chart that follows this rule.

Remember . . .

Plural nouns that are not formed by adding *s* or *es* are called irregular plurals.

Exercise 1

Complete each sentence with an irregular singular or plural noun from the chart on page 281.

1. One _______ isn't enough to pull the farmer's plow.
2. He needs two _______ to pull the plow.
3. Ten _______ formed a circle to play a game.
4. One _______ stood in the center as the leader.
5. The dentist cleaned Len's _______ .
6. The dentist pulled only one _______ .
7. A family of four _______ swam across the lake.
8. One old _______ flew ahead of the others.
9. One _______ was the mother of the children.
10. The other two _______ were the children's aunts.
11. A few small _______ scurried around the barn.
12. The cage was only big enough for one _______ .

Practice Power

▶ **Use the following words to write a short paragraph about a make-believe situation. Use your imagination to make the paragraph exciting!**

woman   women   mouse   mice

Singular Possessives

A possessive noun shows ownership, or possession.

Read these sentences.

We visited Aunt Sarah's farm.
We saw the cow's little calf.

Aunt Sarah's is a singular noun that shows possession. She owns the farm. An apostrophe and *s ('s)* are added to the noun *Aunt Sarah.*

Cow's is a singular noun that shows possession. She has a calf. An apostrophe and *s ('s)* are added to the noun *cow.*

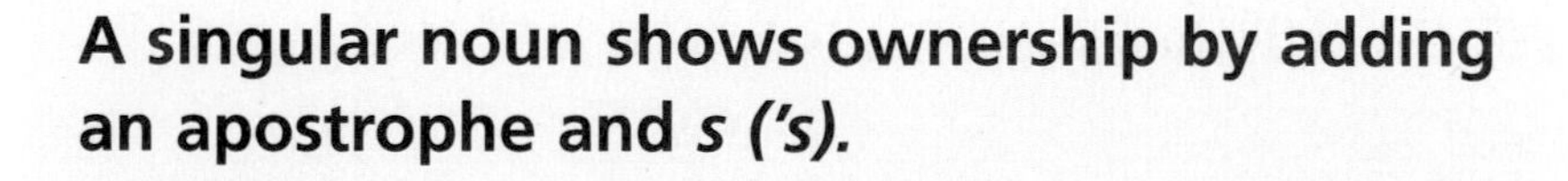

A singular noun shows ownership by adding an apostrophe and *s ('s).*

Name the singular nouns that show possession in these sentences. What is added to these nouns to show possession? What do these nouns own or have?

We touched the lamb's soft wool.
We gathered the brown hen's eggs.
We tasted Mrs. Storm's homemade bread.
We drank the cow's delicious milk.

You are right if you noticed that the following nouns in italics show possession.

lamb's wool	*Mrs. Storm's* bread
hen's eggs	*cow's* milk

An apostrophe and *s ('s)* were added to each noun to show possession.

Exercise 1

Name the noun that shows possession, or ownership, in each sentence.

1. The singer's voice was beautiful.
2. There are strange noises in Lucy's house.
3. A bird landed on the man's head.
4. A monkey sat on the boat's bow.
5. The horse's foal followed her closely.
6. The tire on Sherri's bicycle is flat.
7. I used Dad's tools to build a dollhouse.
8. Our cat ate the dog's food.
9. The girl's jacket hung in the closet.
10. Grandfather's garden is full of rabbits.

Exercise 2

Write the singular noun in italics as a possessive noun. Name what is owned.

Example: the eyes of the *tiger* *tiger's eyes*

1. the music of the *band*
2. the cage of the *hamster*
3. the desk of the *librarian*
4. the feathers of the *dove*
5. the hockey stick of *Gary*
6. the name of the *doctor*
7. the brush of the *painter*
8. the tractor of the *farmer*
9. the shoes of the *dancer*
10. the bus of the *driver*

Exercise 3

Write the singular noun at the left as a singular possessive noun. Underline what the owner possesses.

Elaine	**1.** We found _______ books.
lion	**2.** The _______ paw was full of thorns.
skunk	**3.** A _______ fur is black and white.
butterfly	**4.** We counted the _______ colors.
catcher	**5.** A _______ mitt is well padded.

Practice Power

▶ **Look around you. What things do you see? Who do these things belong to? Write five sentences that tell who these things belong to. Use singular nouns that show possession in your sentences.**

NOUNS

LESSON 6

Plural and Irregular Plural Possessives

Plural Possessives

A singular possessive noun shows one person or thing owning something.

A plural possessive noun shows more than one person or thing owning something.

SINGULAR	one bird
SINGULAR POSSESSIVE (one owner)	one bird's nest
PLURAL	two birds
PLURAL POSSESSIVE (more than one owner)	two birds' nests

The singular noun *bird* does not end in *s*. To show possession, add *'s*.

one *bird's* nest

The plural noun *birds* already ends in *s*. To show possession, just add an apostrophe (').

two *birds'* nests

Remember . . .

To form the plural possessive

1. **Write the plural form.** ***boys***
2. **Add the sign of possession.** ***boys' team***

WRITE THE PLURAL	ADD THE SIGN OF POSSESSION
two foxes	Two foxes' dens had pups in them.
two players	Two players' trophies were given.
two girls	Two girls' bikes are outside.

NOUNS

Irregular Plural Possessives

Irregular plurals do not end in *s.* These few irregular nouns form the plural possessive by adding an apostrophe and *s ('s).*

SINGULAR	PLURAL	PLURAL POSSESSIVE
child	children	the children's game
woman	women	the women's department
mouse	mice	the mice's nest

Remember . . .

Regular plural possessive—
six ducks' feathers

Irregular plural possessive—
three children's toys

Exercise 1

Write the plural possessive form of each word.

	PLURAL POSSESSIVE
lion	**1.** two ________ paws
bear	**2.** two ________ teeth
king	**3.** two ________ crowns
shark	**4.** two ________ fins
boy	**5.** two ________ ideas
girl	**6.** two ________ books
cat	**7.** two ________ tails
scout	**8.** two ________ canoes

Exercise 2

Look for clues that tell whether the nouns should be singular or plural. Which possessive nouns are correct?

1. Many (cook's, cooks') aprons are white.
2. Some (hiker's, hikers') tents are empty.
3. That (pig's, pigs') tail was curled.
4. The (lion's, lions') paw had a thorn in it.
5. Most (elephant's, elephants') trunks are strong.
6. The home (team's, teams') cheers were heard.
7. The (shopper's, shoppers') bag was filled.
8. The (artist's, artists') brush was still wet.
9. All (musician's, musicians') instruments must be tuned before a concert.
10. One (grasshopper's, grasshoppers') legs can create music.

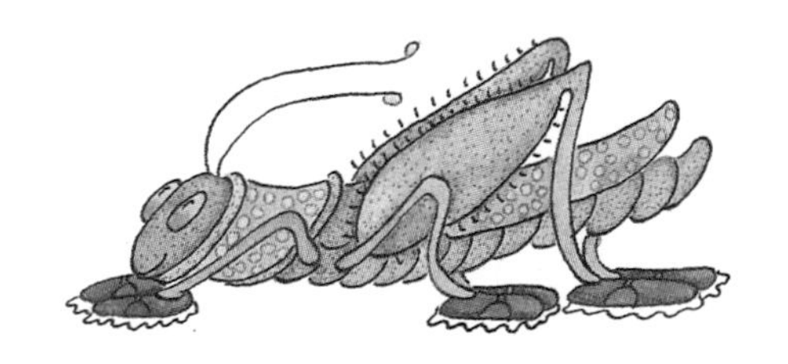

Exercise 3

Write the plural nouns at the left as plural possessives. Underline what the owners possess.

players	1. The _______ uniforms are green and white.
mice	2. _______ tails have almost no hair.
children	3. The _______ toys were in the sandbox.
hens	4. All the _______ eggs were collected.
Native Americans	5. The _______ pottery is useful and beautiful.
sisters	6. My _______ voices are loud.
puppets	7. I sewed the _______ clothes.
men	8. _______ socks are on sale.
turtles	9. The _______ race was slow.
bands	10. The _______ music filled the air.

NOUNS

Exercise 4

An apostrophe has been left out of each word group. Write each group to show that one person or thing is the owner.

1. my aunts pies
2. Teds skates
3. Jessicas buttons
4. Glorias necklace
5. the principals keys
6. the dolls dress
7. my cousins apartment
8. the doctors advice
9. the childs pool
10. the chicks wings
11. Juans shoes
12. the zebras stripes

Exercise 5

An apostrophe has been left out of each word group. Write each group to show that more than one person or thing is the owner.

1. the turkeys tails
2. many birds nests
3. the policewomens uniforms
4. some hikers campfires
5. the scarecrows patches
6. two mens ties
7. the mices cheese
8. the acrobats tricks
9. the ladies perfumes
10. the students books
11. the childrens playground
12. the boys neckties

Putting It All Together

With a small group of classmates, write ten nouns on separate cards or slips of paper. Include proper and common nouns. Include people, places, and things. Place all the nouns in a box or hat and exchange them with another group.

Use the nouns to help you write a silly story. Work together as a group to begin writing a story. When you come to a place in the story that needs a noun, pull one out of the hat or box. Write down the noun. After you have used up all the nouns, read your story aloud.

Chapter Challenge

These sentences tell a story. Read each sentence carefully, and then answer the questions about each sentence.

1. On Labor Day, there was a big parade in Cedar Grove.
2. Mother and the twins stayed home and watched it on TV.
3. Sam and his father went downtown and watched it from the steps of city hall.
4. Visiting bands from New York City marched to music.
5. Fire trucks, old cars, and clowns passed by.
6. For a little while, Sam sat on his father's shoulders to see everything.
7. Now Sam could see the clowns' costumes much better.
8. After the parade, men, women, and children returned to their homes by city buses.
9. When they got home, Dad asked his family, "Did you see Sam and me on TV?"
10. They said, "We did! You were the tallest person on the steps."

SENTENCE NUMBER	QUESTION
1.	Name two proper nouns.
2.	Name a plural noun.
3.	Name four common nouns.
4.	Name two common nouns and one proper noun.
5.	Are these three nouns singular or plural?
6.	Name a noun that shows ownership.
7.	Is *clowns'* a singular or plural possessive noun?
8.	Name three irregular plural nouns.
9.	Name three common nouns and two proper nouns.
10.	Find a noun that names a place.

NOUNS

Creative Space

A drop of rain!
The frog wiped his forehead
With his wrist.

Nobuyuki Yuasa

Explore the Poem . . .

Some poems are long, and some are short. This poem has only three lines. Some poems rhyme, and some do not. This poem does not rhyme.

An exclamation point is used at the end of the first line. Do you think the frog in the poem may have been surprised by the raindrop? Maybe it was not supposed to rain that day. What do you think?

Unexpected things happen to us all the time. Many times we are very surprised by them. We each show this surprise in different ways.

Can you remember something that surprised you?

- A gust of wind!
- A clap of thunder!
- A shadow in the night!
- A flake of snow!
- A flash of lightning!

Use one of these ideas or one of your own ideas for the first line of a poem. Then think of an action that someone or something might do.

Before you begin, read these poems written by students.

A windy day!
The leaves hugged themselves
In the doorway.

A flake of snow!
A rabbit twitched its nose
Just to make sure.

CHAPTER 11

PRONOUNS

Identifying Pronouns

A pronoun is a word that takes the place of a noun.

Read this story, and then follow the directions.

Rose threw the ball to Jack.

1. *Jack* tossed *the ball* to Hannah.
2. *Hannah* caught the ball.
3. Rose and Jack cheered *Hannah* for tagging the runner.
4. By working together, *Rose, Jack,* and *Hannah* helped their team.
5. No wonder the fans cheered *Rose, Jack,* and *Hannah.*

Pretend you are a coach. The nouns in italics in the story are tired players. Send in the pronoun substitutes. Choose the best substitute for each noun.

they them she her he him it

About the Photograph

These children are reading a globe. Use pronouns in a sentence that tells what they may be learning about.

You are a good coach if you said in sentence number:

1. For *Jack,* use *he.* For *the ball,* use *it.*
2. For *Hannah,* use *she.*
3. For *Hannah,* use *her.*
4. For *Rose, Jack,* and *Hannah,* use *they.*
5. For *Rose, Jack,* and *Hannah,* use *them.*

Now read the same story with the pronouns.

Remember . . .

A word that takes the place of a noun is called a pronoun.

The pronouns are listed here.

I	me	we	us
he	him	they	them
she	her	you	
it			

Exercise 1

Find the pronoun in each sentence.

1. The puppy belongs to them.
2. The thunder scared us.
3. You must find the lost puzzle piece.
4. We paddled the canoe.
5. She walked across the gym floor.
6. Give the library card to him.
7. I found a penny on the sidewalk.
8. Where did Karen find it?
9. They look for shells on the beach.
10. A judge gave the blue ribbon to me.

Exercise 2

Use pronouns to take the place of the nouns in italics.

1. Carrie's sister made *Carrie* a pinwheel.
2. Give Paul's snapshot to *Paul.*
3. Max and Shawn flew the plane. *Max and Shawn* are good pilots.
4. Sue and Tina go surfing. Those surfboards belong to *Sue and Tina.*
5. Sara tripped on the jump rope. *Sara* fell.
6. Two wolves howled across the valley. That's how *wolves* talk.
7. Dave was walking his beagle. *His beagle* kept tugging at the leash.
8. Kitty jumped on the trampoline. *The trampoline* was in the gym.
9. A snowman stood in the field. *The snowman* melted in the sun.
10. Mr. Wilder collects maple sap. Then *Mr. Wilder* boils it.
11. Mr. Wilder carried *the bucket of maple sap* into the house.
12. The horses pulled the heavy cart. *The horses* were tired.
13. Mrs. Wilder worked in the kitchen. *Mrs. Wilder* was busy.
14. Four inches of snow fell on the countryside. *The countryside* looked peaceful.
15. Mr. Wilder and his son did the chores. *Mr. Wilder and his son* were tired.

Exercise 3

Complete each sentence with a pronoun that fits.

1. Dana and I go to the movies together. _______ enjoy the same kinds of films.
2. Lee is wearing a purple scarf. _______ got _______ as a gift.
3. Miss Minniver held up the tiny kitten. _______ trembled in her hands.
4. Tom's friends painted the fence. _______ painted _______ white.
5. The subway was crowded with people. _______ were on their way home from work.
6. Take LaTrice home. _______ is tired from the pony ride.
7. Let's ask Susan to the cookout. _______ likes hamburgers and hot dogs.
8. Flies are walking on the ceiling. Don't _______ ever get dizzy?
9. Give these baseball cards to Alex and Jay. _______ asked me for _______ .
10. The children ran to the Ferris wheel. _______ jumped into the small seats.

Practice Power

▶ **Pretend you have friends who are brother and sister. Their names are Roger and Janet. They want to buy a birthday gift for their father, but at first they can't agree on what to buy. Write four sentences that tell a story about what gifts they thought about and what gift they finally decided to buy. Use names in some sentences and pronouns in some sentences.**

Pronouns as Subjects

PRONOUNS

Some pronouns may be used as subjects in a sentence. They take the place of subject nouns.

Which list of sentences sounds correct?

LIST A	LIST B
I play soccer.	*Me* play soccer.
We play soccer.	*Us* play soccer.
He plays soccer.	*Him* plays soccer.
She plays soccer.	*Her* plays soccer.
They play soccer.	*Them* play soccer.

You are right if you said list A. These pronouns are called subject pronouns. They are used before a verb.

Here is a list of subject pronouns.

SINGULAR	PLURAL
I	we
you	you
he, she, it	they

Sometimes a sentence has two subjects. One or both subjects may be pronouns. These pronouns must be subject pronouns.

Skip and *I* rode the train.
He and *I* rode the train.

Exercise 1

Choose the subject pronoun in each sentence. Tell whether the pronoun is singular or plural.

1. Pepper and (I, me) went for a walk.
2. (He, Him) barked all the way down the street.
3. (Them, They) thought Pepper saw something.
4. (Us, We) all tried to calm Pepper.
5. (I, me) thought Pepper saw a squirrel.
6. (Him, It) was eating a nut by the tree.
7. (He, Him) chased the squirrel away from the tree.
8. (Him, It) was faster than Pepper.
9. (Them, They) took turns petting Pepper.
10. Soon (he, him) was very quiet.
11. Pepper and (me, I) didn't see the squirrel anymore.
12. (We, Us) could continue our walk.

Exercise 2

Use subject pronouns to take the place of the words in italics.

1. *The mountains* were covered with snow.
2. *Bev and I* went sledding.
3. Every day *Mike* buys his lunch at school.
4. Sometimes *Sally* buys hers, too.
5. *The chimp* smiled at us.
6. *Many children* feed the chimp peanuts.
7. *The clock* doesn't tick.
8. *Mr. Adams* is able to fix anything.
9. In the evening, *my mom* reads the newspaper.
10. *My brother and I* do our homework.

PRONOUNS

Practice Power

▶ **What do you and your friends or brothers and sisters do on weekends? Write a short paragraph that tells about the things you do together. Use subject pronouns in some of your sentences.**

LESSON 3

Pronouns Used After Verbs

Some pronouns are used only after verbs.

Which list of sentences sounds correct?

LIST A	LIST B
Carla gave *I* a gift.	Carla gave *me* a gift.
Carla gave *we* a gift.	Carla gave *us* a gift.
Carla gave *she* a gift.	Carla gave *her* a gift.
Carla gave *they* a gift.	Carla gave *them* a gift.

You are right if you said list B. These pronouns are used after a verb. Here is a list of pronouns used after a verb.

SINGULAR	PLURAL
me	us
you	you
him, her, it	them

Sometimes a sentence has two nouns or pronouns after the verb. One or both words may be pronouns.

Scout followed Ned and *me.*
The bus passed *him* and *her.*

The pronouns *you* and *it* may be used before or after a verb.

You eat interesting lunches. (subject pronoun)
It crawled along the rock. (subject pronoun)
Grandma sent *you* a package. (after a verb)
She sent *it* on Thursday. (after a verb)

Exercise 1

Choose the correct pronoun in each sentence. Tell whether the pronoun is singular or plural.

1. Those pretzels delighted Sheila and (she, her).
2. Joan gave (him, he) half of her sandwich.
3. Turn (them, they) around.
4. My friend took (I, me) to the movies.
5. It took (we, us) ten minutes to walk to school.
6. Manny gave Dave and (you, I) his best pens.
7. Don't forget to return (she, it).
8. The puppets made (us, we) laugh.
9. The dog followed (them, they).
10. Terry sang Diane and (I, me) a song.
11. My mom made (us, she) dinner last night.
12. (They, I) are going to the movies today.

Exercise 2

Use pronouns to take the place of the words in italics. Use the list of pronouns used after a verb on page 302.

1. The principal took *Jason and Jim* to the auditorium.
2. My rabbit eats *lettuce.*
3. The flight attendant helped *Nancy and me.*
4. I threw *Chuck* the football.
5. The teacher read *the class* a poem.
6. Kate gave *Carol* the new crayons.
7. The zookeeper let *Missy and me* feed the goats.
8. I like *brussels sprouts.*
9. The whale sprayed *Trish* with water.
10. The clown gave *Luke* his autograph.

Exercise 3

Use pronouns to take the place of the words in italics.

1. Joe's older sister Clare took *Joe* to the pet store.
2. *Clare* wanted to help select a gift.
3. They wanted *the gift* for Felix, their pet kitten.
4. *Felix* is six months old today.
5. The pet store manager said, "Can *the manager* help you?"
6. "*Joe and Clare* need a gift for our kitten," Joe and Clare said.
7. The manager showed *Joe and Clare* the pet toys.
8. *Joe and Clare* selected a cute catnip toy.
9. Felix loved *the catnip toy.*
10. *Felix* carried it around all day in his mouth.
11. *The catnip toy* was hidden under the couch.
12. However, *Joe and Clare* found the toy.

Practice Power

▶ **Write a short paragraph about a special person in your life. Use pronouns to talk about this person. Tell who this special person is in your last sentence.**

Possessive Pronouns

Pronouns that show who owns something are called possessive pronouns.

You have learned that a pronoun takes the place of a noun. A possessive pronoun also takes the place of a noun. It takes the place of a person and the object that is owned.

Read these sentences carefully.

	COLUMN A	COLUMN B
1.	Carol's cup is on the table.	*Hers* is on the table.
2.	Our garden has vegetables.	*Ours* has vegetables.
3.	Your hair is curly.	*Yours* is curly.
4.	My raincoat is green.	*Mine* is green.
5.	Doug's mitt is made of leather.	*His* is made of leather.
6.	Mom and Dad's car is new.	*Theirs* is new.

Each word in italics in column B is a possessive pronoun. It takes the place of a person and the object that is owned in column A. Can you tell the word or words that each possessive pronoun takes the place of?

You are right if you said that in sentence number:

1. *Hers*	takes the place of	*Carol's cup.*
2. *Ours*	takes the place of	*Our garden.*
3. *Yours*	takes the place of	*Your hair.*
4. *Mine*	takes the place of	*My raincoat.*
5. *His*	takes the place of	*Doug's mitt.*
6. *Theirs*	takes the place of	*Mom and Dad's car.*

Exercise 1

Find the possessive pronouns in these sentences.

1. Hers is the one in the corner.
2. I don't think I have yours.
3. Maybe it is his.
4. I might have lost mine.
5. Ours is blue and purple with white spots.
6. Theirs is yellow and red with red spots.
7. What color is yours?
8. I like his best of all.
9. Yours is better than mine.
10. Ours is prettier than theirs.
11. Ours has a dog on it.
12. Theirs has a cat on it.
13. Ours has a rectangle rug underneath it.
14. Theirs has an oval rug underneath it.
15. Mine is the most comfortable.

Exercise 2

Complete each sentence with a possessive pronoun.

1. My hat covers my ears. _______ sits on his head.
2. This one is Meg's box. It isn't _______ .
3. Today is Lynn's birthday. I didn't know it was _______ .
4. I think this belongs to Ted and Ed. Yes, it must be _______ .
5. The cat licked my face. Did it lick _______ ?
6. Tamica and I want a kite, too. We want _______ to look like a dragon.
7. Pat's puppet does not have strings like mine. _______ is worn on her hand.
8. Leslie's pencils are sharp. _______ are sharp, too.
9. You have a nice scooter. It's just like _______ .
10. Carlos is my friend, but he is _______ , too.

PRONOUNS

Practice Power

▶ **Here are ten sentences. Write a second sentence for each that uses a possessive pronoun in place of the words in italics.**

Example: I found *Mike's soccer ball.* I found *his.*

1. *Kit's popcorn* spilled on the floor.
2. *Al's bicycle* is broken.
3. *Brian and Kurt's books* are on the desk.
4. *My shoes* are too tight.
5. *Your pet snake* is very long.
6. That is *my bicycle.*
7. *Your room* is filthy.
8. *My hair* is very long.
9. *His grades* are excellent.
10. *Her athletic ability* is amazing.

LESSON 5

The Correct Use of *I* and *Me*

The Correct Use of *I*

I **is used before a verb.** ***I*** **is a subject pronoun.**

Which sentence sounds correct?

Me went to the parade.
I went to the parade.

You are right if you said

I went to the parade.

Which sentence sounds correct?

José and *me* went to the parade.
José and *I* went to the parade.

To be sure, cover the words *José and.* Then ask yourself

Me went to the parade?
I went to the parade?

You are right if you said

José and *I* went to the parade.

When you use *I* and another person's name, it is polite to put the other person's name first.

Nancy and *I* play cards.

The Correct Use of *Me*

Me is used after a verb.

Which sentence in each set sounds correct?

A. Will you take *me* to the circus?
Will you take *I* to the circus?

B. Did you find *me* a white horse?
Did you find *I* a white horse?

You are right if you said

A. Will you take *me* to the circus?

B. Did you find *me* a white horse?

Me is used after a verb.

Which sentence sounds correct?

He gave *Barbara and me* a popsicle.
He gave *Barbara and I* a popsicle.

To be sure, cover the words *Barbara and*.
Then ask yourself

He gave *me* a popsicle?
He gave *I* a popsicle?

You are right if you said

He gave Barbara and *me* a popsicle.

When you use *me* and another person's name, it is polite to put the other person's name first.

Jillian wished Brad and *me* a happy birthday.

Exercise 1

Choose the correct pronoun.

1. (I, me) wrote a poem.
2. Pete and (I, me) wrote a poem.
3. (I, me) watched the kangaroos.
4. Jess and (I, me) watched the kangaroos.
5. In summer (I, me) swim in the pool.
6. Mitch and (I, me) swim in the pool.
7. (I, me) play baseball.
8. Anthony and (I, me) play baseball.
9. (Julie and I, I and Julie) swim at our local pool.
10. Natalie and (me, I) went to the movies last night.
11. (Jerry and I, I and Jerry) act in our school plays.
12. (I and Ted, Ted and I) saw a raccoon.

Exercise 2

Choose the correct pronoun.

1. Lucy bought (me, I) ice cream.
2. Lucy bought Gina and (me, I) ice cream.
3. Michelle saw (I, me) at the store.
4. Michelle saw Stan and (I, me) at the store.
5. Pass (me, I) the blue paint.
6. Pass Fred and (me, I) the blue paint.
7. Uncle Bill telephoned (I, me).
8. Uncle Bill telephoned my parents and (me, I).
9. Mrs. Swanson rewarded (me and Josh, Josh and me).
10. The drawing pleased (Alice and me, me and Alice).

Exercise 3

Complete each sentence with the pronoun *I* or *me*. Use *I* before the verb and *me* after the verb.

1. _______ lost an umbrella.
2. Kelly and _______ lost our umbrellas.
3. _______ baked bread.
4. My mother and _______ baked bread.
5. Show _______ your baseball cards.
6. Show Harry and _______ your baseball cards.
7. The news reporter greeted _______ .
8. The news reporter greeted Regina and _______ .
9. _______ covered my giant pretzel with mustard.
10. Wally and _______ covered our giant pretzels with mustard.
11. _______ gave my father a Christmas present.
12. My father gave _______ a wonderful present.
13. _______ love to walk my dog around the block.
14. My sister and _______ take turns walking him.
15. My brother and _______ will wash the dishes.
16. "Thank you for washing the dishes for _______ ," my mom said.
17. My dad and _______ washed our car.
18. My dad asked _______ to help him wash our car.
19. Chris took _______ to see the museums.
20. Chris and _______ went to the museums.

Putting It All Together

Draw a grid like the one below with four rows and four columns. Write sixteen different pronouns in any order on the grid. With a partner, write a sentence for each pronoun on a separate sheet of paper. Cut the sentences apart and place them in a hat or box.

Take turns pulling out a sentence and reading it. Color in the square that contains the same pronoun as the sentence. The first player to color a row of four pronouns shouts, "Pronoun bingo!"

Chapter Challenge

These sentences tell a story. Read each sentence carefully and then answer the questions.

1. On Friday, we were going to have a popcorn party at school.
2. It would be the first party of the year.
3. On Monday, Mrs. Duffy told me to put a handful of corn in the jar.
4. On Tuesday, she told Billy to put some in it.
5. He almost filled the jar.
6. By Wednesday, it was full.
7. On Thursday, Mrs. Duffy asked, "Which of you will bring cups?"
8. "We can," Kristen and me said.
9. On Friday we all watched as Mrs. Duffy showed us how to pop the corn.
10. She filled the cups so full that mine was overflowing.
11. We all enjoyed our first party of the year.
12. I learned how to make popcorn for myself!

SENTENCE NUMBER	QUESTION
1.	Find a subject pronoun.
2.	Is *it* a singular or plural pronoun?
3.	Is *me* used before or after the verb?
4.	*She* takes the place of what noun?
5.	Is *he* singular or plural?
6.	*It* takes the place of what noun?
7.	Find a pronoun that can be singular or plural.
8.	Is *me* used correctly?
9.	Is *we* used before or after a verb?
10.	Find a possessive pronoun.
11.	To whom does *we* refer?
12.	Is *I* used before or after a verb?

Creative Space

Clapping
slapping
finger-snapping
folding
holding
modeling
molding
writing
fighting
stroking
poking
itching
stitching
shaking
taking
squeezing
teasing
pleasing
HANDS!

Bobbi Katz

Explore the Poem . . .

Did you think your hands could do so much? Choose five words from the poem and think.

What do hands write?
a letter

What do hands stroke?
a puppy

Many of the words in this poem rhyme.

What words rhyme with *clapping?*

What words rhyme with *folding?*

What words rhyme with *squeezing?*

Can you find other rhyming words?

Most of the words end in *ing.* Can you think of other *ing* words that describe what hands can do? The only word that does not end in *ing* is the last word. It tells the part of the body that does the action.

Now think of other parts of your body that can do many things—feet, nose, eyes. Can you name others?

Write a poem using five *ing* words. Don't tell the part of the body until the end of the poem. Try to use two rhyming words in your poem.

Before you begin, read this poem written by a student.

Groaning
moaning
growling
gurgling
tumbling
rumbling
STOMACH!

CHAPTER 12 VERBS

LESSON 1 Action Verbs

Many verbs express action.

Grade Three had a Show-and-Tell class at school. Tim brought his pet hamster in a cage. He read this poem to the class.

> My hamster Wally *plays* with me.
> He *jumps* and *swings* as you can see.
> He *chews* his food without a sound.
> He *turns* the wheel round and round.

Find the words that tell what Wally the hamster does.

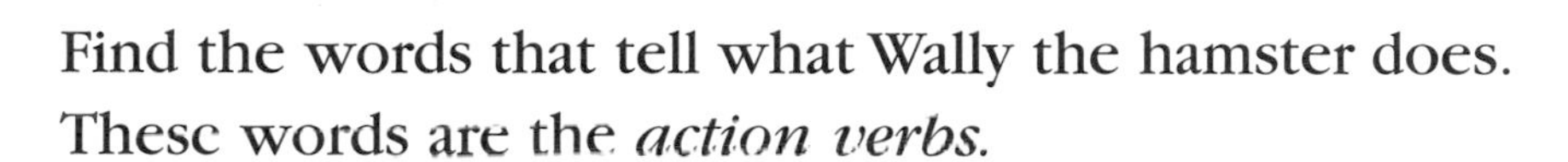

These words are the *action verbs.*

You are right if you noticed that Wally

plays jumps swings chews turns	These are action verbs.

Can you think of other action verbs for a hamster? Try to think of three, and turn each into a sentence.

About the Photograph

These children are sledding down a hill. *Sledding* is an action verb. What activities do you enjoy doing?

Read these sentences about other students' pets. Name the action verb in each sentence.

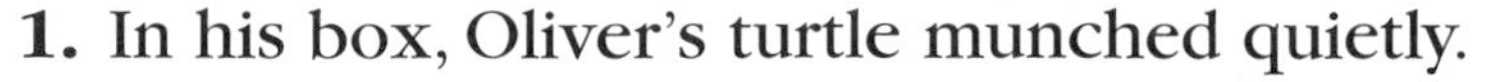

1. In his box, Oliver's turtle munched quietly.
2. Laura's puppy snuggled in her lap.
3. Ned's little kitten purred softly.
4. Juan's dog fetched his ball.
5. Jim's fish swam in a pretty bowl.

You are right if you picked out these action verbs:

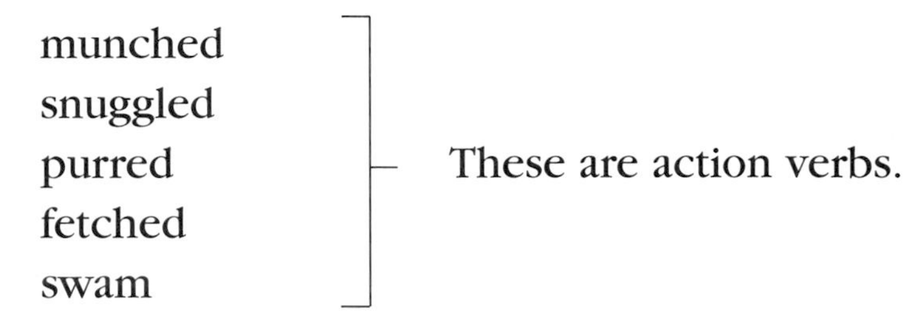

munched
snuggled
purred — These are action verbs.
fetched
swam

Action verbs are also called predicate verbs. Predicate verbs tell what the subject nouns do. Can you name the subject nouns that go with each of the predicate verbs above?

You are right if you matched up:

1. turtle munched
2. puppy snuggled
3. kitten purred
4. dog fetched
5. fish swam

Exercise 1

Find the action verb that completes each sentence below. Use each verb only once. The letter clue in each sentence will help you.

chews	helps	spares
climbs	repays	stretches
falls	roars	struggles
grabs	runs	walks
hears	scurries	wriggles

1. A great lion w_______ through the thick jungle.
2. Feeling tired, he s_______ out to take a nap.
3. Not seeing him, a tiny mouse c_______ over him.
4. Angrily the lion g_______ the frightened mouse.
5. The mouse begs and the lion s_______ him.
6. The lion f_______ into a hunter's trap.
7. He s_______ in the heavy net.
8. The great beast r_______ angrily.
9. The mouse h_______ the roar.
10. He r_______ right to the trap.
11. Then he s_______ up the net.
12. With his sharp teeth, he c_______ a hole in the net.
13. Gratefully the lion w_______ through the hole.
14. A small friend h_______ a trapped lion.
15. One good turn r_______ another.

Exercise 2

Name the action verb in each sentence.

1. The football flew through the air.
2. Some frogs croaked loudly from the pond.
3. The wolves howled at a full moon.
4. Dad works in a factory downtown.
5. Spiders spin webs around the old peach tree.
6. Mary read four books last month.
7. Wild mustangs galloped across the prairie.
8. I called Joey from a phone booth.
9. The porcupine growled at its enemies.
10. He jumped from the canoe.
11. Sara stepped away from the alligator.
12. Tigers swim on hot days.
13. The mail carrier rang the doorbell.
14. The hikers walked along the path.
15. Some ants ate the crumbs on the table.

Practice Power

▶ **From the sentences above, match four subject nouns with different predicate verbs. Tell if the picture the new sentence paints could be real or imaginary.**

Examples: Sentences 15 and 13—Some *ants rang* the doorbell. (imaginary)

Sentences 8 and 6—*I read* four books last month. (real)

Being Verbs

Verbs that do not express action are being verbs.

Many verbs express action.
Some verbs do not express action.
Verbs that do not express action are being verbs.

Which verbs express action? Which verbs express being?

Tyrone *talks* loudly.	Tyrone *is* tall.
Winnie *walks* to work.	Winnie *was* a waitress.
Sam and Sara *skated* fast.	Sam and Sara *are* here.
Karen and Ken *cook* eggs.	Karen and Ken *were* absent.

You are right if you noticed that

- the action verbs are *talks, walks, skated,* and *cook.*
- the being verbs are *is, was, are,* and *were.*

Study this list.

BEING VERBS

is	was	am	has been	have been
are	were	be	had been	will be

VERBS

Exercise 1

Name the being verbs in these sentences.

1. The sand was very hot.
2. Edwin had been captain of the team.
3. *The Velveteen Rabbit* is a beautiful story.
4. Tomorrow Mark will be home.
5. Yesterday Rita was sick.
6. The clouds are very high.
7. The red building is large.
8. Ali has been careful.
9. The twin lakes were icy.
10. Soon summer will be here.

Exercise 2

The verb in each sentence is in italics. Tell if it is an action verb or a being verb.

1. Alex *found* a sand dollar on the beach.
2. Bugs Bunny *is* a funny cartoon character.
3. Daffodils *are* beautiful flowers.
4. Cows *run* in the rain.
5. This *is* a good mystery book.
6. Daniel Boone *was* a brave pioneer.
7. Steve *won* a game of table tennis.
8. The monster movie *was* great.
9. Francisco *ate* a giant ice cream sundae.
10. My brother *will be* a taxi driver.

Exercise 3

Complete each of these sentences with the being verb *is* or *are*.

1. On the bookcase _______ a large globe.
2. Globes _______ like maps.
3. Countries and continents _______ different colors.
4. On the globe, water _______ blue.
5. Some parts of the globe _______ rough, and some parts _______ smooth.

Complete each of these sentences. Use each of these action verbs once.

look	touch	visit
travel	think	spin

6. When you _______ the globe with your hands, the mountains feel high.
7. When you _______ it around, it turns like the planet Earth.
8. When I _______ at the globe, I _______ of the future.
9. Someday I will _______ all the countries of our planet.
10. Then I will _______ to another planet!

▶ **Think about sentence 10 in Exercise 3. Pretend now is the future. Write a few sentences about your visit to another planet. How is this new planet different from Earth? When you are finished, underline the verbs in your story. Then draw a picture to go with your story.**

Helping Verbs

**A predicate verb can have two parts—
a helping verb and a main verb.**

The predicate verbs in these sentences are in italics. Notice how many words are in each predicate verb.

A. Lily *is talking* to Sean.
B. Lily *has been talking* to Sean.

You are right if you noticed that there are

- two words in the predicate verb in sentence A.
- three words in the predicate verb in sentence B.

Some predicate verbs have two or more words. They have a main verb and one or two helping verbs. Helping verbs *help* the main verb.

In sentences A and B, the main verb is *talking.*

> How many helping verbs are in sentence A?
> How many helping verbs are in sentence B?

You are right if you noticed that

- sentence A has one helping verb—*is.*
- sentence B has two helping verbs—*has* and *been.*

Study this list.

	HELPING VERBS		
am	was	has	will
is	were	have	can
are	been	had	might
be			

Exercise 1

The predicate verbs are in italics in each sentence. Name the main verb and the helping verbs.

1. Susan *will sing* in the play.
2. Theresa *is feeding* her fish.
3. I *have been working* every day.
4. Ed *has missed* the bus.
5. My friends *have eaten* all the watermelon.
6. The turkey *was running* across the field.
7. We *are painting* a picture of the lake.
8. The squirrel *has been hiding* its nuts.
9. The scouts *were building* a campfire.
10. These igloos *are made* of snow and ice.

VERBS

Exercise 2

Complete each sentence with a main verb. The helping verbs are given.

1. Joel has been _______ the plants every Monday.
2. The leaves were _______ in the breeze.
3. In the morning, I am _______ to the grocery store.
4. Sharon and I are _______ a sweater.
5. Marty has _______ a clever poem.

Complete each sentence with one helping verb. The main verbs are given.

6. The sweater _______ made of wool.
7. Paula _______ flown her kite each morning.
8. The bear _______ hiding inside the cave.
9. Zeke _______ play football with his friend.
10. A monkey _______ swing by its tail.

Practice Power

▶ **Here are five main verbs. Add one helping verb to each main verb. Write a sentence for each predicate verb.**

Example: tumble—is tumbling
Maura *is tumbling* on the mat.

1. hide
2. fall
3. think
4. dream
5. spin
6. jump

Forms of Verbs

Verbs have different forms.

The form of these two crayons is alike in some ways. The form of these two mice is alike in some ways.

The forms are different in one way. How are the crayons different? How are the mice different?

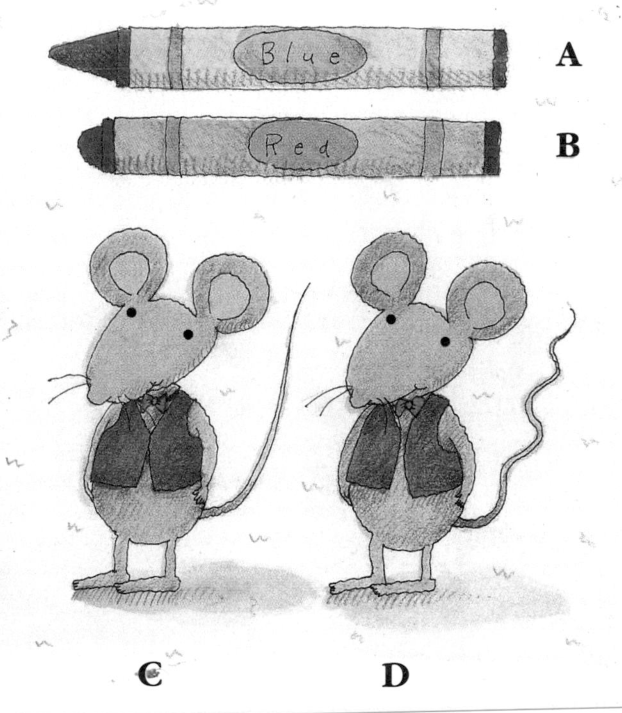

You are right if you noticed that

- blue crayon A is *pointed* in form.
- red crayon B is *blunt* in form.
- mouse C has a *straight* tail.
- mouse D has a *curly* tail.

When verbs are different in form, different names are used. Look at the three forms of the verb *cook.* Notice the different name for each form.

Kim *cooks* carrots.	(present form)
Kim *cooked* carrots.	(past form)
Kim *has cooked* carrots.	(past participle form)
Kim and I *have cooked* carrots.	(past participle form)
Kim *had cooked* carrots.	(past participle form)

What differences do you notice among these verb forms?

You are right if you noticed that

- in *cooks, s* can be a clue to the present form.
- in *cooked, ed* can be a clue to the past form.
- in *has cooked, has* can be a clue to the past participle form.
- in *have cooked, have* can be a clue to the past participle form.
- in *had cooked, had* can be a clue to the past participle form.

Use this chart to remember some clues. This mark ≈ means "can be a clue for."

CLUES TO REMEMBER

s ≈ present form
d or *ed* ≈ past form
has, have, had ≈ past participle form

Exercise 1

Tell if each verb in italics is present, past, or past participle. Use the Clues to Remember on page 328 to help you.

1. The children *played* hockey at Baker Field.
2. The farmer *grows* corn.
3. The robot *has moved* across the room.
4. I *looked* everywhere for my skates.
5. The crowds *have clapped* for every act.
6. Brian *had marked* the path for us.
7. Fred *works* in the grocery store.
8. The boys *rowed* across the lake.
9. Yesterday we *painted* the room.
10. Lauren *fills* her bucket with sand.

Exercise 2

Complete this chart on a sheet of paper. Fill in the past and past participle forms.

PRESENT	PAST (use *d* or *ed*)	PAST PARTICIPLE (use *has* or *had*)
1. Karl clowns	Karl ________________	Karl ________________
2. Jack waits	Jack ________________	Jack ________________
3. Beth jogs	Beth ________________	Beth ________________
4. Ben jumps	Ben ________________	Ben ________________
5. Matt listens	Matt ________________	Matt ________________
6. Marie looks	Marie ________________	Marie ________________
7. Kate cleans	Kate ________________	Kate ________________
8. Jill watches	Jill ________________	Jill ________________
9. Ted bakes	Ted ________________	Ted ________________
10. Tess bounces	Tess ________________	Tess ________________

Practice Power

▶ **Choose five sets of nouns and verbs from Exercise 2. Write five sentences using the nouns and verbs. Use only the past form of the verbs.**

Example: Karl *clowned* around with me.

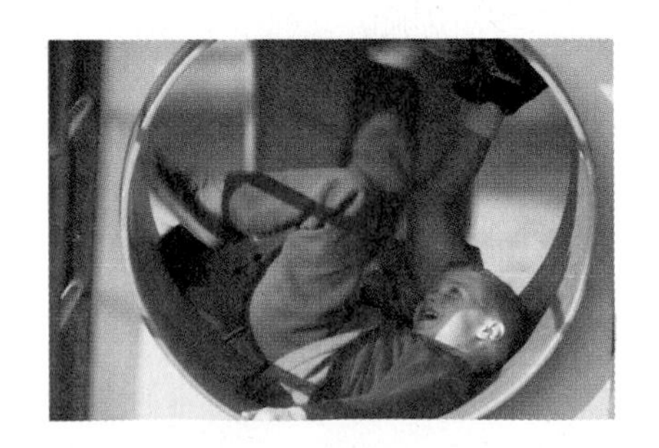

Regular and Irregular Verbs

Some verbs are formed in a regular way.
Some verbs are formed in an irregular way.

Which balloon is different or irregular? Which flower is different or irregular?

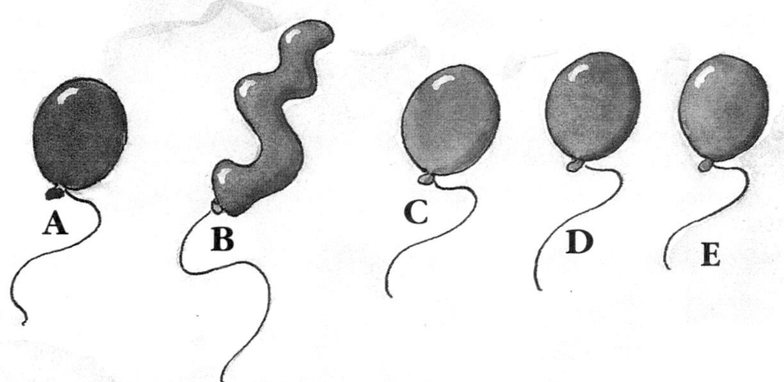

You are right if you noticed that

- balloon B and flower C are different.
- balloon B and flower C are irregular.

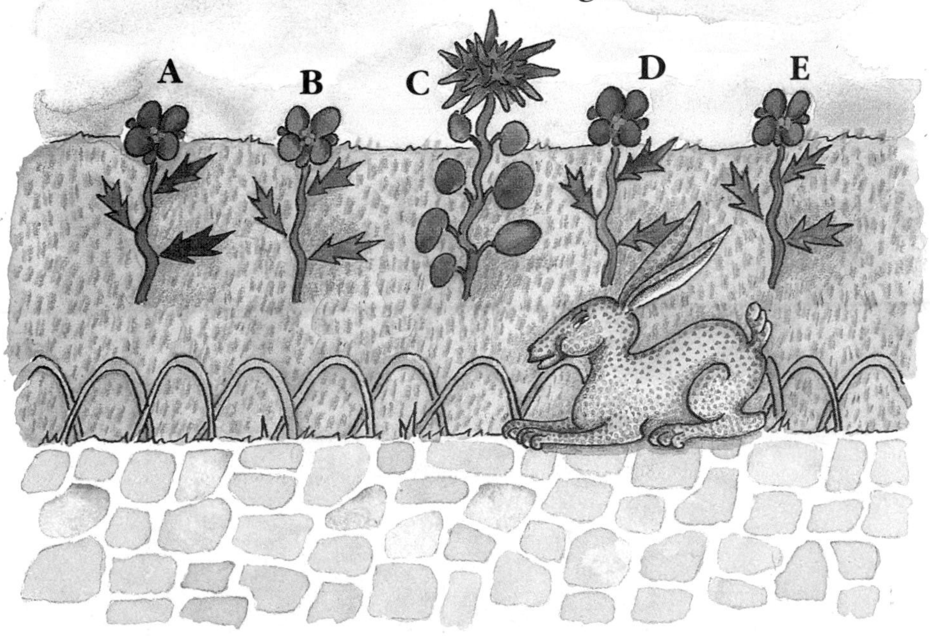

Study this group of past verb forms. Which verb is different or irregular?

We walked.
We jumped.
We ran.
We skated.
We rested.

You are right if you noticed that

- *ran* is different or irregular.
- the other verbs are similar or regular (walked, jumped, skated, rested).

Remember . . .

Verbs that form the past with *d* or *ed* are regular verbs.

Verbs that do not form the past with *d* or *ed* are irregular verbs.

Some Regular Verbs

PRESENT	PAST	PAST PARTICIPLE (use *has, have,* or *had*)
jump	jumped	(has, have, had) jumped
play	played	(has, have, had) played
skate	skated	(has, have, had) skated
walk	walked	(has, have, had) walked

Some Irregular Verbs

PRESENT	PAST	PAST PARTICIPLE (use *has, have,* or *had*)
bring	brought	has brought
buy	bought	has bought
come	came	has come
do	did	has done
eat	ate	has eaten
give	gave	has given
go	went	has gone
is (am)	was (were)	has been
know	knew	has known
run	ran	has run
see	saw	has seen
sit	sat	has sat
take	took	has taken
tear	tore	has torn
write	wrote	has written

VERBS

Exercise 1

Label each verb in the past form *regular* if it ends in *d* or *ed*. Label each verb *irregular* if it does not end in *d* or *ed*. The verbs are in italics. The chart on page 333 will help you.

1. Rosa and Andrew *saw* pictures of hungry children in a magazine.
2. They *decided* to earn some money to help the children.
3. Together they *bought* cookie mix and chocolate chips.
4. Andrew's mother *helped* them as they *mixed* the batter.
5. After they *poured* the batter on trays, she *placed* the trays in the oven.
6. They *baked* them until they were light brown.
7. When they *took* the cookies out of the oven, they *ate* the crunchy, broken ones.
8. Then they *wrapped* small packages with three cookies in each pack.
9. The next day their teacher *explained* to the class why Rosa and Andrew *wanted* to earn money.
10. Many children *bought* small packages of cookies to eat.
11. Rosa and Andrew *counted* the money and *gave* it to Andrew's mother.
12. She *wrote* a check for the amount.
13. Rosa and Andrew *mailed* the check to a fund called "Children Helping Children."
14. They *received* a special letter thanking them.
15. They *knew* they had *helped* a hungry child.

Exercise 2

Complete each sentence with *bring* or *brought*.

1. Last October students _______ photos of their pets.
2. For two years I *have* _______ my lunch to school.
3. Let's _______ old costumes from the attic.
4. Lisa, please _______ my mail.
5. Dennis *has* _______ his softball.
6. Last week a man in a gorilla suit _______ the message.
7. _______ me the newspaper.
8. *Has* Dave _______ a camera?
9. Last summer farmers _______ fresh vegetables to the city.
10. Scuba divers *had* _______ their oxygen tanks.
11. Christian, _______ your coin collection to school.
12. The birds in that nest _______ their chicks worms every day.
13. Who _______ their puppy to school this morning?
14. Susanna *had* _______ two books with her on vacation.
15. The pioneers of olden days _______ all their belongings in covered wagons.

Exercise 3

Complete each sentence with *buy* or *bought*.

1. Yesterday Aunt Mamie _______ fresh eggs from a farmer.
2. We *have* _______ chocolate milk every day.
3. Our class *has* _______ a gerbil.
4. Where is the basket that I _______ ?
5. I *have* _______ a model airplane kit.
6. The baseball team *had* _______ a trophy for their coach.
7. Marge _______ balloons for her experiment.
8. We _______ a bell for the cat.
9. Let's _______ a book about goldfish.
10. What *have* you _______ ?
11. Mrs. Mayer *has* _______ the last ticket.
12. _______ two hamburgers and save fifty cents.
13. Sarah, _______ two tickets for the movie.
14. They *have* _______ all the eggs at the store.
15. Please _______ peaches for our ice cream.

Exercise 4

Complete each sentence with *come* or *came*.

1. _______ roller-skating with me.
2. Our friends *have* _______ to this museum before.
3. _______ over and play our video game.
4. Yesterday Jerome _______ to see the play.
5. A strange noise _______ from the cave.
6. *Has* the train _______ yet?
7. " _______ and see for yourself," said the magician.
8. Julie *has* _______ for the computer club meeting.
9. Our books _______ last week.
10. _______ before the crowd gets here.
11. Betty _______ to the piano recital.
12. Last year six judges _______ to our science fair.
13. My family _______ to this restaurant last week.
14. Henry, _______ to the museum with us.
15. My uncle _______ by train.

Exercise 5

Complete each sentence with *eat, ate,* or *eaten.*

1. We _______ Thanksgiving dinner at my grandparents' farm last year.
2. The dog *had* _______ two slices of wheat bread.
3. We _______ dinner at six o'clock yesterday.
4. Justin _______ yogurt for lunch every day last week.
5. _______ slowly.
6. The seagulls *had* _______ bread crumbs on the beach.
7. Goldilocks _______ all of Baby Bear's porridge.
8. Frogs and turtles often _______ insects.
9. *Has* Al _______ any carrot cake?
10. A trout _______ the wiggling worm.
11. Could you _______ a pound of chocolate?
12. Eddie *had* _______ too many green apples.
13. _______ your vegetables!
14. *Have* you _______ octopus?
15. Does a bear _______ all day?

Exercise 6

Complete each sentence with *go, went,* or *gone.*

1. _______ find out what that noise was!
2. Last year our family _______ to Disneyland.
3. _______ to the trunk, and look inside.
4. The girls *had* _______ the night before.
5. Wild geese _______ south every winter.
6. Aston *has* _______ in the stagecoach.
7. Dawn _______ to the pottery class.
8. They _______ to the movies last night.
9. *Had* the bears _______ before sunrise?
10. I _______ to the museum every Saturday.
11. _______ to bed.
12. The boys *have* _______ to the soccer game.
13. Let's _______ to the park.
14. Last summer I _______ to camp.
15. The class *has* _______ to the school fair.
16. *Had* you ever _______ swimming before today?
17. I _______ into my room after dinner last night.
18. Cinderella _______ to the ball in a pumpkin coach.

Exercise 7

Complete each sentence with *see, saw,* or *seen.*

1. With my glasses, I _______ much better.
2. *Have* you _______ my colored pens anywhere?
3. After the storm, I _______ a rainbow.
4. *Has* André _______ those old circus wagons?
5. Who _______ the full moon last night?
6. I *have* _______ bear tracks in the snow.
7. Monique _______ a famous actress yesterday.
8. We _______ the signs and followed them.
9. *Have* you _______ any stars yet?
10. Lucy *had* never _______ the ocean.
11. _______ what has happened!
12. We never _______ bluebirds in the winter.
13. Please _______ if it is raining.
14. My father *has* _______ the Amazon River.
15. The scouts _______ a long, black snake in the woods.

Exercise 8

Complete each sentence with *take, took,* or *taken.*

1. The witch _______ Hansel's hand in hers.
2. Peggy, _______ off your coat and hat.
3. Angela *has* _______ piano lessons for one year.
4. _______ care of your teeth.
5. *Has* Sir Kevin _______ the dragon to the king?
6. We *had* _______ our kites outside before the rain started.
7. _______ my picture for our class scrapbook.
8. He would only _______ the medicine with a spoonful of sugar.
9. I _______ our poodle for a haircut.
10. Did you _______ binoculars for bird-watching?
11. _______ sugar cubes for the pony.
12. Neil _______ the baby seal to the park ranger.
13. Who _______ that photograph?
14. Carl, _______ two cookies.
15. The explorer _______ a canoe trip on the river.

Exercise 9

Complete each sentence with *tear, tore,* or *torn.*

1. The cats _______ the lace on the curtain.
2. Last week the workers _______ down the old building.
3. Our class *has* _______ this paper for an art project.
4. Kim *had* _______ the paper in half already.
5. Lennie, please _______ the label off this can.
6. The wind _______ shingles off the roof.
7. Rachel *has* _______ a photo from the magazine.
8. _______ a sheet of paper from this pad.
9. The men moved the piano and _______ the rug.
10. Did the baby _______ this page?
11. My parents *have* _______ the paper off the wall.
12. Marnie _______ her art paper into little pieces.
13. Please _______ along the dotted line.
14. Leslie _______ the note in half after she read it.
15. We _______ the rags to make a kite tail.

Exercise 10

Complete each sentence with *sit* or *sat*.

1. A spider *has* _______ beside Miss Muffet.
2. Let's _______ in front of the campfire.
3. We _______ quietly in the stalled taxi.
4. Please _______ in the middle of the theater.
5. Humpty Dumpty _______ on the wall.
6. We'll _______ together on the roller coaster.
7. I *have* _______ behind Virginia for a long time.
8. Bobby _______ and listened to the radio.
9. Let's _______ in the shade.
10. _______ where you _______ yesterday.
11. Three robins _______ in the pine tree this morning.
12. The German shepherd *has* _______ beside the blind man since morning.
13. Don't _______ on the railing.
14. We _______ in the bleachers during yesterday's game.
15. Little Jack Horner _______ in the corner.

VERBS

Exercise 11

Complete each sentence with *write, wrote,* or *written.*

1. In school today, I _______ a story about Martians.

2. George _______ his homework neatly last night.

3. Always _______ the word *I* with a capital letter.

4. Please _______ your name on the first line.

5. Most campers *had* _______ letters to their parents before noon.

6. The poet _______ a silly poem.

7. Chris, _______ the Roman numeral for ten.

8. Abraham Lincoln _______ his lessons on a slate.

9. I *have* _______ about a brave lion.

10. Can you _______ with your left hand?

11. Michelle *has* _______ in her diary.

12. Larry _______ a note on his computer.

13. The students _______ letters yesterday.

14. Anna *has* _______ a play for our class.

15. Kwan can _______ in Chinese.

Practice Power

▶ **Imagine that you and your brother went to a birthday party together. When you arrived, your brother started eating everything in sight.**

Write a story about what happened. In your story, answer some of these questions.

- How did you feel when your brother started eating so much?
- How did you control his behavior?
- How was your brother eating?
- What snacks did he eat?
- Why was he eating so much?

▶ **After you have completed and shared your story, pick out some verbs you have used. Put them in a chart like this.**

REGULAR	IRREGULAR
(*d* or *ed*)	(different)

VERBS

Present Tense

The tense of a verb tells when the action happens.

A verb in the present tense tells about action that is happening now or that happens again and again.

Some verbs in the present tense end in *s*. Some verbs do not end in *s*.

Which verbs sound correct with singular (one) nouns?

Which verbs sound correct with plural (more than one) nouns?

One snake (*wiggles* or *wiggle?*)
Two snakes (*wiggles* or *wiggle?*)

One baby (*giggles* or *giggle?*)
Two babies (*giggles* or *giggle?*)

One puppy (*snuggles* or *snuggle?*)
Two puppies (*snuggles* or *snuggle?*)

You are right if you noticed that these verbs sound correct.

One snake *wiggles.*
One baby *giggles.*
One puppy *snuggles.*

Two snakes *wiggle.*
Two babies *giggle.*
Two puppies *snuggle.*

In the present tense

- if the subject is singular, the verb ends in *s.*
- if the subject is plural, the verb does not end in *s.*

Exercise 1

Copy the nouns listed below the poem on a sheet of paper. Write the verbs that match them. If the verb ends in *s,* underline the *s.*

Fun at the Zoo

A kangaroo *hops* in the funniest way.
The tiger *growls* at her kitten's rough play.
Some beautiful snakes *crawl* up a tree.
Admiring persons *stop* just to see.

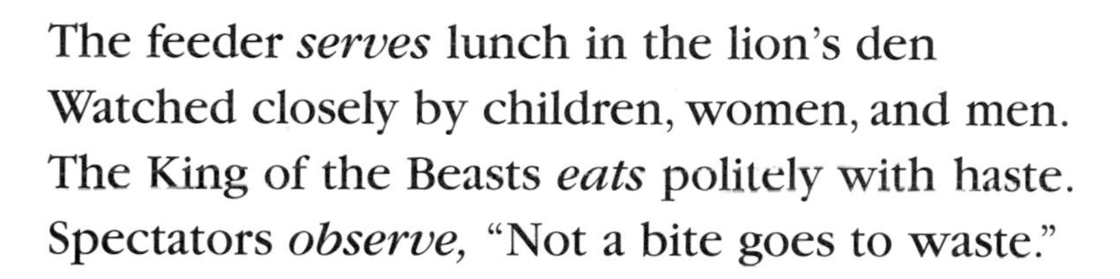

The feeder *serves* lunch in the lion's den
Watched closely by children, women, and men.
The King of the Beasts *eats* politely with haste.
Spectators *observe,* "Not a bite goes to waste."

Nibbling a treetop is a graceful giraffe.
Monkeys *do* tricks just to see people laugh.
Strange voices were heard as we all left the zoo,
"Please come again. It was nice to watch you."

SINGULAR	PLURAL
a kangaroo _______	snakes _______
the tiger _______	persons _______
the feeder _______	spectators _______
the King _______	monkeys _______

Exercise 2

Choose a verb to match the singular noun. The singular noun is in italics.

1. Before dinner, *Rita* (empty, empties) the dishwasher and (set, sets) the table.
2. *Mother* usually (cooks, cook) the meal.
3. *Dad* (clear, clears) the table.
4. *Laura* (sweep, sweeps) the kitchen floor.
5. *Tom* (prepares, prepare) the lunches for the next day.

Exercise 3

Choose a verb to match the subject noun or pronoun.

1. My friend and I (collect, collects) spiderwebs.
2. We (look, looks) for a web without a spider.
3. We (find, finds) them along fences and bushes.
4. My friend Dan (spray, sprays) them with a little spray paint.
5. He (place, places) a piece of paper against the web.
6. The web (stick, sticks) to the paper.
7. Then we (cut, cuts) the web loose.
8. The web (dry, dries) in a short time.
9. We (hang, hangs) the paper with the web on the wall.
10. Dan and I (have, has) fun collecting spiderwebs!

Practice Power

▶ **Choose five of the noun-verb pairs you found for Exercise 1 on page 347. Write five sentences of your own using the nouns and the verbs in the present tense.**

Past Tense

Remember, the tense of a verb tells when the action happens.

A verb in the past tense tells about action that has already happened.

The lights *flashed* on and off.
Nicole *wrote* a letter to her pen pal.

These verbs tell you that the actions *flashed* and *wrote* happened sometime in the past.

VERBS

Exercise 1

Give the past tense of each verb.

1. need _______
2. touch _______
3. feed _______
4. sing _______
5. begin _______
6. cry _______
7. drop _______
8. listen _______

Exercise 2

Complete each sentence with a verb in the past tense.

1. Our third grade (goes, went) on a field trip.
2. We (took, take) a big, yellow bus to the city.
3. We (arrived, arrive) at the museum just as it opened.
4. The guard (smiles, smiled) as we entered.
5. In a large room, we (see, saw) lifelike dinosaurs.
6. Then our guide (told, tells) us about these amazing animals.
7. Some dinosaurs (eat, ate) meat, and some (ate, eat) plants.
8. Some dinosaurs (moved, move) slowly, and some (move, moved) quickly.
9. Before long we (returned, return) to school.
10. We (discuss, discussed) what we (learned, learn) about these fascinating creatures.

Exercise 3

Give a verb in the past tense for each noun.

1. One icicle _______ .
2. The birds _______ .
3. A star _______ .
4. The wind _______ .
5. Six ants _______ .
6. My pen _______ .
7. Six fish _______ .
8. This lion _______ .

Practice Power

▶ **Choose four noun-verb pairs in Exercise 3. Then write four sentences using the verbs in the past tense.**

Example: One icicle *melted* in the warm sun.

LESSON 8

Correct Use of *Is* and *Are*, *Was* and *Were*

Use *is* and *was* with a singular subject. Use *are* and *were* with a plural subject.

Study these sentences.

Kim *is* a third grader.
Last year Kim *was* a second grader.

The twins *are* in sixth grade.
Last year the twins *were* in fifth grade.

Which two verbs match the singular noun *Kim?*
Which two verbs match the plural noun *twins?*

You are right if you noticed that

- *is* and *was* match *Kim* (singular).
- *are* and *were* match *twins* (plural).

Remember . . .

***Is* and *was* are used with singular subjects.**
***Are* and *were* are used with plural subjects.**

VERBS

Exercise 1

Complete each sentence with *is* or *are*.

1. Many clouds _______ floating in the sky.
2. What a great book this _______ !
3. The coats _______ hanging in the closet.
4. My sister _______ shopping at the mall.
5. Warm sweaters _______ on sale.

Exercise 2

Complete each sentence with *was* or *were*.

1. The puppies _______ in the basket.
2. Those soap carvings _______ on display.
3. Robin _______ visiting her cousin.
4. _______ Luis working on his project?
5. Steve and Susan _______ in computer class.

Putting It All Together

On a sheet of paper, write a short story of five sentences. Make sure some sentences use action verbs and others use being verbs. Underline or circle the verbs in each sentence. Then write the story again, leaving blanks for the verbs.

Give the first copy of the story to a partner. Practice reading your story aloud, leaving blanks for the verbs. Have your partner act out the verbs. Challenge the class to guess what verbs the story uses.

Chapter Challenge

These sentences tell a story. Read each sentence carefully. Then answer the questions below.

1. Last summer our family *visited* Disneyland.
2. My best friend *went* with us.
3. We *saw* the Magic Castle first.
4. Then a smiling Mickey Mouse *waved* to us.
5. He *was* so friendly.
6. We *rode* our favorite rides many times.
7. Before we knew it, our week *had ended.*
8. In my opinion, our visit to Disneyland *tops* every vacation so far.

SENTENCE NUMBER	QUESTION
1.	Is the verb *visited* regular or irregular?
2.	Is the verb *went* regular or irregular?
3.	Is the verb *saw* present or past tense?
4.	Is the verb *waved* past or past participle?
5.	Is the verb *was* an action or a being verb? Is *was* singular or plural?
6.	Is the verb *rode* an action or a being verb?
7.	Is the verb *had ended* past or past participle?
8.	Is the verb *tops* singular or plural? Is *tops* present or past tense?

VERBS

Creative Space

Rose, where did you get that red?

Dog, where did you get that bark?
Dragon, where did you get that flame?
Kitten, where did you get that meow?
Rose, where did you get that red?
Bird, where did you get those wings?

Desiree Lynne Collier

Explore the Poem . . .

What are five things the speaker wonders about in this poem? When you think of a dog or a rose, do you wonder about the same things? Use the same animals and flower in this poem, but change the last word. Use the word *that* or *those.*

Dog, where did you get
that tail?

Dragon, where did you get
________ ?

Kitten, where did you get
________ ?

Rose, where did you get
________ ?

Bird, where did you get
________ ?

How did the poet title this poem?

Have you ever wondered where animals or other things in nature get their color, size, shape, or smell?

What would you like to know about a tree, the wind, or the sea?

Think about four or five things in nature. Then think about what makes them special. Write a poem that asks a question about each one. Give your poem a title.

Before you begin, read this poem written by a student. This student began each line with the same letter.

Donkey, where did you get
those ears?
Daffodil, where did you get
that yellow?
Dolphin, where did you get
that nose?
Donkey, where did you get
those ears?
Duck, where did you get
those feet?

CHAPTER 13

ADJECTIVES

Adjectives That Describe

Many adjectives describe nouns.

Read these sentences.

This banana has *thick, yellow* skin.
The fruit is *soft* and *white.*

What noun is described by the adjectives *thick* and *yellow?* What noun is described by the adjectives *soft* and *white?*

You are right if you noticed that

- *thick* and *yellow* describe the noun *skin* (thick, yellow skin).
- *soft* and *white* describe the noun *fruit* (soft, white fruit).

Where are adjectives placed?

- Some adjectives come before nouns—*yellow* skin.
- Some adjectives come after verbs like *is*—fruit is *soft* and *white.*

Adjectives can come after verbs such as *is, are, was,* or *were.*

The fruit *is* soft. The fruits *are* soft.
The fruit *was* soft. The fruits *were* soft.

ADJECTIVES

About the Photograph

What words would you use to describe the people and things you see? Adjectives help describe the world around us.

Read these sentences.

These apples have *shiny, red* skin.
These fruits are *firm* and *crunchy.*
These plums have *smooth, purple* skin.
These fruits are *sweet* and *juicy.*

Which adjectives come before a noun?
Which adjectives come after the verb *are?*

You are right if you noticed that in these sentences

- *shiny, red* and *smooth, purple* come before a noun.
- *firm* and *crunchy* and *sweet* and *juicy* come after the verb *are.*

Remember . . .

Many adjectives describe nouns.
orange **pumpkins.**

Some adjectives come before nouns.
scuffling **noise.**

Some adjectives come after verbs.
Father is ***brave.***

Exercise 1

An adjective comes before a noun in each of these sentences. The noun is in italics. Name the adjective.

1. Fluffy *clouds* floated in the sky.
2. Keith climbed the creaky *stairs.*
3. José wore a striped *jacket.*
4. The old *doll* lay on the floor.
5. Tall *trees* line the pond.
6. Sandra watched graceful *butterflies.*
7. Loud *music* filled the room.
8. We hiked to the green *hills.*
9. Trucks carried the new *cars.*
10. Busy *elves* gathered firewood.

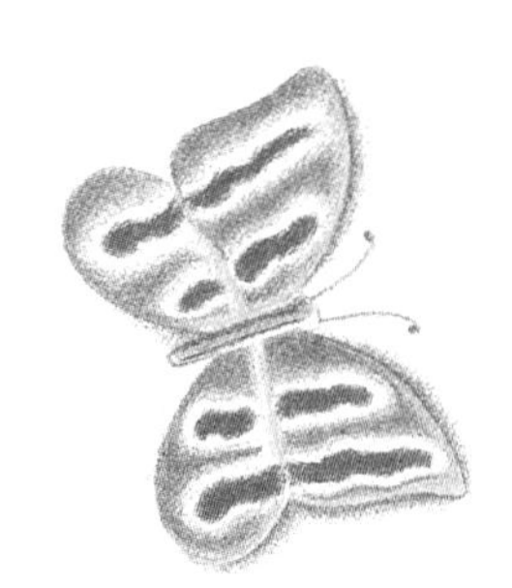

Exercise 2

In these sentences, an adjective comes after the verb *is, are, was,* or *were.* The nouns the adjectives describe are in italics. Name the adjectives.

1. The *stars* in the sky are sparkling.
2. Their *puppies* were sleepy.
3. Kelli's *bedroom* in the basement was green.
4. Our *classroom* is warm.
5. The *salsa* on the table is spicy.
6. Tom's *socks* are striped.
7. Before the bake sale, *Mrs. Kramer* was busy.
8. The *sailboat* was colorful.
9. Lori's *report card* was excellent.
10. The *toys* he found were broken.

Exercise 3

Name the adjective or adjectives that describe the noun in italics in each sentence.

1. Walt brought sour *lemonade.*
2. The *cat* was playful.
3. Mr. Lopez carried the heavy *ladder.*
4. Shiny *books* stood together on the shelf.
5. The *jelly* is sweet.
6. Yellow *finches* sing in their cage.
7. The fuzzy *blanket* is on the bed.
8. The *classroom* was bright and neat.
9. Our *rug* is thick and shaggy.
10. Mark lifted two sacks of red *potatoes.*

Exercise 4

Use an adjective to describe the noun in italics in each sentence.

1. Gene and Sandy flew some _______ *kites.*
2. We painted the _______ *house.*
3. Lynn ate some _______ *ice cream.*
4. We baked two _______ *pies.*
5. We saw a _______ *movie.*
6. The _______ *car* is parked outside.
7. A pair of _______ *scissors* is on the desk.
8. The gifts were wrapped in _______ *paper.*
9. The _______ *sweaters* belong to Kit.
10. At the pet store, we heard _______ *birds.*

Exercise 5

Use an adjective after *is, are, was,* or *were* to describe the noun in italics in each sentence.

1. The *kites* Gene and Sandy flew were _______ .
2. The *house* we painted is _______ .
3. The *ice cream* Lynn ate was _______ .
4. The *pies* we baked are _______ .
5. The *movie* we saw was _______ .
6. The *car* parked outside is _______ .
7. The pair of *scissors* on the desk is _______ .
8. The *paper* around the gifts was _______ .
9. Kit's *sweaters* are _______ .
10. The *birds* we heard were _______ .

Exercise 6

Name the nouns that the adjectives in italics describe in these sentences.

1. Our *biking* club planned a trip.
2. We decided to climb to the top of a *big* hill.
3. Our *tired* group finally reached the top.
4. The hikers were *exhausted* and *hungry.*
5. We rested on the *soft* grass.
6. Then we ate *jelly* sandwiches.
7. The sandwiches were *delicious.*
8. Most hikers were *thirsty,* too.
9. *Cool* water refreshed us.
10. The *happy* hikers walked down the hill.
11. The trip down the hill was *easier.*
12. Our parents were *proud* of us.
13. Next year we plan to climb a *bigger* hill.
14. Each hiker will be *older* and *stronger.*
15. We'll pack a *larger* lunch!

Practice Power

▶ **Pretend that you were one of the hikers that climbed the hill. Imagine that something strange and wonderful happened while you and your friends were resting at the top of that big hill. Write five sentences that tell about what happened. Underline the adjectives in your sentences.**

Adjectives That Compare

Some adjectives can compare two or more persons or things.

In my fishbowl, the goldfish are *larger* than the neon fish.

In my fishbowl, the angelfish is the *largest* of all the fish.

How many kinds of fish are mentioned in these two sentences?

Which adjective in italics compares two kinds of fish?

Which adjective compares three or more kinds of fish?

You are right if you noticed that

- three kinds of fish are mentioned.
  goldfish, neon fish, and angelfish
- *larger* compares two kinds of fish.
  goldfish, neon fish
- *largest* compares three or more kinds of fish.
  angelfish, goldfish, neon fish

Remember . . .

Many adjectives that end with *er* compare two nouns.

larger smaller faster

Many adjectives that end with *est* compare three or more nouns.

largest smallest fastest

Exercise 1

Complete each of these sentences. If the sentence compares two things, choose the *er* adjective. If the sentence compares three or more things, choose the *est* adjective.

1. The corner house is the (bigger, biggest) of the five buildings.
2. Is the fan (louder, loudest) than the air conditioner?
3. The black kitten is the (prettier, prettiest) of the whole litter.
4. In New York, October is (cooler, coolest) than June.
5. This pancake is the (flatter, flattest) in the whole stack.
6. The ocean is (deeper, deepest) than a lake.
7. Is metal (stronger, strongest) than plastic?
8. Your thermos is (larger, largest) than mine.
9. Doughnuts are (sweeter, sweetest) than bagels.
10. That orange is the (juicier, juiciest) of all the fruit.

Exercise 2

Match each adjective pair with a sentence pair. Use both adjectives to compare the two nouns and complete the sentences. The first pair of sentences is done for you.

ADJECTIVES

louder–quieter

smaller–larger

taller–shorter

shallower–deeper

smoother–rougher

1. A river is deeper than a puddle.

   A puddle is shallower than a river.

2. A whisper is ______________________________ .

   A shout is ______________________________ .

3. Cotton is ______________________________ .

   Sandpaper is ______________________________ .

4. A giraffe is ______________________________ .

   A penguin is ______________________________ .

5. A mouse is ______________________________ .

   A camel is ______________________________ .

ADJECTIVES

Exercise 3

Compare the nouns in italics in Part A. Use the adjective that best describes the noun in each sentence. Do the same with Part B.

PART A

roughest	spiciest	cheesiest
smallest	saltiest	sharpest

1. *Grains of sand* are the ________________ .
2. *Pretzels* are the ________________ .
3. *Scissors* are the ________________ .
4. *Pizzas* are the ________________ .
5. *Sidewalks* are the ________________ .
6. *Mustard* is the ________________ .

PART B

woolliest	coldest	juiciest
warmest	fuzziest	tallest

7. *Skyscrapers* are the ________________ .
8. *Lambs* are the ________________ .
9. *Snow* is the ________________ .
10. *Peaches* are the ________________ .
11. *Sunshine* is the ________________ .
12. *Caterpillars* are the ________________ .

Practice Power

▶ **Write sentences to answer any five of these questions about your supermarket. Use an *er* or *est* adjective in each sentence.**

A. Which supermarket is *nearest* your home?

B. Do you go shopping with someone *older* or *younger* than you?

C. What do you buy from the *coldest* aisle in the market?

D. Which needs to be *fresher*—a gallon of milk or a gallon of apple juice?

E. Which is *cheaper*—a dozen eggs or a dozen apples?

F. Which is *heavier* to carry home—a big box of cereal or a big box of cookies?

G. Which is *lighter* to carry home—a bag of potato chips or a bag of potatoes?

H. Which checkout line do you choose—the *shortest* line or the *longest* line?

I. Does your market have one checkout line that is the *fastest* line of all? What is it called?

J. Who is the *happiest* family member when you arrive home with the groceries? Why?

Adjectives That Tell Number

Some adjectives answer *how many* about the noun.

Read these sentences.

In the first half of the game, we scored only ten points.

Some fans were sad.

In the second half of the game, we scored forty points.

Many fans cheered wildly.

What adjectives tell about number?
In other words, what adjectives answer *how many* about the nouns?

You are right if you noticed that these adjectives tell about number.

first half	*some* fans	*forty* points
ten points	*second* half	*many* fans

Remember . . .

Some adjectives tell *exactly* how many.
first ten second forty

Some adjectives tell *about* how many.
some many few

Exercise 1

The nouns in this grocery list are in italics. Name the adjective that tells *how many* about each noun.

At the store we need to buy:

1. ten *pounds* of potatoes
2. a couple of *onions*
3. a dozen *eggs*
4. several *tomatoes*
5. four *gallons* of milk
6. two *jars* of jelly
7. a few *loaves* of bread
8. some *boxes* of cereal
9. many *jars* of baby food
10. one *head* of lettuce

Exercise 2

Make a chart like the one below. Place each adjective from Exercise 1 in the correct column.

ADJECTIVES THAT TELL EXACTLY HOW MANY	ADJECTIVES THAT TELL ABOUT HOW MANY

ADJECTIVES

Exercise 3

One noun in each sentence is in italics. Select the adjective that tells *how many* about this noun. Does it tell exactly or about how many?

1. While we were on vacation, we had several rainy *days.*
2. One rainy *day* we decided to play Chinese checkers.
3. Each player arranged ten colored *marbles* in the home triangle.
4. Pat moved one yellow *marble.*
5. Soon the center of the board had many colored *marbles.*
6. Paul's blue marble jumped six *marbles* in a row.
7. Regina's red marble followed by jumping four *times.*
8. Then Pat's yellow marbles made a few amazing *jumps* on the way to home.
9. Soon only two lonely *marbles* were left.
10. What color do you think got ten *marbles* home first?

Practice Power

▶ **Imagine a visit to the zoo. Select any five of these questions. Write a sentence to answer each question. In each sentence, include an adjective that tells *how many.* Use some adjectives that tell exactly how many. Use some adjectives that tell about how many.**

A. How many monkeys swung from branch to branch?

B. How many peacocks spread their tail feathers?

C. How many polar bears went for a swim?

D. How many elephants asked for a peanut?

E. How many zebras nibbled on grass?

F. How many parent animals played with their babies? Tell what kind of animals played.

G. How many animals took a nap? Tell what kind of animals napped.

H. Did you see animals you would like to take home as a pet? Tell which ones and why.

Articles

The adjectives *the, an,* and *a* are called articles.

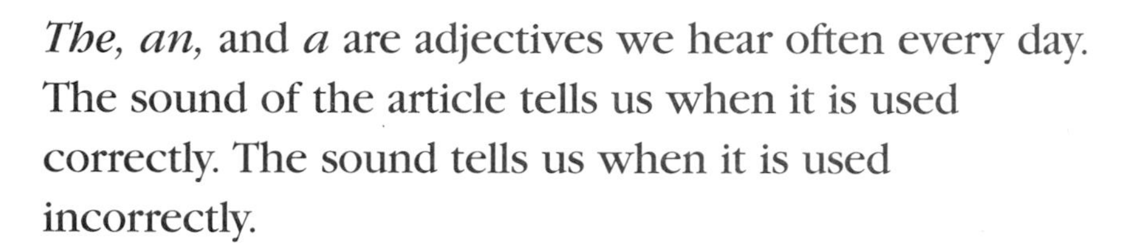
The, an, and *a* are adjectives we hear often every day. The sound of the article tells us when it is used correctly. The sound tells us when it is used incorrectly.

Which sounds correct? Which sounds incorrect?

a camel   the camel   an camel

You are right if you noticed that

- *a* camel and *the* camel sound correct.
- *an* camel sounds incorrect.

Remember . . .

Do not use *an* before words that begin with a consonant sound. Use *a* or *the* before words that begin with a consonant sound.

a desert   a caravan   the sand   the camel

Which sounds correct? Which sounds incorrect?

an onion   a onion   the onion

You are right if you noticed that

- *an* onion and *the* onion sound correct.
- *a* onion sounds incorrect.

Remember . . .

Do not use *a* before words that begin with vowel sounds. Use *an* or *the.*

an onion the onion an hour the hour

Exercise 1

Name the article and the noun in each sentence.

1. The dog barked loudly.
2. Sadie rode an ox.
3. I pushed the wheelchair.
4. Sir Kent wants to catch a dragon.
5. The eggs were cracked.
6. Emily picked up an acorn slowly.
7. Would you like an orange?
8. The rain beat on my window.
9. Ronnie gave me a football.
10. We found blackberry bushes along the stream.

Exercise 2

Decide if *a* or *an* fits the noun. Then name the article and the noun.

1. ___ tugboat pulled the ship up the river.
2. ___ monster led us into the castle.
3. ___ ape swung from branch to branch.
4. ___ snowbird stood on the hill.
5. ___ icicle hung from the rock.
6. ___ otter played under the waterfall.
7. ___ funny cartoon made us laugh.
8. ___ horse ran past our house.
9. ___ flower grew in the crack in the sidewalk.
10. ___ elevator was stuck between floors.

Exercise 3

Tell which sentence in each pair is expressed correctly. Correct the sentence that is incorrect. The first pair is done for you.

1. An old horse ran by our house. (correct)
2. An young horse ran by our house. (incorrect)
(A young horse ran by our house.)

3. A kindly monster welcomed us.
4. A angry monster welcomed us.

5. An courteous ape swung on the branch.
6. An impish ape swung on the branch.

7. A unsmiling bus driver stood on the hill.
8. A smiling bus driver stood on the hill.

9. An enormous icicle hung from the rock.
10. An tiny icicle hung from the rock.

Practice Power

▶ **Play the WHY game. Read any four sentences from Exercises 1, 2, or 3 on pages 373–374. Ask yourself WHY about the sentences. Use your imagination to write the answers. Use adjectives that describe as well as articles.**

Examples: 1. An old horse ran by our house. Why?
The old, gray horse was playing tag with my little sister.

2. The dog barked loudly. Why?
The little dog heard heavy footsteps on the porch.

Adjectives That Point Out

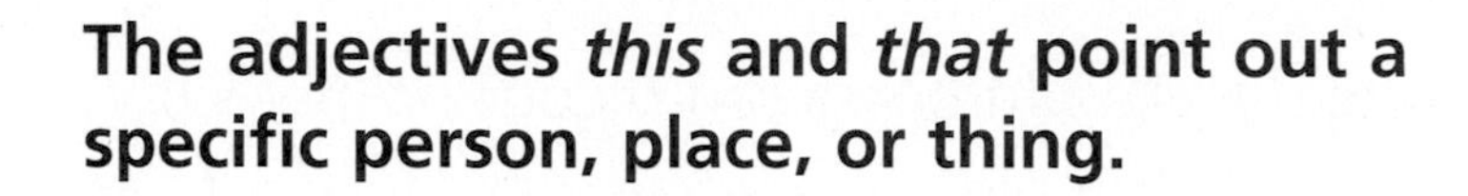

The adjectives *this* and *that* point out a specific person, place, or thing.

A zookeeper visited our school. She brought animals to show us. She said

> *This* raccoon is called Rudy.
> *That* raccoon is named Randolf.

Which raccoon is *nearer* to the zookeeper?
Which raccoon is *farther* away from the zookeeper?

Which adjective pointed to the raccoon *near* at hand?
Which adjective pointed to the raccoon *farther* away?

You are right if you noticed that

- Rudy is nearer to the zookeeper.
  This pointed to Rudy.
- Randolf is farther away.
  That pointed to Randolf.

Remember . . .

***This* points to nouns that are near.**
***That* points to nouns that are farther away.**

Exercise 1

Answer each question by choosing one of the two sentences that follow it.

1. Which bus is *closer?*
   This bus travels south to the city.
   That bus travels north to the suburbs.

2. Which kitten is *farther* away?
   This striped kitten is playful.
   That white kitten is sleepy.

3. Which quilt is *closer?*
   Aunt Marie made this quilt with different colored patches.
   Aunt Rita made that blue and red quilt.

4. Which farm is *farther* away?
   The family who lives on that farm raises cows.
   The family on this farm raises wheat.

5. Which cow is *closer?*
   This cow is big.
   That cow is black and white.

Exercise 2

The nouns are in italics. Use *this* or *that* correctly in each sentence pair.

1. I'm painting _______ small *picture* of a clown.
   I'm copying from _______ large *picture* on the wall.
2. I'm going to buy _______ green *sweater* in the store window.
   I'm wearing _______ brown *sweater* now.
3. We have lived in _______ old *house* for ten years.
   Tomorrow we're moving to _______ new *house* across the street.
4. Now I'm going to get _______ jigsaw *puzzle* from the shelf.
   I've solved _______ crossword *puzzle.*
5. This year I'm riding _______ small, blue *bike.*
   Next year I'll ride _______ large, silver *bike* in our garage.

Exercise 3

The nouns from Exercise 2 are given in this chart. Give the adjective that tells more about the noun and the adjective that points out.

	NEARER		FARTHER AWAY	
1.	_______________	picture	_______________	picture
2.	_______________	sweater	_______________	sweater
3.	_______________	house	_______________	house
4.	_______________	puzzle	_______________	puzzle
5.	_______________	bike	_______________	bike

Putting It All Together

You are going to make a list of adjectives. Number a sheet of paper 1–6. For each number, write the following kinds of adjectives:

1. describing adjective
2. describing adjective
3. describing adjective
4. adjective that tells number
5. describing adjective
6. adjective that compares more than three

Now use your adjective list to complete the story below. Once you stop laughing, make a new list of adjectives to complete the story in a more serious way.

My family and I decided to head south for vacation. We piled into our (1) _______ , (2) _______ car and sped off. Riding along a (3) _______ road we must have seen (4) _______ cows. Two (5) _______ ones told us to stop staring and "mooove" on. When I got to our hotel, I was the (6) _______ vacationer.

Chapter Challenge

Read these sentences carefully. Then answer the questions on page 381. Use only one or two adjectives or nouns for each answer.

1. Jude, Maria, and Nina like to play in their large backyard.
2. Each of the four seasons spreads a pretty carpet for them.
3. Jude likes autumn's rug of colorful leaves.
4. The children rake some leaves into huge piles to play in.
5. The winter carpet is soft and white.
6. The children use this carpet to build several snowmen.
7. Maria thinks winter's rug is even prettier than autumn's rug.
8. Spring's rug is fresh and green.
9. All games are fun with the gentle spring sun shining.
10. In summer, Maria holds the hose while the other two children run through the cool, soft spray.
11. Nina thinks summer's rug is the prettiest of all.
12. No wonder this yard is the children's favorite place.

SENTENCE NUMBER	QUESTIONS
1.	In what kind of backyard do the children play?
2.	How many seasons spread carpets?
3.	What kind of leaves are part of autumn's rug?
4.	How many leaves are raked into a pile?
5.	What adjectives follow *is* and describe winter's carpet?
6.	How many snowmen do the children build in winter?
7.	What adjective compares two seasons' rugs?
8.	What adjectives follow *is?* Which rug do they describe?
9.	How many games are fun in the spring?
10.	How many children run through the spray? What kind of spray is it?
11.	What adjective compares the four seasons' rugs? What are the four seasons?
12.	What adjective means the yard is near?

Creative Space

Automobile Mechanics

Sometimes
I help my dad
Work on our automobile.
We unscrew
The radiator cap
And we let some water run—
Swish—from a hose
Into the tank.

And then we open up the hood
And feed in oil
From a can with a long spout.
And then we take a lot of rags
And clean all about.
We clean the top
And the doors
And the fenders and the wheels
And the windows and floors. . . .
We work hard
My dad
And I.

Dorothy Baruch

Explore the Poem . . .

In this poem, Dad is working with someone. Who is it? What are Dad and this person doing? Can you find three things they do on this project?

Read the last three lines of the poem. Do you think the speaker likes working with Dad?

Have you ever worked with someone on a project or a chore—your mom, brother, sister, friend, teacher? What are some of the things you did together? Write a poem beginning with

Sometimes
I help my ______

Write about two or three things you do on this project. Finally, end your poem with the words

We work hard
My ______
And I.

Before you begin, read this poem written by a student.

Sometimes
I help my mom
Plant flowers in the garden.
We dig the holes
And carefully put in the plants.
Then we sprinkle them with water
Slurp—from the watering can
Into the ground.
We work hard
My mom
And I.

CHAPTER 14 ADVERBS

Kinds of Adverbs

Adverbs tell more about verbs.

Adverbs can tell *when, where,* or *how* about an action.

Read these sentences.

Laura *often* walks to the library.
She goes *upstairs.*
There she reads books *quietly.*
Later she *happily* writes her own stories.

Tell what word in italics answers each of these questions.

When does Laura walk to the library?
When does she write her stories?
Where does she go?
Where does she read books?
How does she read books?
How does she write stories?

You are right if you answered the questions with these words.

walks *often*	goes *upstairs*	reads *quietly*
writes *later*	reads *there*	writes *happily*

About the Photograph

How do you read? Do you read silently? Quickly? Eagerly? What is something else you do? Use adverbs to tell how, where, or when you do it.

These words are called adverbs. Adverbs tell about verbs. Here are lists of adverbs. The question they answer is at the top of each list.

WHEN?	WHERE?	HOW?
today	above	happily
tomorrow	down	loudly
yesterday	far	quickly
always	here	quietly
first	inside	roughly
never	nearby	sadly
now	out	safely
sometimes	outside	slowly
soon	there	softly
later	up	fast

Remember . . .

Adverbs can tell *when, where,* or *how* about verbs.

Exercise 1

The verbs are in italics. Find the adverbs that tell *when.*

1. The cats *sang* late at night.
2. We *will pick* peppers tomorrow.
3. Joanne *went* to the dentist yesterday.
4. A Native American tribe once *camped* here.
5. Our class *made* fortune cookies today.
6. The fire chief *will visit* us soon.
7. Let's *play* a game next.
8. Sometimes I *count* the stars.
9. Never *leave* a campfire.
10. First *peel* the apples.

Exercise 2

The adverbs that tell *when* are in italics. Find the action verb that each adverb tells about. Write the verb and the adverb in each sentence.

1. I'll finish my homework *now.*
2. Bill went *twice* to the clock museum.
3. We *often* visit my grandparents.
4. Our paintings will dry *soon.*
5. Paul *never* forgets to feed the hamster.
6. Ed *always* walks home from school.
7. I hope the rain stops *soon.*
8. We built a tree house *yesterday.*
9. He came *late* to class.
10. Shelley hears sleigh bells *again.*

Exercise 3

The adverbs that follow each sentence tell *when*. Choose the one that fits better.

1. Our family _______ lives in an apartment. (now, before)
2. Finish the dishes _______ , Pam. (now, yesterday)
3. I visited the library _______ . (often, tomorrow)
4. _______ jump on the stairs. (Never, Yesterday)
5. The plane is delayed and will leave _______ in the morning. (soon, later)
6. David finished _______ . (tomorrow, yesterday)
7. The girls went to the party _______ . (soon, early)
8. Most farmers get up _______ . (early, tomorrow)
9. _______ the painting was finished. (Always, Finally)
10. After weeks of waiting, my birthday _______ came. (early, finally)

Exercise 4

The verbs are in italics. Find the adverbs that tell *where.*

1. The tall ships *sailed* proudly away.
2. A busy carpenter *is working* outside.
3. The small alligator *slid* forward.
4. Please *come* out to play.
5. The hungry seagulls *swooped* down.
6. *Carry* the corn inside.
7. Granny *ran* downstairs with a broom.
8. The acrobat *jumped* back.
9. The stagecoach driver *stepped* down.
10. *Leave* your skateboard there.

Exercise 5

Choose an adverb to complete each sentence.
Use each adverb once.

down outside up far away

1. Pick _______ your comic books.
2. Jane put _______ her baseball bat.
3. If it rains, we can't go _______ .
4. The young birds flew _______ .
5. Morgan is only three and can't go _______ .

everywhere backward below here close

6. Put the birdhouse plans _______ .
7. The officer on the ship's deck said we could go _______ .
8. I looked _______ for the hidden eggs.
9. The baby chimp stood _______ to its mother.
10. The car moved _______ into the garage.

ADVERBS

Exercise 6

The adverbs that tell *where* are in italics. Find the action verb each adverb tells about. Write the verb and the adverb.

1. Who let the cats *in?*
2. The elephant walked *backward.*
3. Bring your bike *inside.*
4. Angelo went *upstairs* quickly.
5. The jellyfish floated *away.*
6. The dog looked *everywhere* for a bone.
7. We ate our picnic lunch *here.*
8. Dandelion seeds travel *far.*
9. An eagle flew *high.*
10. The balloons sailed *up* and *away.*

Exercise 7

The verbs are in italics. Find the adverbs that tell *how.*

1. The popcorn *popped* loudly.
2. Jason carefully *signed* his name.
3. Andrea slowly *sipped* the thick milkshake.
4. The team *splashed* noisily in the pool.
5. Sue quickly *tore* a piece of paper from her notebook.
6. The toddler *walked* clumsily across the room.
7. Kim easily *solved* the math problems.
8. We *played* gently with the kittens.
9. I nervously *waited* for my turn at bat.
10. The lion *tiptoed* quietly through the jungle.

Exercise 8

The verbs are in italics. Find the adverbs that tell *how.* Write the verb and the adverb.

1. A duck *swam* slowly past the dock.
2. Her babies *hurried* nervously after her.
3. The mother *quacked* loudly at the people on the dock.
4. Jay *knew* certainly what she wanted.
5. They roughly *broke* bread into crumbs.
6. The children *threw* the crumbs carefully where the ducks could reach them.
7. The mother duck *scurried* directly toward the crumbs.
8. Her babies *paddled* quickly to keep up.
9. They *dropped* their beaks carefully to eat the crumbs.
10. After the meal, the family *swam* happily away.

Exercise 9

The adverbs in italics answer the question *how, when,* or *where.* Tell which question each adverb answers.

1. *Yesterday* Ben washed his dog Sam.
2. He washed him *outside* near the steps.
3. He rinsed him *carefully* and *gently.*
4. *Then* Ben took his clean pet for a walk.
5. Both of them walked *proudly* down the street.
6. *Today* we'll visit the art museum.
7. We'll walk *inside* and *outside.*
8. We'll *carefully* examine the paintings and statues.
9. *Tomorrow,* in school, we'll talk about our trip.
10. *Then,* we'll write a report about it.

Exercise 10

Choose the adverb that fits the story better. Then decide whether the adverb tells *when, where,* or *how.*

1. When Ken went to sleep, his tooth was throbbing (dully, sharply).
2. The next morning he awoke (early, late).
3. Now the pain was worse. His tooth throbbed (dully, sharply).
4. His mom called the dentist (later, immediately).
5. Ken walked (nervously, gladly) to the dentist's office.
6. Ken took the elevator (up, down) to the fifth floor.
7. The office music played (loudly, softly).
8. The dentist spoke (calmly, angrily) to him.
9. She fixed his sore tooth very (roughly, gently). The pain stopped.
10. Now that his tooth didn't hurt, Ken walked home (sadly, happily).

Practice Power

▶ **Does the story of Ken's toothache remind you of a time when you hurt yourself or felt some pain? Write a short story about it. Try to answer some of these questions.**

When did the pain start?
How did it feel?
Who helped you?
What did you do when the pain stopped?
How did you feel then?

▶ **After you finish, underline the words that tell *when, where,* or *how* in your story.**

Using Words Correctly

Good* and *Well

Good is an adjective that describes nouns.
***Well* is an adverb that tells about verbs.**

Good is an adjective. It describes nouns.

The blue ones are *good* crayons.
That was a *good* movie.
Is this *good* popcorn?

Well is an adverb. It tells about verbs.

Ella sings *well.*
Fish swim *well.*
Mrs. Jenkins tells a story *well.*

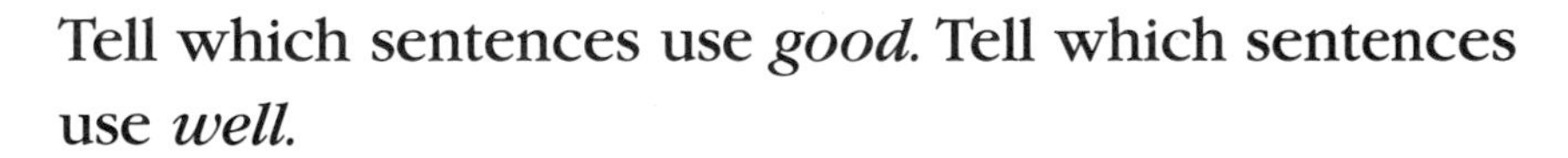
Tell which sentences use *good.* Tell which sentences use *well.*

1. Joan colors (good, well).
2. That is (good, well) soup.
3. Rain is (good, well) for flowers.
4. Mark skates (good, well).

You are right if you said

1. Joan colors *well.* (adverb)
2. That is *good* soup. (adjective)
3. Rain is *good* for flowers. (adjective)
4. Mark skates *well.* (adverb)

Exercise 1

Complete each sentence with *good* or *well.*

1. What a (good, well) idea!
2. Matt is a (good, well) shortstop.
3. Betsy can do a cartwheel (good, well).
4. Did you beat the eggs (good, well)?
5. Noon is a (good, well) time to eat lunch.
6. Jody writes (good, well) poems.
7. My grandmother speaks Italian (good, well).
8. The bus driver turns this big bus (good, well).
9. This is a (good, well) newspaper to read in the morning.
10. Peanuts are a (good, well) snack.
11. The market had a (good, well) selection of meat.
12. My grandmother said I behaved (good, well) in the market.
13. The clerk gave me a (good, well) piece of cheese.
14. My father said milk is (good, well) for you.
15. The clerk packed our groceries (good, well) in large boxes.

To, Too, and *Two*

***To, too,* and *two* are homophones.**

Read these sentences.

Let's go *to* the ice cream shop.
Susan wants *two* scoops of ice cream.
She wants chocolate sauce, *too.*
These sundaes are *too* big!

What word in italics tells

- where they are going?
- how many scoops of ice cream?
- what Susan also wants?
- that the size of the sundaes is more than enough?

You are right if you noticed that

- *to* tells *where.*
- *two* tells *how many.*
- *too* means *also* or *more than enough.*

ADVERBS

Exercise 2

Tell whether the word in italics shows *how many, where, also,* or *more than enough.*

1. Can you eat *two* hot dogs?
2. Anthony threw the ball *too* hard.
3. Take these flowers *to* your teacher.
4. I found *two* nickels in my pocket.
5. My dog is a cocker spaniel, *too.*

Complete each sentence with *two, too,* or *to.*

6. Is it Maria's birthday, _______ ?
7. I read _______ books this week.
8. Joey and Stan rode _______ the park.
9. The turtle moves _______ slowly to win the race.
10. Do you like going _______ the car wash?

Their and *There*

Their and _there_ are homophones.

Read these sentences.

> The children let go of *their* balloons.
> Look at the balloons over *there!*

What word in italics tells

- what the children own?
- where the balloons are?

You are right if you noticed that

- *their* tells *what is owned.*
- *there* tells *where.*

ADVERBS

Exercise 3

Tell whether the word in italics shows *what is owned* or *where.*

1. Put your muddy shoes *there.*
2. *Their* cat likes dog food!
3. They did *their* homework together.
4. We went *there* to see the baby polar bear.
5. Who brought *their* lunch today?

Complete each sentence with *their* or *there.*

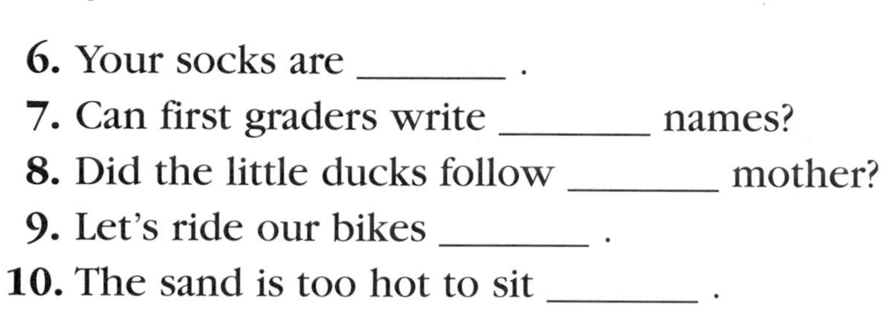

6. Your socks are _______ .
7. Can first graders write _______ names?
8. Did the little ducks follow _______ mother?
9. Let's ride our bikes _______ .
10. The sand is too hot to sit _______ .

Putting It All Together

Look at the example below and write your own simple sentence describing an action. After the sentence, write adverbs telling when, where, and how. Act out the sentence with one of the adverbs, and challenge a partner to guess what the sentence is. Take turns acting out and guessing sentences.

Example: He makes his bed quickly.
upstairs.
roughly.

Chapter Challenge

Read this story carefully and then answer the questions with adverbs. The verbs are in italics.

1. Yesterday Martin and Anne *took* their dog Lucky to the beach.
2. Here they *played* Frisbee with Lucky.
3. Each time they tossed it, Lucky *ran* eagerly after the Frisbee.
4. Her black coat *glistened* brightly in the waves.
5. She always *carried* the Frisbee back proudly.
6. Martin and Anne *patted* her excitedly.
7. Finally the children *knew* Lucky was getting tired.
8. Carefully they *spread* out the beach blanket.
9. All three *rested* quietly.
10. Later they *played* Frisbee again.

SENTENCE NUMBER	QUESTION
1.	*When* did Martin and Anne take Lucky to the beach?
2.	The children and Lucky played *where?*
3.	Lucky ran *how?*
4.	Her black coat glistened *how?*
5.	*When* did Lucky carry the Frisbee back? *How* did she carry the Frisbee back?
6.	*How* did the children pat Lucky?
7.	*When* did the children know Lucky was tired?
8.	*How* did the children spread the blanket?
9.	*How* did they rest?
10.	*When* did they play again?

Creative Space

Jump or Jiggle

Frogs jump
Caterpillars hump

Worms wiggle
Bugs jiggle

Rabbits hop
Horses clop

Snakes slide
Sea gulls glide

Mice creep
Deer leap

Puppies bounce
Kittens pounce

Lions stalk—
But—
I walk!

Evelyn Beyer

Explore the Poem . . .

This poem has seven stanzas. A stanza is a group of lines.

How many lines are there in each stanza in this poem?

Each stanza has two words that rhyme. What line rhymes with

- Frogs jump?
- Worms wiggle?
- Snakes slide?
- Puppies bounce?

Now write a poem like this one. Use the second word from each line, but change the first word. Can you think of other animals or insects that

- jump and hump?
- wiggle and jiggle?
- hop and clop?
- slide and glide?
- creep and leap?
- bounce and pounce?

Then write another poem, using your own ideas. Write two stanzas. Before you begin, read this poem written by a student.

Tigers run
Hippos sun

Sparrows cheep
Roadrunners beep

CHAPTER 15 PUNCTUATION AND CAPITALIZATION

End Punctuation

End punctuation helps you to write clear sentences.

You and your friend are taking a walk. You are surprised to see an old castle, and you decide to explore. You push open the heavy, creaking door and find a large, dark, dusty room. When you brush away the cobwebs, you see a boy sitting on a chair in the middle of the room. Now you can see why he is so still and quiet. His hands and feet are tied to the chair. You try unsuccessfully to untie the knots. He nods toward a note on a nearby desk.

we are in great danger there is a monster upstairs don't make any noise can you find the scissors in the desk drawer hurry cut me loose

About the Photograph

The pom-pom and megaphone tell us this girl has a lot of school spirit. How do we know when a sentence has strong feelings? How do we know when a sentence is asking a question?

Just as you figure out the jumbled message, you hear the monster returning. You quickly untie the boy just in time for all of you to make a narrow escape.

Imagine that the boy handed you this note:

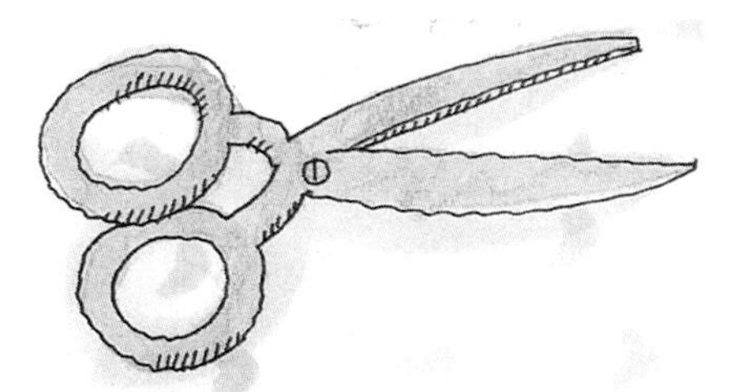

> *We are in great danger! There is a monster upstairs. Don't make any noise. Can you find the scissors in the desk drawer? Hurry. Cut me loose.*

Each sentence begins with a capital letter. Each sentence has an end mark. They help you read more quickly and understand the message. With this note, you could have untied the boy and escaped before the monster returned.

Look at the end marks in the second note.

Sentences that tell strong feelings end with an exclamation point.

> *We are in great danger!*

Sentences that ask end with a question mark.

> *Can you find the scissors in the desk drawer?*

Sentences that command end with a period.

> *Cut me loose.*

Sentences that tell facts end with a period.

> *There is a monster upstairs.*

Exercise 1

Use the end mark of punctuation as a clue. Tell if each sentence tells, asks, commands, or exclaims.

1. For the first time, my little brother Charles stayed overnight with his friend Anthony.
2. Charles was so excited about packing!
3. Should I take my turtle with me?
4. I'd better take my favorite cereal, Crunchy Nut.
5. My mother calmed him down.
6. Don't take your turtle, Charles.
7. Eat the cereal that Anthony likes.
8. When Charles came home, he told us all about his visit.
9. Anthony's Apple Crunch cereal is the greatest!
10. Best of all, we played with Anthony's puppy.
11. When can Anthony come visit me?
12. When can I go back and visit him?

Exercise 2

Tell whether each sentence is a telling sentence, an asking sentence, a commanding sentence, or an exclaiming sentence. Then place the correct mark of punctuation at the end.

1. The smell of lilacs filled the room
2. May I borrow the tape
3. How dark the sky is
4. Nina's hobby is collecting coins
5. What is the password
6. Pass the ketchup, please
7. What a tall bean stalk
8. Why do baby deer have spots

Exercise 3

Tell what end mark of punctuation should follow each of these sentences. Tell what word should begin with a capital letter.

1. look at the parrot
2. how cold the water is
3. our class will visit the planetarium
4. he took his turtle on a trip
5. can you stay awhile
6. finish quickly, please
7. can you pat your tummy and rub your head
8. why did David go
9. how juicy the peaches are
10. oh, the dog stole my candy
11. rub your tummy and pat your head
12. the farmer raises hogs

Practice Power

▶ **Shopping at the mall with a friend, you see many exciting toys in a store window. What question might you ask your friend? Write an asking sentence. Once inside, what might you tell your friend to do? Write a commanding sentence. How would you feel about being in the toy store? Write an exclaiming sentence.**

Capital Letters

Some words always begin with capital letters.

Here are examples of words that always begin with capital letters. Think of why each capital letter is used.

A. Jennifer, Luis, and Lucky
B. Elm Avenue, Chicago, Ohio, Canada
C. Memorial Day
D. Tuesday, August 10
E. I
F. the Empire State Building, Beaver Bridge

Name the example that fits the rule below.

1. Names of holidays begin with a capital letter.
2. Names of people and pets begin with a capital letter.
3. Names of days and months begin with a capital letter.
4. Names of streets, cities, states, and countries begin with a capital letter.
5. Names of buildings and bridges begin with a capital letter.
6. The personal pronoun *I* is a capital letter.

Exercise 1

Read each group of words. Tell which rule from page 407 goes with each group of words.

1. Betsy Ross Bridge
2. London, Los Angeles, Cairo
3. Patsy, Rob, Fido
4. Library of Congress
5. When I'm hot
6. Friday, Sunday, Thursday
7. Veteran's Day, Father's Day
8. January, March, June
9. Independence Hall
10. Marsh Street, Lawrence Boulevard

Exercise 2

Find the words that need a capital letter.

1. Our cat puff is afraid of mice.
2. What interesting facts do you know about abraham lincoln?
3. Smoke rose from aladdin's lamp.
4. A mosquito buzzed in winnie's ear.
5. They named the little dog moose.
6. We make popcorn on saturdays.
7. During the game, i tagged her out.
8. The crutches belong to kathy.
9. Repairs are being made on shady lake bridge.
10. Every labor day my family has a reunion.

Exercise 3

Tell the reason each word in italics begins with a capital letter.

1. *Philadelphia* is an important port.
2. *London Bridge* is falling down.
3. The students at *Hudson School* made snow statues.
4. Jan rode six miles in the bike race on *Wednesday*.
5. Do you live on *Shadow Lane?*

Find the words that need a capital letter. Tell why.

6. florida has lots of sunshine.
7. My brother mark lives at colby college.
8. Can i sit in the front row?
9. The pigeon flew from dallas to houston.
10. We saw the golden gate bridge in san francisco.

Exercise 4

Complete each sentence with a word or words from this list. Remember to use capital letters.

MONTHS		DAYS
January	July	Sunday
February	August	Monday
March	September	Tuesday
April	October	Wednesday
May	November	Thursday
June	December	Friday
		Saturday

1. Every week we begin school on _______ .
2. We don't go to school on _______ or _______ .
3. Valentine's Day is in _______ .
4. Thanksgiving is in _______ .
5. The third day of the week is _______ .
6. New Year's Day is _______ 1.
7. Independence Day is _______ 4.
8. My birthday is in _______ .
9. The sixth day of the week is _______ .
10. Summer vacation begins in _______ .

Exercise 5

Write each sentence correctly. Use capital letters where they are needed. Use this list to help you.

New Year's Day	Independence Day
Arbor Day	Labor Day
Washington's Birthday	Columbus Day
Mother's Day	Father's Day
Christmas Day	Dominion Day

1. we planted a tree on arbor day.
2. father's day is celebrated in summer.
3. on mother's day, we baked cinnamon rolls.
4. on washington's birthday, we had cherry cheesecake.
5. who is honored on columbus day?
6. in canada, people celebrate dominion day.
7. rachel visited her aunt on new year's day.
8. did your family have a picnic on labor day?
9. snow fell on christmas day.
10. let's watch the fireworks on independence day.

Practice Power

▶ **Write the following sentences. Use capital letters where they are needed.**

- **Write one sentence about your favorite holiday.**
- **Write one sentence about a friend of yours.**
- **Write one sentence about your favorite month.**
- **Write one sentence about a famous city.**
- **Write one sentence about your town or city.**

LESSON 3

Abbreviations

Abbreviations are short ways of writing some words. Some abbreviations begin with capital letters and end with periods. Some do not begin with capital letters.

Study this list of abbreviations.

DAYS OF THE WEEK			
Sunday	Sun.	Thursday	Thurs.
Monday	Mon.	Friday	Fri.
Tuesday	Tues.	Saturday	Sat.
Wednesday	Wed.		

MONTHS OF THE YEAR			
January	Jan.	September	Sept.
February	Feb.	October	Oct.
March	Mar.	November	Nov.
April	Apr.	December	Dec.
August	Aug.		

May, June, and July are not abbreviated.

OTHER ABBREVIATIONS			
inch	in.	Street	St.
foot	ft.	Road	Rd.
yard	yd.	Avenue	Ave.
pint	pt.	Boulevard	Blvd.
quart	qt.	South	S.
gallon	gal.	North	N.
East	E.	West	W.

Do all of these abbreviations begin with a capital letter?
Do all of these abbreviations end with a period?
Which months are not abbreviated?
Which abbreviations do not begin with a capital letter?

Exercise 1

Write the abbreviation for each of these words.

1. January
2. inch
3. August
4. gallon
5. Tuesday
6. North
7. December
8. Boulevard
9. Saturday
10. February

Exercise 2

Look at a calendar for this year. Find the day of the week for each of these dates. Then use abbreviations to write the month, date, and day.

1. April 1
2. December 12
3. September 5
4. August 14
5. March 5
6. November 6
7. October 7
8. January 29
9. February 3
10. May 18

Exercise 3

Use an abbreviation for each word in italics. Rewrite this shopping list.

1. a six *inch* ruler
2. one *yard* of ribbon
3. five *feet* of wire
4. one *pint* of cream
5. one *quart* of milk
6. one *gallon* of ice cream

The stores are in different places. Rewrite the addresses, using abbreviations for the words in italics.

7. 16 *South* Maple *Road*
8. 101 *North* Ship *Boulevard*
9. 222 *South* Washington *Avenue*
10. 403 *East* Newport *Street*

Practice Power

▶ **Here is a memo that Cathy wrote to herself.**

Jan. 15

Thurs.

Send Tom a birthday card.

31 N. Adams St.

People write memos to remind themselves of important things. Write five memos to remind yourself of things you must do. Use abbreviations.

Titles and Initials

Titles and initials are also abbreviations.

Look at these names.

Dr. Alice R. Gates
Mr. Sam D. Robbins

Dr. and *Mr.* are titles that come before these names. These titles are abbreviated. *R.* and *D.* are abbreviations for names. Letter abbreviations for names are called initials. These initials could stand for what names?

Did you notice that most titles and initials begin with a capital letter and end with a period?

Study this list. Which title does not end with a period?

TITLES	USE BEFORE THE NAMES OF	EXAMPLES OF TITLES AND INITIALS
Dr.	doctors and dentists	Dr. P. Sanchez
Mr.	single or married men	Mr. Larry S. Rogers
Mrs.	married women	Mrs. W. Bennett
Miss	single women	Miss Amelia D'Amico
Ms.	single or married women	Ms. K. Donnelly
Gov. (governor)	leaders or heads of state	Gov. Grace Sears
Capt. (captain)	leaders of groups	Capt. Terry Hunter
Rev. (reverend)	some religious men or women	Rev. Thomas S. Cox

Exercise 1

Write the abbreviation for the title each of these people would have.

1. a married woman
2. a doctor
3. a governor of a state
4. a single man
5. a dentist
6. a single woman
7. a religious man or woman
8. a married man
9. a leader of a group

Exercise 2

Here is a list of friends and relatives of Toby's. Use each name once to answer the questions.

Miss M. Teesdale	Ms. L. Teesdale	Dr. M. Patel
Mr. E. Coleman	Mrs. R. Coleman	Capt. S. Garrett

1. Which person might be Toby's dentist?
2. Which person might be a leader of a group of police officers in the city where Toby lives?
3. Which person might be Toby's Uncle Ed?
4. Which persons might be Toby's two single aunts?
5. Which person might be married to Toby's Uncle Ed?

Read the above list of Toby's friends and relatives. Think of some names that the initials stand for. Rewrite the list, using names instead of initials.

Example: Miss Mary Teesdale

Exercise 3

Put the correct title before each name. Use capital letters and periods correctly.

1. e b white (a married man)
2. jean brown field (a single woman)
3. florence o chang (a married woman)
4. j h hawkins (doctor)
5. harold terry (a single man)
6. p kolarik (a police captain)
7. j d dawson (a religious person)
8. jorge m delgado (a single man)
9. nancy p addison (a single woman)
10. kathleen cadden (a married woman)

Practice Power

▶ **Look at the six characters pictured below. Make up a name for each character. Include a title and first initial for each name.**

1. 

2. 

3. 

4. 

5. 

6. 

Titles of Books and Poems

Titles of books are underlined. Titles of poems have quotation marks around them.

Study these titles.

The Wizard of Oz (book)

"The Pied Piper of Hamelin" (poem)

In titles

- the first word and all important words begin with capital letters.
- little words like *of, to,* and *for* do not begin with capital letters unless they are the first word.
- titles of books are underlined.
- titles of poems have quotation marks around them.

Exercise 1

Copy the titles of these poems and books. Use capital letters where they are needed. Then tell which titles are books and which are poems.

1. the little house on the prairie
2. goldilocks and the three bears
3. "sing a song of people"
4. the red balloon
5. pippi longstocking
6. "wynken, blynken, and nod"
7. "the gingham dog and the calico cat"
8. whistle for willie

Exercise 2

Put quotation marks around each of these poem titles. Use capital letters where they are needed.

1. the snail's dream
2. who has seen the wind?
3. the city mouse and the country mouse
4. the barefoot boy
5. to an insect

Underline each of these book titles. Use capital letters where they are needed.

6. the trouble being eight
7. dotty's suitcase
8. the discontented ghost
9. marcia gets some braces
10. what happened to the eggs?

Practice Power

▶ **Find three books in the library. Write the titles correctly and underline them. Find three poems you like. Write the titles correctly and put quotation marks around them.**

Commas

Commas help you to write clear sentences. Commas are used to separate nouns in a series.

The teacher asked Judy to write a sentence that names four kinds of transportation. Judy wrote:

> Cars trains ships and airplanes are four kinds of transportation.

The teacher then asked Gary to write a sentence that names three desert animals. Gary wrote:

> Camels lizards and snakes are three kinds of desert animals.

Both Judy and Gary need to write their sentences more clearly. They need to use commas in their sentences. Judy and Gary rewrote their sentences this way:

> Cars, trains, ships, and airplanes are four kinds of transportation.
>
> Camels, lizards, and snakes are three kinds of desert animals.

Judy and Gary wrote their nouns in a series. This means they wrote the nouns one after the other. Judy and Gary had to use commas to separate the nouns. They learned that if you use three nouns in a series, a comma is used after the first two nouns. If you use four nouns in a series, a comma is used after the first three nouns.

Exercise 1

Use commas to separate the nouns in a series.

1. I collected sand shells and seaweed from the beach.
2. We grilled hamburgers hot dogs chicken and sausage at the picnic.
3. Daisies daffodils and roses are my favorite flowers.
4. We saw bears tigers giraffes and zebras at the zoo.
5. Pluto Mars Venus and Earth are planets.
6. I had soup a sandwich and cookies for lunch.
7. The ring the watch and the wallet were on the table.
8. John Jean and Joan are fourth graders.
9. Regina needed glue scissors and paper for the project.
10. My dad bought chairs tables and lamps.

Exercise 2

Complete each sentence with three or four nouns. Use commas where they are needed.

1. I saw _______ _______ and _______ in the sky.
2. Around our house, there are _______ _______ and _______ .
3. Mom said to buy _______ _______ _______ and _______ at the store.
4. _______ _______ and _______ were piled on the chair.
5. Down the street came _______ _______ and _______ .
6. They served _______ _______ and _______ at the Pasta House Restaurant.

Commas are used to separate the names of persons spoken to from the rest of the sentence.

Sometimes when you talk to a person, you want to use that person's name. When you speak directly to a person, it is called *direct address.*

If the person addressed is the first word in the sentence, a comma is placed after the name.

> Andy, we'll meet you at the park.

If the person addressed is the last word in the sentence, a comma is placed before the name.

> We'll meet you at the park, Andy.

If the person addressed is not the first or last word in the sentence, a comma is placed before and after the name.

> We'll meet you, Andy, at the park.

Exercise 3

Use commas to separate the words in direct address.

1. Feed the goldfish Jason.
2. Karen let's go to the movies.
3. I think Mary we should stop at Grandma's.
4. I got a cold Sergio on the first day of school.
5. Miles red mixed with yellow makes orange.
6. Let's build a snow fort class.
7. Elena bring your flute to the party.
8. The cuckoo clock is broken Paul.
9. Hurry Brian or we will be late.
10. What mark of punctuation Clare should I use?

Exercise 4

Complete each sentence with a word in direct address. Use commas where they are needed.

1. Draw a picture _______ about your story.
2. _______ look through the telescope.
3. Look at the sword swallower _______ .
4. There is an inchworm on your sleeve _______ .
5. _______ don't bark at Maureen.

Practice Power

▶ **Imagine you are in your favorite toy store. Write two sentences addressing your friends about what you see. Then write two sentences that name some toys you would like to buy.**

Example: Brendan, look over here at the games.
I wish I could buy rockets, robots, and race cars.

Direct Quotations

A direct quotation contains the exact words of a person.

For the class newspaper, Amy interviewed her classmates about their favorite after-school snacks. Beth told Amy she likes apples. Bud told Amy that he likes to eat cookies. When Amy wrote about the interview with Beth, she couldn't decide which of these two sentences to use.

A. Beth said, "After school, I eat an apple."

or

B. Beth said, "After school, she eats an apple."

Sentence B does not tell Beth's exact words. Sentence A is correct. It tells Beth's exact words.

Study sentence A: Beth said, "After school, I eat an apple."

Notice that

- exact words need quotation marks before (") and after (") them.
- the first word of what is said begins with a capital letter.
- a comma separates what is said from the rest of the sentence.

Which sentence tells Bud's exact words?

A. Bud said, "He likes to eat cookies."

B. Bud said, "After school, I like to eat cookies."

C. Bud said that he likes to eat cookies.

Sentence B is correct: Bud said, "After school, I like to eat cookies."

Sentence B has

- Bud's exact words.
- quotation marks before and after what is said.
- a capital letter to begin the first word of what is said.
- a comma separating what is said from the rest of the sentence.

Exercise 1

Here are sentences that tell what Beth's other classmates like to eat after school. Put quotation marks and capital letters in the correct places.

1. Henry said, after school, I often eat crackers.
2. Joyce said, after school, I munch on muffins.
3. Laura remarked, after school, I like an orange.
4. Our teacher replied, after school, my snack is tea and toast.
5. Anita said, after school, I drink milk.

Exercise 2

Put commas in the correct places. Remember, commas always come before the quotation marks.

1. "Let's play ball" said Joan.
2. "I'm afraid to go in the attic" said Andy.
3. The coach said "Watch what I do."
4. "I'm going to the store" said Uncle Joe.
5. "Please wait here" said Kent.

Exercise 3

Put commas and quotation marks in the correct places. Remember, commas always come before the quotation marks.

1. Tom promised I'll try again.
2. Marge asked Is it going to rain?
3. Jim remarked I like to play checkers.
4. The little girl asked When will we get there?
5. The cab driver said I'll take you to the stadium.

Sometimes the exact words of a speaker are a question. Use a question mark at the end of the exact words.

> "Who is in that costume?" asked Rosa.
>
> "Will you play ball with me on Saturday?" asked Bart.

Sometimes the exact words express a strong feeling. Use an exclamation point at the end of the exact words.

> "I can't wait for the circus to come!" said Carlos.
>
> "What big sandwiches these are!" cried Dominic.

Exercise 4

Put question marks and exclamation points in the correct places. The question marks and exclamation points come before the quotation marks.

1. "You scared me" exclaimed Aunt May.
2. "Who won" called the girls.
3. "What a surprise" they shouted.
4. "How tall are giraffes" asked Juan.
5. "Have you ridden in a plane" asked Henry.

Putting It All Together

With a partner, make up a movement to go with each punctuation mark. Also make up a movement that means capitalization. Just for fun, read aloud the story below. Whenever you come to capital letters and punctuation, perform the movements you made up.

> Yesterday, the doorbell rang. I ran to the door, opened it, and saw Mr. P. L. Swift!
>
> "Hi, Mr. Swift," I said. "Do you have my copy of Ramona the Pest?"
>
> "Yes," he said. "I rang your bell because I knew you were waiting for it."

Chapter Challenge

These sentences tell a story. Read each sentence carefully. Then answer the questions on page 429.

1. On thursday, the third graders would be making holiday wreaths for their families.
2. They would need eight candy mints, a paper clip, and their school picture.
3. Kelly and Steven were so excited!
4. They thought they would send their wreaths to their grandparents in Miami.
5. If they mailed them by Wednesday, December 8, they would arrive in time for the holidays.
6. The day finally came to make the wreaths.
7. "Does everyone have all the things they need?" questioned Ms. Talbot.
8. Ms. Talbot told the class to unwrap their mints and put them in a circle on a piece of waxed paper.
9. Then they put a paper clip under one of the mints and baked them until they melted.
10. "Kelly and Steven, can you tell where you will put your pictures?" asked Ms. Talbot.

SENTENCE NUMBER	QUESTION
1.	What word should begin with a capital letter?
2.	Why is a comma used after *mints* and after *clip?*
3.	What kind of sentence is sentence 3?
4.	Why is the first letter in *Miami* capitalized?
5.	What is the abbreviation for *December?*
6.	What kind of sentence is sentence 6?
7.	Why are quotation marks used before *Does* and after *need?*
8.	Why do *Ms.* and *Talbot* begin with capital letters?
9.	What kind of sentence is sentence 9?
10.	What two names are in direct address.

Grammar and Writing Handbook

Grammar

ADJECTIVES

An adjective is a word that describes a person, place, or thing. An adjective tells *which one, what kind, how many,* or *how much.*

Adjectives That Compare

Some adjectives compare two or more persons or things.

Many adjectives that end with *er* compare two nouns.

An apartment building is *taller* than a house.

Many adjectives that end with *est* compare three or more nouns.

A skyscraper is the *tallest* building in the city.

Adjectives That Describe

Many adjectives describe nouns.

Some adjectives come before nouns.

The *fuzzy* caterpillar clings to the green leaf.

Some adjectives come after verbs like *is, are, was,* or *were.*

The caterpillar is *fuzzy.*

Adjectives That Point Out

The adjectives *this* and *that* point out a specific person, place, or thing.

This points to nouns that are near.

This is the path to my home.

That points to nouns that are farther away.

That path will take you out of town.

Adjectives That Tell Number

Some adjectives answer *how many* about the noun.

Some adjectives tell exactly how many.

Please give each child *four* magnets.

Some adjectives tell about how many.

Each child should also have a *few* paper clips.

Articles

The adjectives *the, an,* and *a* are called articles.

Use *a* or *the* before words that begin with a consonant sound.

a desert *the* sand

Use *an* or *the* before words that begin with vowel sounds.

an onion *the* hour

ADVERBS

An adverb is a word that tells more about a verb. Adverbs can tell *when, where,* or *how* about an action.

Adverbs That Tell How

Some adverbs answer the question *how* or *in what manner.*

The chorus sang *loudly* and *cheerfully.*

Adverbs That Tell When

Some adverbs answer the question *when* or *how often.*

My library book is due *tomorrow.*
I *always* choose a new book.

Adverbs That Tell Where

Some adverbs answer the question *where.*

Sarah cleaned *under* her bed.

NOUNS

A noun is a word that names a person, place, or thing.

Common Nouns

Common nouns name any of a group of persons, places, or things.

student	states	book
teacher	mountains	vegetables

Plural Nouns

Plural nouns name more than one person, place, or thing.

Many nouns form the plural by adding *s* to the singular noun.

doll	dolls
kite	kites

Nouns ending in *s, x, z, ch,* and *sh* form the plural by adding *es* to the singular.

guess	guesses	lunch	lunches
box	boxes	radish	radishes

Plural nouns that are not formed by adding *s* or *es* are called irregular plurals.

child	children	man	men
foot	feet	cavity	cavities

Possessive Nouns

Possessive nouns show ownership or possession.

Irregular Plural Possessives

Irregular plurals do not end in *s*.

To form the plural of an irregular plural noun, add an apostrophe and an *s* (*'s*).

children	children's chairs
women	women's shoe department

Plural Possessives

A plural possessive noun shows more than one person or thing owning something.

To form the plural possessive:

1. Write the plural form.

2. Add the apostrophe only.

six horses	six horses' saddles
five teams	five teams' coaches

Singular Possessives

A singular possessive noun shows one person or thing owning something.

To show ownership by a singular noun, add an apostrophe and an *s* (*'s*).

one dog	one dog's collar
one lady	one lady's purse

Proper Nouns

Proper nouns name a particular person, place, or thing.

Katie Johnson	(person)
Chicago, Illinois	(place)
Girl Scouts of America	(thing)

Singular Nouns

Singular nouns name only one person, place, or thing.

sister	(person)
city	(place)
boat	(thing)

Subject Nouns

Subject nouns tell who or what does the action.

The subject noun and predicate verb are the most important words in a sentence.

The *moon* glowed brightly.

PRONOUNS

A pronoun is a word that takes the place of a noun.

Object Pronouns

Object pronouns are used only after verbs.

Object pronouns are *me, us, you, him, her, it,* and *them.*

Joshua sent *me* a letter.
He asked *us* to visit him.
Please give *her* the notebook.
The alarm will wake *them* at 7 o'clock.

Possessive Pronouns

Possessive pronouns show who owns something.

Possessive pronouns are *mine, ours, yours, his, hers,* and *theirs.*

This blanket is *mine.*
This baseball bat is *his.*
Our car is bigger than *theirs.*

Subject Pronouns

Subject pronouns may be used as subjects in a sentence. They take the place of subject nouns.

Subject pronouns are *I, we, you, he, she, it,* and *they.*

We hurried to the car.
You brought flowers.
She climbed the stairs.
It is a nice day.

SENTENCES

A sentence is a group of words that expresses a complete thought.

This is a sentence:	George Washington was our first president.
This is not a sentence:	our first president

Asking Sentences

Some sentences ask. Asking sentences are called questions.

An asking sentence begins with a capital letter and ends with a question mark (?).

Is your homework finished?

Commanding Sentences

Some sentences command. They tell you what to do. They are called commanding sentences.

A commanding sentence begins with a capital letter and usually ends with a period (.).

Toss the ball.

Exclaiming Sentences

Some sentences exclaim. They express strong or sudden feelings. They are called exclaiming sentences.

An exclaiming sentence begins with a capital letter and ends with an exclamation point (!).

This is the best day ever!

Telling Sentences

Some sentences tell thoughts. Telling sentences are called statements.

A telling sentence begins with a capital letter and ends with a period (.).

Horses eat oats.

The children play soccer.

VERBS

A verb is a word used to express action or being. Without a verb there can be no sentence.

Action Verbs

Verbs that express action are action verbs.

The dog *ran* quickly.

Being Verbs

Verbs that do not express action are being verbs.

The bus *is* here.

Forms of Verbs

Verbs have different forms. Each form has a different name.

PRESENT FORM

If a verb ends in *s,* it might be in the present form.

Sue *talks* on the phone.

PAST FORM

If a verb ends in *d* or *ed,* it might be in the past form.

Sue *talked* on the phone yesterday.

PAST PARTICIPLE FORM

If a predicate verb includes *has, have,* or *had,* it might be in the past participle form.

Sue *has talked* on the phone every day.

Helping Verbs

Some predicate verbs have two or more words—a main verb and one or more helping verbs.

The deer *are running* fast.

Irregular Verbs

Some verbs are formed in an irregular way. Verbs that do not form the past with *d* or *ed* are irregular verbs.

All the school bells *ring* at 9:00 A.M.
Last year the bells *rang* at 8:30 A.M.

Predicate Verbs

The subject noun and predicate verb are the most important words in a sentence.

A predicate verb is the main action word in a sentence.

Frank *swung* at the ball.

Regular Verbs

Some verbs are formed in a regular way. Verbs that form the past with *d* or *ed* are regular verbs.

Joy and Kim *walk* to the library each day.
The boys *walked* to the library this morning.

Tense of a Verb

The tense of a verb tells when the action happens.

Past Tense

A verb in the past tense tells about action that has already happened.

The baby *smiled* today for the first time.

Present Tense

A verb in the present tense tells about an action that is happening now or that happens again and again.

The baby *smiles* at everyone.

Writing

CAPITALIZATION AND PUNCTUATION

Abbreviations

Some abbreviations begin with capital letters and end with periods. Some do not begin with capital letters.

Abbreviations are short ways of writing some words.

Sunday	Sun.	inch	in.
January	Jan.	foot	ft.
North	N.		

Capital Letters

Some words always begin with a capital letter.

NAMES OF HOLIDAYS

Fourth of July

NAMES OF PEOPLE AND PETS

Linda Sparky

NAMES OF DAYS AND MONTHS

Tuesday May

NAMES OF STREETS, CITIES, STATES, AND COUNTRIES

Grove Street Detroit Florida Canada

NAMES OF BUILDINGS AND BRIDGES

Wrigley Building Tower Bridge

PERSONAL PRONOUN *I*

May I be excused from the table?

Commas

Commas are used to separate nouns in a series.

Please bring your *crayons, scissors, and glue* to art class.

Commas are used to separate the names of persons spoken to from the rest of the sentence.

Mrs. Belue, is it time for gym?

Direct Quotations

A direct quotation contains the exact words of a person.

Exact words need quotation marks before and after them. The first word of what is said begins with a capital letter. A comma separates what is said from the rest of the sentence.

The zoo director said, "I want you to look closely at this snake."

End Punctuation

The end mark of a sentence is a question mark (?), period (.), or exclamation point (!).

Who will take attendance?
I will take attendance.
Everyone is here!

Titles of Books and Poems

All the important words in the title begin with capital letters. The small words are not capitalized.

Titles of books are underlined or written in italics.

The Cat in the Hat by Dr. Seuss
The Cat in the Hat by Dr. Seuss

Titles of poems have quotation marks around them.

"Stopping by Woods on a Snowy Evening" by Robert Frost

Titles and Initials

A title comes before a name. A title begins with a capital letter and ends with a period.

Titles and initials are abbreviations that help name a person.

Dr. Margaret Levy
Mr. Patrick Doyle
Prof. Ann Manning

An initial is one capital letter followed by a period.

I. M. Pei
B.J. Armstrong

USING WORDS CORRECTLY

Good and *Well*

Good* is an adjective that describes nouns. *Good* describes persons, places, or things and answers *what kind.

Pete is a *good* tennis player.

***Well* is an adverb that describes the actions of verbs.**

He plays tennis *well.*

I and *Me*

***I* is used before a verb. *I* is a subject pronoun.**

I swim at the pool.

***Me* is used after a verb.**

Bob gave *me* a towel.

Is and *Are, Was* and *Were*

***Is* and *was* are used with singular subjects.**

This tomato *is* ripe.
This tomato *was* picked yesterday.

***Are* and *were* are used with plural subjects.**

We *are* very good friends.
The kittens *were* soft and cuddly.

Their and *There*

***Their* tells what is owned.**

This new school is *their* school.

***There* tells where.**

The house over *there* is empty.

To, Too, and *Two*

***To* tells where.**

Let's go *to* Bobby's house.

***Too* means "also" or "more than enough."**

Bobby's new jacket is *too* big.

***Two* tells how many.**

Bobby can wear *two* sweaters under his jacket.

Index

Steps in THE WRITING PROCESS are set in capitals for easy reference.

A/an, 372-375, 432
Abbreviations, 412-417, 441
Acceptance, writing letters of, 158-159
Action verbs, 67-69, 317-320, 438
A Day in Your Life paragraph
  DRAFTING, 63
  PREWRITING, 62
  PROOFREADING, 65
  PUBLISHING, 65
  REVISING, 64
  writing, 62-65
Addressing, envelope, 163-165, 178
Adjectives, 356-381, 430-432
  articles as, 372-375, 432
  good, 393-394
  that compare, 363-367, 430
  that describe, 357-362, 431
  that point out, 376-379, 431
  that tell number, 368-371, 431
  using colorful, 70-71
Adverbs, 385-399, 432
  kinds of, 385-392
  that tell how, 385-386, 390-392, 432
  that tell when, 385-388, 391-392, 432
  that tell where, 385-386, 389-392, 433
  well, 393-394
Aldis, Dorothy, 188-189
"Alligator Pie" (Lee), 197
Alphabetical order
  of books in library, 234-235
  in dictionary, 213-215
  in index, 226-227
And, combining sentences with, 78-80
Antonyms, 57, 85-86, 111-112, 137-138, 171-172, 203-204
Apostrophes
  in contractions, 60-61, 114-115, 140-141, 174-175, 206-207
  in possessive nouns, 283-290
Are/is, 351-352, 444
Articles *(a/an/the),* 372-375, 432
Asking sentences, 246-250, 260-262, 404-406, 437
Ate/eight, 87
Atlas, 229, 231
"Automobile Mechanics" (Baruch), 382

Baruch, Dorothy, 382
Beat/beet, 173-174
Be/Bee, 113-114
Beet/beat, 173-174
Beginning sentences, 41-46, 102-105
Being verbs, 321-323, 438
Beyer, Evelyn, 400
Body, in friendly letter, 147, 150, 176
Book reports, writing, 131-132, 142-145
  DRAFTING, 143
  PREWRITING, 142
  PROOFREADING, 145
  PUBLISHING, 145
  REVISING, 144
Books
  kinds of, 232-233
  parts of, 221-228
  reference, 229-231
  titles of, 418-419, 443
  writing about characters in, 133-135, 236-239
Breathing, exercises for, 185
Brooks, Gwendolyn, 201
Buy/by, 58-59

C

Call number, 234–235
Capital letters, 407–419
  for abbreviations, 412–417, 441
  for first words in sentences, 78, 248–249, 253, 257
  for *I,* 78
  for initials, 415–417, 443
  for personal titles, 415–417, 443
  for proper nouns, 276–277, 407–411, 441
  in titles of books and poems, 418–419, 443
Card catalog, 234–235
Cent/sent, 173–174
Character, in a story, 133–135
Character sketch
  DRAFTING, 237
  guidelines for writing a, 237
  PREWRITING, 236
  PROOFREADING, 239
  PUBLISHING, 239
  REVISING, 238
  writing a, 133–135
Choral speaking, 184–191
Closing, in friendly letter, 147, 150, 176
Coatsworth, Elizabeth, 187
Collier, Desiree Lynne, 354
Comma, 78–79, 420–426, 442
Commanding sentences, 251–255, 260–262, 404–406, 437
Common nouns, 276–277
Comparison, adjectives in, 363–367
Compound predicates, 75–77
Compound sentences, 78–80
Compound subjects, 72–74
Contractions, 60–61, 114–115, 140–141, 174–175, 206–207

D

Dear/deer, 86–87
Definitions, in dictionary, 218–220
Describing a place, in writing,
  DRAFTING, 91
  PREWRITING, 90
  PROOFREADING, 93
  PUBLISHING, 93
  REVISING, 92
Dictionary skills, 213–220
Direct address, commas in, 422–423, 442
Directions, listening to, 194–195
Direct quotations, 424–426, 442
DRAFTING
  a Day in Your Life paragraph, 63
  book report, 143
  character sketch, 237
  describing a place, 91
  friendly letters, 177
  nature poem, 209
  personal narrative, 20–22
  report, 117

E

Editor's Workshop, 64–65, 92–93, 118–119, 144–145, 178–179, 210–211, 238–239
Eight/ate, 87
Encyclopedia, 229–231
Ending sentences, 41–43, 50–53, 102–105
End punctuation, 403–406. *See also* Exclamation point; Period; Question mark
Entry word, in dictionary, 213
Enunciation, exercises for, 185
Envelope, addressing, 163–165, 178
Exclaiming sentences, 256–262, 437–438
Exclamation point, 256–262, 404–406, 449
Exercises
  for breathing, 185
  for enunciation, 185

F

Fiction books, 232–233
Field, Rachel, 196

"Flowers Are a Silly Bunch" (Spilka), 200
For/four, 205
Forms, filling out, 166-169
Four/for, 205
Friendly letters
  DRAFTING, 177
  parts of, 147-153, 176
  PREWRITING, 176
  PROOFREADING, 179
  PUBLISHING, 179
  REVISING, 178
  writing, 176-179
"Fun at the Zoo," 347

Glossary, in books, 224, 227-228
Good/well, 393-394
"The Grasshoppers" (Aldis), 188-189
Greeting, in friendly letter, 147, 149, 176
Guide words, in dictionary, 216-217

H

Heading, in friendly letter, 147, 149, 176
Headline, in news story, 121-123
Hear/here, 113-114
Helping verbs, 324-326, 439
Here/hear, 113-114
"Hey, Bug!" (Moore), 190
Hole/whole, 173-174
Homophones, 58-59, 86-88, 113-114, 138-139, 173-174, 204-205, 395-398, 445
Hour/our, 113-114
How-to paragraph, writing a, 124-126

I, capitalizing, 78
I/me, 308-311, 444
Index, in books, 224, 226-227
Initials, 415-417, 443
Invitation, writing letters of, 154-157
Irregular verbs, 331-345, 439
Is/are, 351-352, 444
Italics, 443

"Jump or Jiggle" (Beyer), 400-401

Katz, Bobbi, 314
Know/no, 58-59
Kuskin, Karla, 186, 191

Lee, Dennis, 197
Lessac, Frané, 11
Letters, 146-165, 176-179
"Lewis Has a Trumpet" (Kuskin), 186
Library skills, 221-235
Listening. *See also* Speaking
  to directions, 194-195
  to poetry, 196-201, 211
  for sequence, 192-193

Mail/male, 139
Mailing address, 163-165
Meat/meet, 86-87
Me/I, 308-311, 444
Middle sentences, 41-43, 47-49, 102-105
Moore, Lilian, 190
My Little Island (Lessac), 10, excerpted, 11-13, discussed, 14-15

Nature poem
  DRAFTING, 209
  PREWRITING, 208
  PROOFREADING, 211
  PUBLISHING, 211
  REVISING, 210

News story, writing a, 121-123
No/know, 58-59
Nonfiction books, 232-233
Nouns, 270-291, 433-435
  common, 276-277, 433
  identifying, 271-275
  plural, 278-282, 286-290, 433-434
  possessive, 283-290, 434
  proper, 276-277, 435
  singular, 278-280, 283-285, 434-435
  as subjects, 263-266, 435

O

O'Neill, Mary L., 198
Oral presentations, 181-183
Order words, 125-126
Our/hour, 113-114

P

Pair/pear, 205
Paragraphs
  beginning sentences, 41-46, 63, 102-105
  DRAFTING, 63
  ending sentences, 41-43, 50-53, 102-105
  finding and organizing an idea, 35-40
  middle sentences, 41-43, 47-49, 102-105
  PREWRITING, 62
  PROOFREADING, 65
  PUBLISHING, 65
  REVISING, 64, 81-83
  titling, 54-55, 63-64
  writing, 36-40, 62-65
Past tense, 349-350, 440
Pear/pair, 205
Peer conference, 21, 22
Period,
  for abbreviations, 412-417
  to end sentences, 246-249, 253, 404-406, 442
  for initials, 415-417, 443
  for titles, 415-417, 443
Personal narrative, 10, 15-17
  DRAFTING, 20-22
  PREWRITING, 17-19
  PROOFREADING, 26-29
  PUBLISHING, 30-31
  REVISING, 23-25
Plural nouns, 278-282, 286-290
Poems. *See also* Nature poem
  choral reading of, 184-191
  exploring, 268-269, 292-293, 314-315, 354-355, 382-383, 400-401
  listening to, 196-201, 211
  rhyme in, 209, 293, 315
  stanzas in, 401
  titles of, 418-419, 443
  writing, 208-211, 269
"Poemsicle" (Silverstein), 199
Poetry, listening to, 196-201, 211
Possessive nouns, 283-290, 434
Possessive pronouns, 305-307
Predicates
  combining, 75-77
  verbs in, 263-266, 318-320, 440
Present tense, 346-348, 351-352, 440
PREWRITING
  a Day in Your Life paragraph, 62
  book report, 142
  character sketch, 236
  describing a place, 90
  friendly letters, 176
  nature poem, 208
  personal narrative, 17-19
  report, 116
Pronouns, 294-313, 435-436
  definition of, 295, 435
  I/me, 308-311, 444
  possessive, 305-307, 436
  as subjects, 299-301, 436
  used after verbs (object), 302-304, 436

PROOFREADING
a Day in Your Life paragraph, 65
book report, 145
character sketch, 239
describing a place, 93
friendly letters, 179
nature poem, 211
personal narrative, 26-29
report, 119
Proofreading editor's marks, 23, 25, 27, 29
Proper nouns, 276-277
PUBLISHING
a Day in Your Life paragraph, 65
book report, 145
character sketch, 239
describing a place, 93
friendly letters, 179
nature poem, 211
personal narrative, 30-31
report, 119

Q

Question mark, 246-250, 260-262, 404-406, 437
Questions, 246-250, 260-262, 404-406
Quotation marks
for direct quotations, 424-427, 442
for poem titles, 418-419, 443
Quotations, 424-427, 442

R

Read/red, 138-139
Reference books, 229-233
Regular verbs, 331-334, 440
Reports, 94-109, 116-119
choosing an idea and finding facts, 95-97
DRAFTING, 117
planning, 98-101
PREWRITING, 116
PROOFREADING, 119
PUBLISHING, 119
REVISING, 106-109, 118
writing, 102-105, 116-119
Return address, 163-165
REVISING
a Day in Your Life paragraph, 64
book report, 144
character sketch, 238
describing a place, 92
friendly letters, 178
nature poem, 210
personal narrative, 23-25
report, 106-109, 118
Rhyme, in poems, 209, 315
Road/rode, 139
"Rose, where did you get that red?" (Collier), 354-355
"Rudolph Is Tired of the City" (Brooks), 201

S

Sea/see, 58-59
Senses, writing using your, 90
Sent/cent, 173-174
Sentences
beginning, 41-46, 63, 102-105
combining, 78-80
definitions of, 243-245, 437
ending, 41-43, 50-53, 102-105
kinds of, 247-262, 437-438
middle, 41-43, 47-49, 102-105
predicates in, 75-77
subjects in, 72-74
Sequence, listening for, 192-193
Series, commas in, 420-421, 442
Signature, in friendly letter, 147, 151, 176
Silverstein, Shel, 199
Solo, 184, 186, 188-189
"The Sound of Water" (O'Neill), 198
Sources, 95-97
Speaking. *See also* Listening
choral, 184-191
oral presentations, 181-183
Spelling
of homophones, 58-59, 86-87, 113-114, 138-139, 173-174, 204-205, 395-398, 445
of irregular verbs, 331-345
of plural nouns, 278-282, 286-290

Spilka, Arnold, 200
Stanzas, 401
Statements, 246–250, 438
Story about yourself, writing a, 127–130
Subject nouns, 263–266, 318, 320
Subjects
combining, 72–74
nouns as, 263–266, 318, 320
pronouns as, 299–301
"Sudden Storm" (Coatsworth), 187
Synonyms, 56, 84–85, 110–111, 136–137, 170–171, 202, 210

T

Table of contents, in books, 224–225
Telling sentences, 246–250, 260–262, 404–406, 438
Thank-you letters, writing, 160–162
That/this, 355, 376-378
Their/there, 397–398, 445
This/that, 355, 376-378
"Tiptoe" (Kuskin), 191
Titles, 415–419
of books and poems, 418–419, 443
for paragraphs, 54–55, 63-64
personal, 415–417, 443
To/too/two, 395–396, 445
Tuning-up exercises, 185

U

Underlining, of book titles, 418, 443
Unison, 184, 186–187, 190
Usage
ate/eight, 87–88
beat/beet, 173–174
be/bee, 113–114
buy/by, 58–59
cent/sent, 173–174
dear/deer, 86–87
for/four, 205
good/well, 393–394, 444
hear/here, 113–114
hole/whole, 173–174
hour/our, 113–114
I/me, 308–311, 444
know/no, 58–59
mail/male, 139
meat/meet, 86–87
pair/pear, 205
read/red, 138–139
road/rode, 139
sea/see, 58–59
that/this, 355, 376-378
their/there, 397–398, 445
to/too/two, 395–396, 445
you're/your, 204–205

V

Verbs, 316–353, 438–440
action, 67–69, 317–320, 438
being, 321–323, 438
forms of, 327–330, 439
helping, 324–326, 439
irregular, 331–345, 439
main, 324–326
past tense, 349–350, 440
predicate, 440
present tense, 346–348, 440
regular, 331–334, 440
using strong, 67–69
Vocabulary
antonyms, 57, 85–86, 111–112, 137–138, 171–172, 203–204
homophones, 58–59, 86–88, 113–114, 138–139, 173–174, 204–205, 395–398, 445
synonyms, 56, 84–85, 110–111, 136–137, 170–171, 202, 210
Voices
deep, 184–186, 190
falling, 184
light, 184–187, 189, 190
loud, 184, 191
rising, 184
soft, 184, 191

Was/were, 351-352, 444
Well/good, 393-394
Whole/hole, 173-174
Word map, 38-42, 96-97, 100
Word meanings, in dictionary, 218-220
Writer's Workshop, 62-63, 90-91, 116-117, 142-143, 176-177, 208-209, 236-237
Writing
- a Day in Your Life paragraph, 62-65
- beginning sentences, 41-46, 102-105
- book reports, 131-132, 142-145
- character sketches, 133-135, 236-239
- describing a place, 90-93
- ending sentences, 41-43, 50-53, 102-105
- friendly letter, 176-179
- how-to paragraphs, 124-126
- letters of acceptance, 158-159
- letters of invitation, 154-157
- middle sentences, 41-43, 47-49, 102-105
- nature poem, 208-211
- news stories, 121-123
- paragraphs, 36-40, 62-65
- personal narratives, 17-33
- reports, 102-105, 116-119
- stories about yourself, 127-130
- thank-you letters, 160-162

THE WRITING PROCESS, 17-33

You're/your, 204-205
Yuasa, Nobuyuki, 292

Acknowledgments

10 From *My Little Island* by Frané Lessac. Copyright © 1984 by Frané Lessac. Used by permission of HarperCollins Publishers.

186 "Lewis Has a Trumpet" from *In the Middle of the Trees.* Copyright © 1958, renewed 1980 by Karla Kuskin. Reprinted by permission of Scott Treimel New York.

187 "Sudden Storm" Copyright © 1966 by Grosset & Dunlap, Inc., renewed, from *The Sparrow Bush* by Elizabeth Coatsworth. Used by permission of Grosset & Dunlap, Inc., a division of Penguin Putnam Inc.

188 "The Grasshoppers" from *Here, There and Everywhere* by Dorothy Aldis. Copyright 1927, 1928, copyright renewed © 1955, 1956 by Dorothy Aldis. Used by permission of G.P. Putnam's Sons, a division of Penguin Putnam Inc.

190 "Hey, Bug!" from *I Feel the Same Way* by Lilian Moore. Copyright © 1967 Lilian Moore. Copyright renewed 1995 Lilian Moore Reavin. Reprinted by permission of Marian Reiner for the author.

191 "Tiptoe" from *In the Middle of the Trees.* Copyright © 1958, renewed 1980 by Karla Kuskin. Reprinted by permission of Scott Treimel New York.

196 "Barefoot Days," copyright 1926 by Doubleday, a division of Bantam, Doubleday, Dell Publishing Group, Inc., from *Taxis and Toadstools* by Rachel Field. Used by permission of Bantam Doubleday Dell Books for Young Readers.

197 From *Alligator Pie* (Macmillan of Canada, 1974). Copyright © 1974 Dennis Lee. With permission of the author.

198 "The Sound of Water" from *What Is That Sound!* by Mary L. O'Neill. Copyright © 1966 by Mary O'Neill. Copyright renewed 1994 Abigail Hagler and Erin Baroni. Reprinted by permission of Marian Reiner.

199 "Poemsicle" from *A Light in the Attic* by Shel Silverstein. Copyright © 1981 by Evil Eye Music, Inc. Used by permission of HarperCollins Publishers.

200 "Flowers Are a Silly Bunch" from *Once Upon a Horse* by Arnold Spilka. Copyright © 1966 by the author.

201 "Rudolph Is Tired of the City" from *Bronzeville Boys and Girls* by Gwendolyn Brooks. Copyright © 1956 by Gwendolyn Brooks Blakely. Used by permission of HarperCollins Publishers.

268 "Size-wise," "Pencil Pal," and "Letting Go." No authors listed.

292 "A drop of rain!" from *Year of My Life: A Translation of Issa's 'Oraga Haru',* Nobuyuki Yuasa, trans. Copyright © 1972 The Regents of the University of California. Reprinted by permission.

314 "Hands" Copyright © 1978 by Bobbi Katz. Reprinted with permission of the author who controls all rights.

347 "Fun at the Zoo." No author listed.

354 From *Rose, where did you get that red?* by Kenneth Koch. Copyright © 1973 by Kenneth Koch. Reprinted by permission of Random House, Inc.

382 "Automobile Mechanics" from *I Like Machinery* by Dorothy W. Baruch. Copyright © 1933 by Harper & Brothers, New York. Reprinted by permission of Bertha Klausner International Literary Agency, Inc.

400 "Jump or Jiggle" by Evelyn Beyer, from *Another Here and Now Story Book* by Lucy Sprague Mitchell. Copyright 1937 by E.P. Dutton; renewed © 1965 by Lucy Sprague Mitchell. Used by permission of Dutton Children's Books, a division of Penguin Books USA Inc.

All attempts possible have been made to contact author and publisher for cited works in this book.

Art & Photography

Cover: Konstantin Rodko, *Train Station.* SuperStock.

Part One Opener: Jack Savitsky, *Train in a Coal Town,* 1968. National Museum of American Art, Washington, DC/Art Resource, NY.

Part Two Opener: Peter Sickles, *Sailboats Around the Peninsula.* Peter Sickles/SuperStock.

Photographs: CLEO Photography, 34, 242, 356. **PhotoDisc, Inc.,** 1(T), 4(B), 6(B), 7(BR), 10, 13, 19, 25, 40, 42(B), 43, 44, 45, 48, 49, 63, 64, 66, 75, 89, 94, 109, 120, 126, 128, 129, 144, 146, 156, 167, 180, 187, 197, 198, 199, 200, 201, 212, 214, 217, 219, 220, 221(L), 225, 226, 227, 233, 248, 253(B), 254, 255, 259, 268, 270, 284(B), 292, 293, 304, 309, 314, 317, 319, 323, 329(B), 330, 333, 343(T), 348, 351, 352, 354, 358, 368, 371(B), 375, 377, 379, 382, 384, 388, 397(B), 398(B), 400, 402, 405, 409(B), 423, 427. **Skjold Photographs,** 294, 316.

Illustrations: Mary Lynn Blasutta, 50, 51, 70, 71, 107, 185, 196, 243, 244, 251, 252(T), 253(T), 265(T), 266, 272, 274, 278, 279, 283(T), 301(T), 302, 334, 335, 346, 347(B), 367(B), 369, 371(T). **Susan Blubaugh,** 38, 283(B), 328, 338, 339. **Nan Brooks,** 3(B), 154, 155, 160(B), 161, 275. **Ted Carr,** 130, 397(T). **Ralph Creasman,** 52, 256, 263, 412(B). **David A. Cunningham,** 36, 37, 78, 79, 102, 104, 105, 108(B), 222, 223, 230(T), 235, 258, 264, 265(B), 276, 300, 301(B), 337(B), 340, 341, 370, 373(B), 385, 394. **Pat Dypold,** 182, 194(B). **Kerry Gavin,** 159(B), 163, 165. **Linda Gist,** 245. **Jean Cassels Helmer,** 1(B), 2(B), 5(M, B), 7(T), 35, 41, 47, 53(B), 91, 95, 96, 98, 99, 103, 280, 281, 282, 363, 364(B), 365, 376. **Cynthia Hoffman,** 391. **Paul Hoffman,** 359. **Mary Jones,** 124, 125, 188, 189, 218, 257, 286, 288, 289, 325(T), 331, 332(B), 364(T), 403, 408, 409(T), 410(T), 411, 419(T), 424. **G. Brian Karas,** 2(T), 6(T), 68, 69, 121(B), 131, 246, 247, 260, 262, 290, 307, 318, 327, 349, 360, 361, 389, 390, 404, 407. **Carl Kock,** 3(T), 5(T), 42(T), 53(T), 55, 67, 76, 77, 80, 83, 97, 100, 101, 108(T), 121(T), 127, 134, 135, 152, 158, 159(T), 164, 168(T), 169, 179, 181, 183, 184, 213, 216, 232, 234, 250, 261(B), 284(T), 285, 296, 298, 299, 303, 305, 311, 320, 321, 324, 329(T), 332(T), 337(T), 343(B), 344, 345, 347(T), 357, 367(T), 372, 373(T), 374, 386(R), 392, 393, 396(T), 398(T), 418, 425, 426. **Eileen Mueller Neill,** 166, 277, 419(B). **Publishers Resource Group,** 18, 90. **Phil Renaud,** 54. **William Seabright,** 153, 249, 306, 366, 395, 410(B), 421(T). **Slug Signorino,** 4(T), 7(M), 72, 73, 122, 123, 147(B), 148, 149, 150, 151, 157, 190, 191, 192, 193, 252(B), 297, 322, 325(B), 386(L), 396(B), 422. **Mark Ulrich,** 46. **Carl Whiting,** 3(M), 4(M), 6(M), 147(T), 160(T), 162, 168(B), 224, 228, 231, 261(T), 308, 414, 415, 416, 417, 420, 421(B). **Mick Wiggins,** 273.